The Sound of Pictures

The Sound of Pictures

Listening to the Movies, from Hitchcock to *High Fidelity*

ANDREW FORD

Published by Black Inc.,
an imprint of Schwartz Media Pty Ltd
37–39 Langridge Street
Collingwood Vic 3066 Australia
email: enquiries@blackincbooks.com
http://www.blackincbooks.com

Copyright © Andrew Ford 2010.

ALL RIGHTS RESERVED.
No part of this publication may be reproduced, stored in a retrieval system, or transmitted in any form by any means electronic, mechanical, photocopying, recording or otherwise without the prior consent of the publishers.

The National Library of Australia Cataloguing-in-Publication entry:

>   Ford, Andrew, 1957-
>
>   The sound of pictures : listening to the movies, from
>   Hitchcock to High Fidelity / Andrew Ford.
>
>   ISBN: 9781863955102 (pbk.)
>
>   Includes index.
>
>   Motion picture music--Philosophy and aesthetics.
>   Motion picture music--Analysis, appreciation.
>   Motion picture music--Production and direction.
>   Music, Influence of .
>
>   781.542

Book design by Thomas Deverall
Typeset by Duncan Blachford
Index by Michael Ramsden

Contents

Introduction	1.
The Role of Music	7.

Five Composers

Ennio Morricone	29.
Richard Rodney Bennett	41.
Dick Hyman	55.
Lalo Schifrin	66.
Howard Shore	75.

Listening to the Movies

Classical Music in Films	87.
Pop Goes the Score	105.
Pictures of Sound	127.
Listening for Clues in Hitchcock	146.
The Sound of Voices	167.
The Sounds of Silence (and Bumps in the Night)	178.

Five Directors

Bruce Beresford	201.
Sally Potter	218.
Wim Wenders	237.
Peter Greenaway	244.
Peter Weir	261.

Epilogue: The Shared Experience of Sound	279.
Some Further Reading & Acknowledgments	283.
Films Mentioned in This Book	285.
Index	297.

for Elsie

Introduction

When people say to me that they like film music – and I hear this surprisingly often – I never know what they mean. For a start, film music is not all one thing. A film score might be full of the pop hits of the day, or it might sound broadly classical, in any one of a hundred styles from Handel to Wagner to Stravinsky to Philip Glass. In the early twenty-first century, there is a growing chance it might actually have been composed by Philip Glass. Film music isn't a genre and it isn't a style.

My guess is that most people hear the term 'film music' and conjure up one of those epic scores, the sort of thing Maurice Jarre composed for David Lean in *Lawrence of Arabia* (1962) and *Doctor Zhivago* (1965), all big tunes, late-Romantic harmonies and sumptuous orchestration. There are still film composers working in that broad tradition, though few with Jarre's gift for a tune.

Younger filmgoers will be far more familiar with the soundtrack as pop collage, often deriving, one suspects, from the contents of the director's iPod. I have a friend who buys CDs of film soundtracks, sometimes without having seen the film, because he finds it a convenient way to encounter new sounds and new songs, assembled with a story-telling rationale. Until he sees the film in question, the precise rationale will elude him, but I think he at least feels something like an emotional strand running through the musical selections.

Take any film music out of its context and it will lose its filmic rationale, though it might retain some of the associations. Play Jerome Moross's opening title music for *The Big Country* (William Wyler, 1958) in a concert hall, as some of our symphony orchestras are now wont to do, and the audience will very likely see in its mind's eye a panoramic shot of a ranch in a big, empty landscape. It will be the same if the orchestra plays the slow snare-drum rolls from Bernard Herrmann's score for *Taxi Driver* (Martin Scorsese, 1976). We see the yellow cab slowly prowling the night streets of New York, steam rising from the manholes. John Williams's theme for the *Harry Potter* films likewise conjures shadowy sets, an owl or two and a sinister, smirking Alan Rickman.

Famous film music will tend to jog the memory of the listener. A feeling for the film in question, a general idea of the look of the picture, the vivid recollection of a specific image: any or all of these may be swiftly conjured up by the sound of the music, assuming we have first heard the music in the context of the film. In *Jaws* (Steven Spielberg, 1975), Williams successfully evokes the presence of a shark with just two notes. Go to a piano. Somewhere near the bottom of the keyboard play a rising minor second – that's any note followed by the note immediately above it – slurring the two notes and making the second one very short. There it is: the Great White brought to life in music. But only because we've seen the film.

Sometimes it is not musical themes – or not only themes – that impress themselves on our memory, but the style of the music: the swirling bagpipes of *Tunes of Glory* (Ronald Neame, 1960), the ragtime of *The Sting* (George Roy Hill, 1973). It might be the actual sound of the music, for example its orchestration – Bernard Herrmann's strings-only score for *Psycho* (Alfred Hitchcock, 1960), Jerry Goldmith's percussion ensemble in *Seven Days in May* (John Frankenheimer, 1964), the brass band in *Brassed Off* (Mark Herman, 1996). Or it might be the specific timbre of an individual instrument, a distinctive tone-colour that becomes emblematic of a film, summing it up in a matter of seconds: Anton Karas's zither in *The Third Man* (Carol Reed, 1949), Larry Adler's mouth organ in *Genevieve* (Henry Cornelius, 1953), Gheorghe Zamfir's panpipes in

Introduction

Picnic at Hanging Rock (Peter Weir, 1975), the piano in *The Piano* (Jane Campion, 1993). There's the banjo in *Deliverance* (John Boorman, 1972), the tuba in *Close Encounters of the Third Kind* (Steven Spielberg, 1977) and the shamisen in *Ai no corrida* (Nagisa Oshima, 1976). Many people, having bought their ticket for this last movie for entirely other reasons, must have had their first exposure to the sound of the shamisen from Oshima's film.

But it need not be a musical sound at all. All manner of noises can evoke the movies in which they were heard. When I began the final stages of putting this book together, I emailed friends and colleagues I knew to be filmgoers and asked them if they had any favourite film moments in which sound – musical or otherwise – truly stood out. One that came up a lot in the replies was *Apocalypse Now* (Francis Ford Coppola, 1979), not for the 'Ride of the Valkyries' in the famous sequence with the helicopters, but for the opening scene with the sound of the ceiling fan morphing into a helicopter and back again. It is a small detail at the start of a very big film, but it encapsulates much of what follows and quickly explains the state of mind of Captain Willard (Martin Sheen) as he lies there, drunk, staring at the revolving fan blades on his ceiling.

On a far grander scale, the overwhelming factory noise in *Norma Rae* (Martin Ritt, 1979) permeates the whole film, even in the scenes that are not set in the factory, and it stays with you long after you've left the cinema. And sounds that we might normally regard as pleasant can become threatening in a certain context. Certainly Alfred Hitchcock gave the innocent squawk of the seagull a wholly new meaning in *The Birds* (1963).

In the five years I spent watching and listening to films and conducting interviews about movies for this book, I made some documentary features, also called *The Sound of Pictures*, for ABC Radio. One of these was about the role of the sound editor, and involved an interview with the late Rodney Holland discussing some of the films he had worked on. These included *Don't Look*

Now (Nicolas Roeg, 1973), *Barry Lyndon* (Stanley Kubrick, 1975) and *Cross of Iron* (Sam Peckinpah, 1977).

In editing and mixing the script and interview with sounds from the films, my co-producer Jenny Parsonage and I began to feel ill. The problem was *Cross of Iron*. Like all Peckinpah's work, it is extremely violent (of course, it is a war film). The climax shows just how important the work of a sound editor can be to a movie. It is a typical Peckinpah slow-motion massacre, with lots of shooting and screaming on the soundtrack, while body parts are being shot off and spurting arterial blood makes great arcs against the sky. You might think it was the pictures that made us feel ill, but it wasn't. Watching the scene was one thing – maybe the slow-motion artiness ameliorated the effect – but listening was another. As we edited our radio feature with the sound alone, the screams became unbearable. Finally, we decided we could not inflict the sequence on either our radio listeners or ourselves, and we edited out more than half of it. That's the power of sound in films.

There isn't very much literature about film sound, and what has been written over the years is mostly academic, involving lots of jargon and theories. You won't find much jargon in this book, and nothing at all about 'diegetic' and 'non-diegetic' music (that's music played on the screen versus music that we hear only in the composer's score). And I have no grand theories to advance. Theories can be so limiting and things that don't fit the theory so easily disapproved of. (Okay, maybe that was a little theory right there, but there won't be any more.)

My technique in writing this book has been very simple. I have watched and listened to films, often many times over, and tried to identify some links. My hope is that readers of the book will do more or less the same. There are about 400 films mentioned and practically every one is available on DVD. The structure of the book is quite loose and will be readily perceived: there's a general chapter on the uses of music, followed by five interviews with film

Introduction

composers. Then there are six more chapters about specific uses of music and sound, followed by five interviews with film directors. I had intended to include a chapter about film musicals, but in the end it seemed this topic needed a book to itself. The same with animated films.

One of the earliest books on film music, and one of the most provocative, is *Composing for the Films* by Theodor W. Adorno and Hanns Eisler (1947). I discuss some of their ideas in Chapter 1. In the words of my friend the composer Martin Bresnick, their book is 'insightful and stupid in equal measure'. He's right. And one of the most insightful bits is where the authors take aim at people who say that film music should be unobtrusive, that a successful movie score is one you don't notice. They were writing back in the 1940s, but you still hear this claim made today. And it's rubbish.

The purpose of this book is to encourage its readers to listen to films as actively as they watch them – to hear the sound of pictures.

Andrew Ford
Robertson, NSW

The Role of Music

One of my favourite war movies begins conventionally enough for a film of its time. Orchestral music wells up, a rather noble theme emerges, and the credits roll. Ahead of the film's title, we read on individual 'cards' the names of the cast, including Laurence Olivier, Leslie Howard and Raymond Massey. But then convention is broken, for the last card in the sequence reads:

> and the music of
> Ralph Vaughan Williams
> in

The film is *49th Parallel*, made by Michael Powell and Emeric Pressburger in 1941, when it was unusual to give the composer equal billing with the actors, making a star of the music. It is no more usual today.

Naturally, having Vaughan Williams work on your movie was something to brag about. The 69-year-old composer had never before written music for a feature film, and here he did a sterling job. But Powell and Pressburger's use of Vaughan Williams's name above the titles of *49th Parallel* was not simply a matter of boasting.

This intermittently impressive and unfailingly interesting film was in part designed, like Alfred Hitchcock's *Foreign Correspondent* (1940), to encourage the USA to enter the war. Powell said he hoped 'to scare the pants off the Americans' and the movie, which in the United States was called *The Invaders*, ends with a fugitive Nazi U-boat commander momentarily reaching US soil at Niagara Falls.

So the securing of a famous composer for the film, his name proudly proclaimed on screen in the first minute, was part of a propaganda exercise.

Now that its original purpose is behind it, the opening credit sequence of *49th Parallel* jolts its viewers in a different way. It makes 'the music of Ralph Vaughan Williams' look very much like a player, a character in the drama. And, in a way, it is. In a way, music always plays a role.

One of the most basic uses of music is to help the viewer become immersed in a film, to believe in it. This is a paradox, because a score, whether specially composed or assembled from pre-existing tracks, is one of the least plausible aspects of a movie. Even Hitchcock, a director attuned to music and not noted for his insistence on verisimilitude, dispensed with the score in *Lifeboat* (1944), because in a film set entirely in a small boat in the middle of the ocean, he couldn't see where the music would be coming from. The film's composer, Hugo Friedhofer, whose contribution to the picture ended with the two-and-a-half minutes of rather good music he had written for the opening credits, wondered aloud where Hitchcock believed the camera was coming from. And it is a fair point. Once you start worrying about the provenance of the music, nearly everything else about filmmaking invites similar scrutiny. Certainly this was the vale of tears into which the Danish filmmakers of Dogme 95 wandered when they made one of their self-imposed rules the avoidance of any sound that wasn't part of the filming process. This of course included music.

Besides saving money, the motivation of Lars von Trier, Thomas Vinterberg and their colleagues was partly to rid their work of falsity and manipulation and the seductive quality of the score. They were on to something, of course, even if one wouldn't necessarily want to watch their films all the time. It is precisely as a means of seduction that music has been used by filmmakers from the beginning. Even the makers of silent films understood the importance of music. It was played on the set for the actors. In the cinema, music was added live to the movie by a pianist or an organist or even an orchestra. Films have always used music to make comedy funnier, tragedy sadder, tension tenser, but most often to establish the mood, to set the scene. Music in mainstream films invites us to surrender, to lie back and think of Hollywood. Whether it is lulling or energising, creepy or humorous, film music aims to suck us in. And once sucked, we enter the film more or less on its terms. This has been the hope, at least, of film directors throughout history, especially those with an eye to commercial success.

Die Hard (John McTiernan, 1988) is a solid, mainstream example of this. Police officer John McClane (Bruce Willis) flies into Los Angeles to spend Christmas with his children and estranged wife, and within twenty minutes he is saving the world. How can we be made to believe such stuff? How will we ever accept that after being punched and kicked a great deal, mostly in the face, after having his bare feet lacerated with broken glass, falling from significant heights and being shot in the shoulder, McClane is still going around taking out the bad guys? The answer, to a surprising degree, lies with Michael Kamen's resourceful score. The important thing is that the viewer is given no time to think, and the sheer amount of music helps here. The music provides continuity – literally, because it hardly ever stops – and it provides pace, slowing down, speeding up, and controlling the way the audience watches and understands the film.

The score itself is not without interest. We're continually reminded that it is Christmas by the sound of bells and by the use, throughout, of little motifs from 'Winter Wonderland' and 'Let It Snow! Let It Snow! Let It Snow!'. The 'Ode to Joy' theme from Beethoven's ninth symphony is similarly used. This begins as the frankly odd choice of music played by a string quartet at a party, then becomes associated with the German terrorists led by Hans Gruber (Alan Rickman). At the moment the door of a vault swings open to allow Gruber's men access to $640 million, the 'Ode to Joy' comes triumphantly to the fore, choir and all. So there is humour, too, in Kamen's score. But the musical package as a whole is there to manipulate the audience, and one can hardly complain about this, because it is surely manipulation that the *Die Hard* audience is after. If you go to a film like this, you will want to be white-knuckled at the edge of your seat. And, as Hitchcock was among the first to work out, your knuckles won't be white if you're puzzling over the logic of the plot. Music helps us suspend that function of the brain.

But it would be a mistake to believe that only a composed score can manipulate its listeners. Plenty of modern films make regular and strategic use of pop music for similar effect. The romantic comedy *Sliding Doors* (Peter Howitt, 1998) has a score by David Hirschfelder, but more prominently, and more importantly in terms of scene setting, songs on the soundtrack by Jamiroquai, Dido, Blair and other 1990s pop acts.

The film opens on Helen (Gwyneth Paltrow), a busy working girl, leaving her apartment in the morning. Simultaneously, on the soundtrack, the harmless funk of Blair is making 'the Portobello Road' seem like a cool place to be, while advising us to 'Have fun, living in the city'. Helen is late for work, but she's happy (the music tells us this), jogging up the stairs from the underground, dodging the rush-hour commuters and ringing ahead to her favourite café to order a take-away coffee, which is duly waiting for her along with a kiss from the jolly Mediterranean proprietor. In other words, it's the opening titles of a dozen TV sit-coms.

As Helen finally arrives at work, late for her meeting, the credits have finished rolling, Blair's music has faded and the film has established time (the late 1990s), place (London) and mood (cheerful, with a tinge of wistfulness). So in a matter of minutes and with just a single song the audience is primed, disbelief willingly shelved.

In the case of *Sliding Doors* this is just as well, because before long we will be asked to accept two preposterous ideas. The first concerns magic on the underground and the sliding doors of the film's title: with a whoosh of David Hirschfelder's wind chimes, our heroine becomes two people – one making the train, the other missing it – who, for the remainder of the film, will inhabit parallel realities. If you like romantic comedies and you like Gwyneth Paltrow, you will go along with the magic. Rather harder to believe is that one of these Helens, an apparently intelligent and sophisticated woman, might fall for a man who finds it endlessly amusing to recite old *Monty Python* sketches. Sometimes the burden placed on film music is simply too much for it to bear.

The ability, indeed the tendency of film music to manipulate its audience was one of the objections raised by the cultural theorist Theodor W. Adorno and the composer Hanns Eisler in their book *Composing for the Films*, first published in 1947. Both authors, but especially Adorno, were writing from the perspective that the only thing that mattered was what we sometimes call 'high art' or, to put it another way, pure art. In a telling comment referring to the most famous living concert-hall composers of their day, the writers say that they 'cannot imagine Schönberg or Stravinsky stooping to compose genre music'. By genre music, they mean tense, dissonant horror themes, chromatic but ultimately consonant love themes and fast chase music. Apart from the fact that it might be argued that both these composers did indeed 'stoop', and more than once, it is Adorno and Eisler's assumption that film music must remain pure that raises eyebrows today and probably did so even back in 1947.

Film music does not and really cannot function like other music. For a start, there is the simple fact that it always accompanies pictures, often sound effects and sometimes dialogue, so that the music is just one component in the mix, the other elements affecting the way we hear it – that's if we hear it at all. More importantly, though, there is the matter of structure.

A successful piece of music, a musical 'work' – whether it is a three-minute, three-chord pop song or an hour-long symphony by Bruckner – will have a successful structure. To put it too simply, there is a beginning, a middle and an end. But film music is nearly all middle, the beginning and end of the structure belonging to the film itself. Structure is classical music's rationale, but the rationale for film music is the film. Take this music out of its context, then, play it in the concert hall, and an absence is felt. The big tune might remain, likewise the evocative orchestration, and together these will bring back memories, feelings and images if we know a film well, but we will still miss the structure that the film itself provides. This is not the fault of film music. It is not a fault at all. It is simply the way in which music works in this context.

Adorno and Eisler wanted music to retain its structure, advocating that filmmakers should shoot and cut their movies to fit the music. Well, it's certainly a point of view. And, of course, it's been done, at least for individual scenes within films. But it is an extremely restrictive practice that the authors propose, and it hinges on the tacit belief that music is of prime importance in the filmmaking process, not merely one element among many.

Ultimately, the problem with Adorno and Eisler's theories was that they objected so much to commercialisation and mass culture that they were only ever able to approve of what we would call 'art films'. Even Sergei Prokofiev's famous score for Eisenstein's *Alexander Nevsky* (1938), which most people would place up at the arty end of the spectrum, came in for criticism. And yet, while some modern readers might find much of the book too far detached from the real world to be taken seriously, *Composing for the Films* is still worth reading, and many of its authors' criticisms do remain valid.

The authors railed against the clichés of film music, which they felt had a deadening effect on the genre. Clichés should always be rooted out, and Hollywood at its laziest (which is most of the time) abounds in them. Among the clichés that Adorno and Eisler identified were certain types of music. These included not only genre music, but also the obvious use of culturally specific music for certain settings. For example, *Gilda* (Charles Vidor, 1946) is set in Argentina, and tangos continually remind us of this, just as cajun music is ever present in *The Big Easy* (Jim McBride, 1986). And there are individual sonorities that fulfill the same function: an accordion alerts us to the fact that we're in France, the Westminster chimes tell us we're in London, bagpipes place us in Scotland. Music can also inform us about time. Christmas music in Christmas films is an obvious example, from *It's a Wonderful Life* (Frank Capra, 1946) and *The Holly and the Ivy* (George More O'Ferrall, 1952) to *Comfort and Joy* (Bill Forsyth, 1984) and, as already mentioned, *Die Hard*. On a grander scale, there is music to locate a film in history: either music of the period in which the film is set or music in the style of the period. Examples of the former might be the sounds of the High Renaissance that stand shoulder to shoulder with Peter Maxwell Davies's original and very violent score in Ken Russell's *The Devils* (1971), set in the early 1600s; or Handel's music, more or less contemporaneous with the story in Kubrick's *Barry Lyndon*, set in the middle of the eighteenth century. For an example of pastiche, which is altogether more common, one might mention the pseudo-baroquery of George Fenton's music in *Dangerous Liaisons* (Stephen Frears, 1988). In most of these cases, it is not so much the music itself that Adorno and Eisler would have considered clichéd as the use of it.

However there are also plenty of musical clichés. Once the sound of the Western was established, it was never really shrugged off. Fiddles and mouth organs, folksongs and hoedowns, the parlour tunes of Stephen Foster, revivalist hymnody and the rhythmic galloping of horses' feet: stir it all together and you have the classic Western score.

By much the same token, the later *films noirs* all tend to have jazz scores, and not just any sort of jazz: it is slow, sultry and cool, like the films themselves. Miles Davis's trumpet in Louis Malle's *Ascenseur pour l'échafaud* (1958) is a good example. But fast, loud modern jazz is used for representations of mental or physical chaos in, say, *The Naked Kiss* (Samuel Fuller, 1964) or *Repulsion* (Roman Polanski, 1965) or John Cassavetes's *Shadows* (1959).

Rather harder to explain is the quasi-archaic sound regularly concocted by composers to represent ancient civilisations. You hear this music in *Spartacus* (Stanley Kubrick, 1960), *The Fall of the Roman Empire* (Anthony Mann, 1964) and any number of other toga flicks. The melodic lines will be modal, the chords will move in parallel, generally in intervals of fifths and fourths, there will be brass and there will be drums. Strangely enough, it is precisely these same elements that serve to convey the idea of 'natives' or indeed 'savages' – seen or unseen, noble or not. One might compile a very long list of these, but here are four examples offering some ethnic diversity: Nigerian natives in *Sanders of the River* (Zoltán Korda, 1935), Hindu natives in *Black Narcissus* (Powell & Pressburger, 1947), native Americans in *Broken Arrow* (Delmer Daves, 1950), Indian Muslim rebels in *North West Frontier* (J. Lee Thompson, 1959): their music is almost interchangeable.

Another cliché that Adorno and Eisler singled out was the pervasive use of the *leitmotif*. This concept is most often associated with the nineteenth-century music-dramas of Richard Wagner and especially with his operatic cycle *The Ring of the Nibelung*. Individual themes represent individual characters, and so, at its most blatant and least interesting, the *leitmotif* will announce the entrance of a character rather in the manner of a personal fanfare. It often functions like this in Hollywood. Wagner applied his themes more subtly. For example, a *leitmotif* in the orchestra might suggest a character who is not present on stage, letting the audience know (if they're listening hard) that the one singing on stage is thinking of the one whose music we are hearing. Moreover, Wagner used his *leitmotifs* to stand for all manner of abstract concepts and emotions, in all manner of combinations. Claude Debussy, by no means an out-and-out critic of Wagner's works, nevertheless found little subtlety in *The Ring*, objecting to what he heard as a passing parade of musical signposts. For much the same reason, Adorno and Eisler objected strongly to the overuse of the *leitmotif* in film. And this was long before John Williams attempted to out-Wagner Wagner in *Star Wars* (George Lucas, 1977).

*

As a general rule, clichés begin as fashions, and so to understand how some of the more virulent musical habits arose in the movies, it is worth, briefly, looking at where film music came from.

There was a time when virtually all film composers also wrote for the concert hall. Film music grew out of the classical tradition and, especially in Hollywood, most of the great names in early film music were born in Europe, particularly in the old Austro-Hungarian empire. During the 1930s – the first decade of talking pictures – hundreds of exiled Jewish intellectuals and artists arrived in the United States, among them Erich Wolfgang Korngold, Franz Waxman and Miklós Rózsa. These composers brought with them late-Romantic and expressionist styles that were European to the core.

As a child, Korngold had gone, on the recommendation of the late-Romantic composer Gustav Mahler, for lessons with Mahler's friend Alexander Zemlinsky. Another pupil of Zemlinsky's, later his brother-in-law, was the expressionist composer Arnold Schoenberg. As a young man in Vienna, Korngold had written concert music and operas, including *Die tote Stadt* and *Das Wunder der Heliane*, which were admired by two of the greatest opera composers of all time, Richard Strauss and Puccini. After he settled in Hollywood, Korngold applied his operatic skills to the swashbuckling films of Michael Curtiz. *The Adventures of Robin Hood* (1938), *The Private Lives of Elizabeth and Essex* (1939) and *The Sea Hawk* (1940) all sound like operas without the singing. And of course this is how and why those *leitmotifs* got into films.

Franz Waxman composed *Bride of Frankenstein* (James Whale, 1935), *Rebecca* (Alfred Hitchcock, 1940) and *Sunset Blvd* (Billy Wilder, 1950). Rózsa, whose Hollywood career began a little later, was responsible for *Double Indemnity* (Wilder, 1944), *Spellbound* (Hitchcock, 1945) and *The Lost Weekend* (Wilder, 1945). Max Steiner, who had been in America since 1914, composed the scores for *King Kong* (Merian C. Cooper, 1933), *Gone with the Wind* (Victor Fleming, 1939) and *Casablanca* (Curtiz, 1942). And we should add the name of another Jewish exile, the Ukrainian Dimitri Tiomkin. His film credits include Frank Capra movies such as *Lost Horizon* (1937), *Mr Smith Goes to Washington* (1939) and *It's a Wonderful Life*, four middle-period Hitchcock films, and a great many Westerns.

These composers and their imitators dominated Hollywood film-making in the middle of the twentieth century. All but Korngold continued into the 1960s (in Rózsa's case, the 1980s). Steiner and Waxman took their music into television, where the former worked on *Hawaiian Eye* and *77 Sunset Strip*, the latter on *Peyton Place* (Waxman had done the score for the 1957 Mark Robson film so it seemed natural to sign him up for the TV series, too). In particular, these composers established the norm – soon to be another cliché – that any film involving big ideas or big ambitions required an orchestra behind it. Even after film music had developed new tendencies with pop songs under the titles, or jazzy scores from American composers such as Elmer Bernstein, Tiomkin and Rózsa continued to be in demand for epics. Tiomkin composed *55 Days at Peking* (Nicholas Ray, 1963) and *The Fall of the Roman Empire*; Rózsa's best-known film score is *Ben-Hur* (William Wyler, 1959).

Today, there are still very few modern Hollywood blockbusters that lack a lush orchestral score, and the big-name film composers remain broadly in the tradition established by the likes of Steiner and Rózsa. John Williams, obviously, owes a marked debt to Wagner. He also draws on later European composers – Igor Stravinsky for the motor rhythms in *Jaws*, Prokofiev for those bold, unexpected modulations in *E.T.* (Spielberg, 1982). If it all sounds American to our ears, it is possibly because we have begun to associate this style of music with Hollywood (Adorno would have been appalled). Williams's great skill, and it should not be underestimated, is to give Hollywood what it wants, which is more of the same, but to do so with class and skill and subtle originality. Like his illustrious European-born predecessors, Williams has the ability to transform himself from project to project, while continuing to draw on musical styles and gestures from the broad tradition of nineteenth- and twentieth-century classical music.

New fashions will always come along, in film music as in all else, and in time they will turn to clichés. Since Thomas Newman began bringing his distinctive sounds to film music in the mid-1980s, and particularly since his score for *American Beauty* (Sam Mendes, 1999) and theme music for the HBO series *Six Feet Under* (2001–05), other composers for film and television appear to have been drawn to his instrumentation – marimba, tabla, synthesised 'junk' percussion, oboe – as well as his modal melodic writing and use of high, floating piano chords. It is hard to believe that Williams's score for *Catch Me If You Can* (Steven Spielberg, 2002) or Hans Zimmer's music for *Frost/Nixon* (Ron Howard, 2008) would have sounded quite as they do without the example of Thomas Newman. It should be added, however, that film composers as famous and busy as Williams and Zimmer (and probably Newman, too) can only manage their busyness by employing a team of assistants to orchestrate, elaborate and expand their musical ideas, so it might have been a minion and not the Great Men themselves who fell under Newman's spell.

Clichés in film music – and in other areas of film – are not, of course, immutable. One hardly needs to be a card-carrying postmodernist to recognise that it is possible to turn a cliché on its head and even revivify it so that it seems, for a moment, to be a brand new idea. Lawrence Kasdan's *Silverado* (1985) did just this for the Western; Bruce Broughton's score is not only in the tradition of the cowboy scores of yore, but is rather bigger and better than many of them. Similarly *Far from Heaven* (Todd Haynes, 2002) deals in the clichés of the domestic melodramas that Douglas Sirk once used to direct. The film is set in 1950s Hartford, Connecticut, where it's always autumn and red leaves fall elegantly from suburban trees, while behind respectable middle-class walls, respectable middle-class women wrestle with their husbands' homosexuality and their own growing attraction to the black gardener. An eighty-year-old Elmer Bernstein wrote the score for this one, recapturing the same kind of depiction of small-town life that he had created for films such as *To Kill a Mockingbird* (Robert Mulligan, 1962).

Casino Royale (Martin Campbell, 2006) is a film notable for taking the worn-out and increasingly laughable James Bond franchise and bringing to it good writing, good directing and good acting (Daniel Craig). Forty-four years after *Dr No* (Terence Young, 1962), and at least two decades after all but the most dyed-in-the-wool Bond fans had ceased caring about the films, the obvious approach would have been to go for laughs (since the audience was already laughing) and play up the self-parody. After all, the 1967 film called *Casino Royale* (Val Guest et al.), very loosely based on Ian Fleming's book of the same name, had been an early Bond spoof. The clear alternative to making a comedy was to put the beached whale of a franchise out of its misery and stop making the films altogether. It surely can't have crossed many people's minds that James Bond might be made to seem exciting again. But, alongside the elevation of creative standards, Bond was revived by addressing the clichés that had accrued over the years and subverting them one by one.

Part of this was a matter of role reversal. It is Bond, and not the 'Bond girl', who gets naked, just as it's Bond, not the girl, who says – and seems to mean – the words 'I love you'. It is also Bond who walks out of the waves in his swimmers, mirroring the shot of Ursula Andress in a bikini emerging from a shimmering sea as Honey Ryder in *Dr No*. Moreover, when a bartender asks the secret agent whether he would like his martini shaken or stirred, the new Bond replies testily, 'Do I look like I give a damn?'

But the biggest clichés are saved for the end, and this alone helps to freshen them up. Wicked Mr White (Jesper Christensen) answers his phone and a voice says, 'We need to talk.' He replies, 'Who is this?' Simultaneously, he is shot in the leg. Now '007' saunters onto the scene to supply the answer and the film's last line: 'The name's Bond. James Bond.' And, with that, Monty Norman's famous theme erupts over the closing credits. Suddenly this tired old bit of music sounds as thrilling as the first time we heard it, a musical cliché triumphantly reborn.

It was against such a backdrop of musical trends and clichés that the composer Bernard Herrmann shone so brightly. There was no lack of professionalism about Herrmann – he got the job done – but there was also very little of the chameleon. His scores jump out at you, in almost any context, as being the work of Bernard Herrmann. He had such a strong musical idiolect that one can usually spot his music within seconds. He used instruments distinctively and combined them distinctively. Yet more striking, whether one understood the technicalities or not, was his use of harmony, which typically blurred major and minor chords. You can hear these chords in films from *Citizen Kane* (Orson Welles, 1941) to *Taxi Driver*, while in *Vertigo* (Alfred Hitchcock, 1958) Herrmann's music delivers a real-time analytical exposition of the technique as he spells out his chords, note by note, rolling back and forth in contrary motion across the arpeggios. It's as though he is saying, 'See? This is how I do it.'

Herrmann's music is vital to *Vertigo*. This might be one of Hitchcock's greatest films, but it is also one of his least typical. The majority of the director's work is either light comedy masquerading as high suspense, or vice versa. *Vertigo* is neither. It is a profoundly sad picture, a study in hopeless obsession, and the music elevates what is essentially a tawdry narrative to the level of grand, romantic tragedy.

Music can do that to a film. In *Notes on a Scandal* (Richard Eyre, 2006), the story of a jealous middle-aged London school teacher reaches surprising heights of passion, thanks not only to the music of Philip Glass (a composer who owes a thing or two to Herrmann), but also and specifically to the high volume of much of that music. There are moments in the film when the score literally overwhelms the drama, drowning it out and, in the process, making the ordinary mythic.

Like Herrmann, Glass is a very distinctive musical voice and hard to miss. Glass has resisted aligning himself with any one director, but Herrmann will forever be associated with Hitchcock, in spite of scoring only eight of his fifty-odd films, seven if you don't count *The Birds*, which had no score but for electronic bird noises, supervised by Herrmann. Composers with strong musical idiolects can help create a house style for a director, if the partnership lasts long enough. Besides Herrmann with Hitchcock, one thinks of Nino Rota and Federico Fellini, Georges Delerue and François Truffaut, Michael Nyman and Peter Greenaway. And when it is a matter of choosing music from existing sources, a filmmaker's musical preferences can achieve something similar.

It is hard for a seasoned moviegoer to hear Bach's solo cello suites and not think of the later films of Ingmar Bergman. The director's use of music may be minimal, but it is always striking, and the sound of Bach – it was usually a *sarabande*, a slow dance in triple time – sticks in the mind. By the same token, New Orleans jazz or the Benny Goodman orchestra or the tunes of George Gershwin will bring to mind Woody Allen, though it is only the films set in and around New York City that actually feature vintage jazz, and only the comedies, from his first feature, *Take the Money and Run* (1969), to *Whatever Works* (2009). Allen's serious films tend to employ serious music – Varèse's *Ecuatorial* for the dream sequences in *Another Woman* (1988) and Schubert's G-minor string quartet for the murder story in *Crimes and Misdemeanors* (1989) – while films set beyond the Triborough area often use lighter classical music: Mendelssohn in *A Midsummer Night's Sex Comedy* (1982), Italian opera and popular classics in the London films *Match Point* (2005) and *Scoop* (2006) and, for that matter, a specially composed Philip Glass score in *Cassandra's Dream* (2007). There are also genre films, such as *Shadows and Fog* (1991), a comedy in the form of a German expressionist film that is full of the music of Kurt Weill. *Husbands and Wives* (1992) has no music at all except for Bubber Miley's sublime version of 'What Is This Thing Called Love?' over the opening and closing titles. So the vintage jazz association is intermittent. But often a filmmaker who uses strong music well imprints things on our memories that are not strictly accurate. We associate Hitchcock with Herrmann from just eight films, and Woody Allen with jazz from not many more.

Adorno and Eisler complained about films in which music was used simply to reinforce what was on the screen, but right from the beginning there have been examples of the opposite tendency with music used ironically. Cheerful or pretty music in tense situations is something of a favourite. Hitchcock did this memorably in *Strangers on a Train* (1951), associating the murder with the sound of a fairground organ playing 'And the Band Played On', and horror films have made much use of children's songs, musical boxes and other innocent musical sounds. Progressive rock band Goblin's jangly theme at the start of *Suspiria* (Dario Argento, 1977) shares the same instrumental timbres and the same mode – actually the very same notes – as the beginning of Mike Oldfield's *Tubular Bells* heard in *The Exorcist* (William Friedkin, 1973).

Badlands (Terrence Malick, 1973) might not be a horror film, but its two antiheroes, Kit (Martin Sheen) and Holly (Sissy Spacek), commit plenty of murders. The film is set in the American Midwest in 1959, and the recurrent music is from Carl Orff's *Schulwerk*. In the 1930s, Orff composed his rather basic pieces as learning tools for children to play on tuned percussion (xylophones and the like), and they are still used in some classrooms today. In point of fact, Orff had originally written the music in the hope of selling his whole teaching system to the Hitler Youth, but they never bought it. One probably shouldn't make too much of that connection in the context of Malick's film. Kit and Holly are not Nazis, but they are certainly youthful – Holly is just fifteen – and the music reminds us of this with every appearance, its simple innocence at odds with the killing on screen. Similarly, the chic foxtrot that opens Pier Paolo Pasolini's notorious *Salò* (1975) stands in ironic contrast to the shocking scenes of human degradation that follow.

Music has many possible roles in films. It can even be itself. And when music is seen as well as heard, it really becomes a player. As the US soldier Bob Johnson (real-life Sergeant John Sweet) reaches the organ loft of Canterbury Cathedral and sits down at the console in Powell and Pressburger's mystical wartime film *A Canterbury Tale* (1944), he not only fills the historic building with music, but also the whole of the final reel. The sense of attainment, achievement, relief and finally optimism is palpable. In contrast, Charles Aznavour's luckless piano player in *Tirez sur le pianiste* (François Truffaut, 1960) does more than get into trouble through his playing, he allows it to becomes a metaphor for his frustrations and his boredom. We watch him sitting expressionless in the café, tapping out Georges Delerue's infuriatingly catchy little tune.

In Jane Campion's *The Piano*, the instrument is something noble, almost alive. Ada (Holly Hunter) doesn't just express herself through the piano, she lives and breathes through it and will do anything to keep contact with it. In Scott Hicks's *Shine* (1996), the piano comes to symbolise a dangerous dream ('No one's ever been mad enough to attempt the Rakh 3!'), the agent of mental destruction for David Helfgott (Geoffrey Rush) as well as the path to some sort of redemption. *The Soloist* (Joe Wright, 2009) blends all these themes.

The Italian wedding music at the start of *The Godfather* (Francis Ford Coppola, 1972) demonstrates better than words the continuing links of the American Mafia families to their Sicilian homeland and its traditions. All the guests know the tunes. But by *The Godfather: Part II* (Coppola, 1974), at a similar outdoor party a continent away at Lake Tahoe, Michael Corleone (Al Pacino) is at pains to present himself as a model American citizen. The musical corollary of this is that the band no longer has any idea how to play a tarantella. When an old man tries to teach them the rhythm, he is mocked.

There's a similar example of history passing and musical traditions fading in *The Scent of Green Papaya* (Tran Anh Hung, 1993), as the film jumps from 1951 to 1961. In a scene in the early part of the movie, the father (Ngoc Trung Tran) is playing a *đàn nguyệt* – the two-string 'moon lute' – with apparent skill. In a later scene, his son is holding the instrument, turning it over in his hands as though wondering how it might work. Finally, he gives it a bit of a polish.

Tran's film has a very interesting score, part traditional Vietnamese, part Western contemporary, by Tôn-Thât Tiêt – the film was shot in France, and many of the credited musicians on the soundtrack are from the Paris-based contemporary-music specialists Ensemble Intercontemporain. It also features a composer, Khuyen (Vuong Hòa Hôi), as one of the main characters in the second part of the film, and it manages to show his occupation with some fidelity. He improvises, he scribbles (we see a sheet full of musical ideas), he rejects. The conventional Hollywood representation of the composer has inspiration striking, followed by a quick sprint to the piano and then the music pouring, fully imagined, out of the composer's fingers. In the same way, on-screen songwriting teams generally manage to come up with both words and music in little more than the time it takes to sing the finished song.

It is not just Hollywood that makes a poor fist of conveying the act of creating music. Even such celebrated European films as *Death in Venice* (Luchino Visconti, 1971) and *Three Colours: Blue*

(Krzysztof Kieslowski, 1993) don't really get it right. For one thing, we seldom see any work going on. Visconti gives Dirk Bogarde a little pair of glasses to make him look like Mahler (whose music we are listening to) and, in the process, turns Thomas Mann's Aschenbach from a writer into a composer, but apart from a few shots of a piano, there's little to connect him to his trade. Kieslowski at least tries to show us Julie (Juliette Binoche) composing. We see musical notation and hear a synthesised orchestra playing extracts, but somehow it is all too slick and easy. *Amadeus* (Milos Forman, 1984) does it better. At least one senses the work, the effort. We see and hear musical ideas being had, jettisoned, revised and re-orchestrated. If only the modern instruments on the soundtrack matched the eighteenth-century instruments on the screen!

But Hollywood has got the composer right at least once and, what's more, in a solidly mainstream film. As its title predicts, *The Glenn Miller Story* (Anthony Mann, 1954) shows us the main biographical events in the doomed bandleader's life, but, much more impressively, it also allows us to eavesdrop on the process of composition and, in particular, orchestration. In terms of the film's plot, the 'Glenn Miller sound' has been something of a Holy Grail. Anthony Mann shows its creation. Obviously it helps if the audience knows what it is listening for because they will recognise 'the sound' as it emerges.

To start with, there is no distinctive sound at all: the Glenn Miller Orchestra might be any big band. As the film progresses, the instruments proliferate into choirs and the harmonies get closer, but it is only when Joe, the trumpet player, splits a lip in rehearsal and Miller (James Stewart) is forced to rewrite his charts overnight that 'the sound' finally arrives.

'Clarinet lead. And I can harmonise it real tight, all in the same octave,' Miller says to no one in particular, reaching for the manuscript paper and rushing from the room.

Next, we see him seated at a table, writing the walking bass line of 'Moonlight Serenade', and as he does this we hear the line with simple piano chords. Then muted trombones add a syncopated accompaniment, then muted trumpets, and finally unison saxophones join in, playing the last line of the chorus.

As Miller works, the camera pulls back as though to make room for this expanding sonority. At last, that clarinet lead emerges, swathed in close-harmony saxophones, and the picture dissolves to the rehearsal room, beginning tight on the bell of the clarinet. Slowly the camera pulls back, once again, to show us the whole band with Miller conducting. There's a close-up of Miller, listening, looking pensive, looking pleased, before dissolving into another image of him, still conducting, but now in a tuxedo. The band is in a dance hall, scores of young men and women are dancing to 'Moonlight Serenade' and Miller's wife, Helen (June Allyson), is seated at a table looking on. She reaches round to the back of her neck where, we may assume, the hairs are on end.

When the band's trumpets and trombones stand up and the crowd bursts into spontaneous applause, Si Schribman (George Tobias), Miller's backer, turns to Helen excitedly.

'It looks like he's got it, maybe,' says Si. 'Listen to those kids!'

'But there's no maybe about it, Mr Schribman,' Helen replies, firmly. 'That's it. That's the sound.'

Throughout these changing scenes the music hasn't stopped, it has grown. It has gone from a simple bass line to the full Glenn Miller Orchestra sound. It has played a role. Indeed, it has played the principal role.

FIVE COMPOSERS

Ennio Morricone

The composer Ennio Morricone has had a stellar career in films, both in Europe and the United States. One of his achievements is virtually to have invented the sound of the 'Spaghetti Western'. Anyone with even a passing interest in films can whistle the first few notes of his 'coyote' theme from The Good, the Bad and the Ugly *(Sergio Leone, 1966). He lives in Rome, in a spacious apartment near the Campidoglio, and that's where we had this conversation in December 2006.*

ANDREW FORD: I've just been watching the director's cut of *Cinema Paradiso* [Giuseppe Tornatore, 1988], a film that contains much of the history of early Italian cinema, and enjoying once again your music for the film. What drew you to this project?

ENNIO MORRICONE: I was charmed and fascinated by a scene at the end of the film, and this is what persuaded me to write the music. In this scene, there is a kind of history of cinema through clips of kisses from various films, assembled into a sequence which correspond to a logic, not forced by the director, but a natural logic which comes about from the events of the film. This also says something about the recent history of Italy, because the parish priest does not want the people to see the kisses. So they had been edited out of the films, but the projectionist has put them together in a sequence. This scene convinced me I should do the music for this movie.

AF: So is that normally the way you work on a film: you are inspired by a particular scene and that leads you into the sound of the music?

EM: No. Generally not. This was a specific film that hit me. I shouldn't have been able to accept it, and I had already rejected it – I had to do an American movie – but this final scene of kisses convinced me to do this film and to refuse the American film. But it's not a general approach. It's just what happened with this movie. And then when I saw everything that was in the movie – the events leading up to this particular episode – I understood it was a very beautiful film. It was coherent, the way the director pieced everything together, the whole narration: there was nothing left hanging. Afterwards, when I read the script that Franco Cristaldi sent me, that confirmed that the final scene was the important part for me. Then I understood that everything else was important, but that was later on.

AF: Is it possible to describe, either in relation to *Cinema Paradiso* or another film, how you get your initial musical ideas? And also what they are: whether they're thematic or instrumental or what?

EM: It depends a little upon the dialogue that one has with the film director. Later, I reflect on the music, after having spoken with the director, having seen the film, or after having read the script or the summary or the story, and knowing the way the director works. And the idea comes for how to set the music in the film. This is in general. Then there are particular cases where, from seeing the film, the idea arrives quickly and sensationally – like lightning! It almost stuns you the way it comes. When it happens this way, the idea is generally very good, because it comes out of the story or the images. And one example of this is *Novecento – 1900 –* by Bernardo Bertolucci [1976], that I composed practically in the dark! I wrote down my musical ideas in graphic symbols while I watched the film. Of course that was just the starting point. I had to develop the ideas later. But I didn't compose anything new, I only developed the ideas that arrived with this vision in the dark.

AF: In *Ripley's Game* [Liliana Cavani, 2002], music is part of the plot, because Maria, Ripley's girlfriend, plays the harpsichord and she practises and she gives a concert. Does that mean that you are forced to think differently about the music? And does the other music, in a sense, come out of these moments in the film where the music is centre stage?

EM: In all films where an instrument is played by an actor, and the music becomes an integral part of the story, that music also becomes important in the score of the film. The experience I've had over the years (and other composers have had the same experience) is that this music is internal to the film, not external – it's internal because you see the source, and this is not a casual source, like a radio, but it is a source that expresses something of the protagonist, and also the person who plays the music becomes fundamental to the film. In that case the music was fundamental. But we only hear the entire piece in the final scene, and this completes the musical idea that has been proposed in small doses throughout the film, continuing under the closing credits.

AF: Another film I've been watching recently is Almodóvar's *Tie Me Up! Tie Me Down!* [1990]. In that film, it seems to me, the music had almost an active role, and sometimes an ironic role, too. For example, it conjures a sense of innocence at the beginning.

EM: It's certainly ironic, because the film itself was ironic. Ironic and also childlike in some way. This man is in love with this woman, and he ties her up and keeps her captive. But he doesn't want to kill her, or even rape her; he was in love with the girl and his actions were somewhere between the naïve and the paradoxical. That's why I wrote the music in that way – in collaboration with Almodóvar.

AF: When the suspense music comes, it can't be taken completely seriously because it has such strong echoes of Bernard Herrmann's music for Hitchcock. It tells us that this is not really a suspenseful moment.

EM: It's up to you. This story takes us to the limits of the paradoxical. If this is something that you notice, then what you say is correct. How much one discovers in the music will depend upon the individual filmgoer. One notices certain details and misses others. The degree to which certain musical styles will come to light depends a bit on your sensitivity and cultural background, and also on your approach to the film. I didn't notice the Hitchcockian music! Music leaves one free to interpret it. This is both the misfortune and the good fortune of music. It's not explicit.

AF: But the film's dialogue gives your music precise meanings, doesn't it?

EM: Rightly so.

AF: Can you think of any moments when you have put music into a film to say something that is not being said on the screen?

EM: All the time. I am not going to tell what you can already see and what is already being said. I try to enter the psyche of the characters and to express what they have inside them. To sum it up: I make explicit with the music what is implicit in the film.

AF: So it's like opera.

EM: In some ways, yes. Except that the music in a film has long pauses while in opera it runs through the whole story.

AF: In *Days of Heaven* [Terrence Malick, 1978], there is a piece of music by Camille Saint-Saëns – the 'Aquarium' from *Carnival of the Animals* – and your own music comes out of that, almost like a series of variations. Was that your idea?

EM: I took into account the fact that the director wanted to use this piece, so I had to connect my own score to this music somehow.

AF: It must be different for every film, but what sorts of advice do you receive from directors? Someone like Malick knows that he wants a particularly piece of music in his film, but in general do you get strong advice in terms of the kind of music you should write? And do you take it?

EM: There's always a discussion. It depends on the conversation with the director. That piece by Saint-Saëns: Malick wanted it and he put it in. There was no reason for me not to do as he wanted. But it's not always like that. Normally the director doesn't ask for anything like that. We find the way together. Sometimes the composer proposes something that is so obvious the director accepts it; sometimes he doesn't accept it and so we don't get along.

I often tell this episode. In *Lolita* [1997], the director Adrian Lyne came to Rome to listen to the themes that I had written. He told me, 'They are beautiful, these themes. But they are not immortal.' I replied to him, 'For them to be immortal, you have to wait a few years. It takes a bit of time. You can't say today if something is immortal.' Naturally he had to laugh, because it was such an obvious answer. But I wrote the theme again, it became immortal, and we put it in the film. Sometimes directors say things to try to improve what the composer has written, but normally with me that shouldn't be necessary. I write mostly for myself. Even before writing for the movies. I must be pleased with it first of all, and then the director, and then the audience and all the other people. There was another producer many years ago – he wasn't a real producer, he only produced that movie, and he wasn't very good – he put a clause in the contract with three conditions: the music in the film must be Mediterranean; it must be a great success; and it must be beautiful. I told him, 'No, I'm already out of the contract!' You can always object that it's not Mediterranean, nor beautiful nor … what was the other one? A success! How do I know if it's going to be successful? He was very naïve and of course we removed that clause. It was quite ridiculous. The composer must see the film and express himself freely. Naturally he must also have the imprimatur of the director otherwise there is no point in going into the recording studio and wasting money.

AF: Every film composer I've spoken to has complained about directors who use 'temp' tracks [temporary music placed against the film before the composer is brought in]. Some of them have refused to have anything to do with these directors. Have you come across temp tracks very much?

EM: Certainly. And then I always refuse the film. Because I would be feeling too much influenced by music, which may be appropriate – it's not that the choice [of temp track] was silly – but I didn't feel I could accept a film where I was led to imitate that music and it deprived me of the possibility of responding personally to the film. Sometimes something even worse happens. A director who knows that I would refuse a film [with one of these tracks] puts the temporary music in, but when he shows me the film he doesn't play it! This is even more serious, because all the opinions that he will give me about my music, when the time comes to record it, will go through the filter of the music that he has already put with it. I know this happens, and when I know it is happening or I can guess that it's happening, then I ask, 'Have you used temp music?' Then they let me hear it. If it's not very important, I accept the job nevertheless, but if it's too overwhelming I refuse it. But there is this serious danger that its influence remains, and yet I don't know about it. So my ideas are in competition with this music that the director has put there. This can lead to very serious mistakes at the recording stage, because there the director's point of view stems from what he has already edited. It's like a first love: you never forget it! The first application of the music on the film remains imprinted on the director's mind. Even if that music is very ugly, it remains with him like something fundamental that gives a certain impulse to his images. Even if it's worthless. It takes the composer's balls away – excuse the expression. Well, his brain anyway. What we lose is the process of reflection.

AF: Who are the film composers who you admire?

EM: There are films ... I don't want to enter down this path. Because I don't want to name names. As soon as you start naming certain names, you forget others. And also because there is an international tendency in film music for the credited composers not actually to write the music – they get other people to write it for them. They might produce a rough sketch, but the orchestration is left to others. This is one of the most important parts of the job, it can be more important even than the creative phase from the composer. It's a very serious thing. I never heard that Beethoven would have an orchestrator, or Musorgsky or Rimsky-Korsakov. Orchestration is part of the profession and the creativity of the composer. This habit in the movies started with songs in musicals where the orchestration and the arrangements are done by others, and now it extends to film scores. We can see it in the cinema in the final credits. At the start of a film we see the name of a composer, but in the closing credits we find that the orchestration, arrangements, et cetera are the work of others. This, to me, is a very serious handicap and stops me from being able to give real judgments. Certainly I hear beautiful things and things that are less beautiful. But if something is beautiful, who is responsible? The use of orchestrators in the cinema can only be for one of three possible reasons: either the composer cannot compose, or else he's lazy – he has the ability, but he's too busy and so he leaves it up to others – or he's accepted too much work … They should accept only the jobs they can do – that's if they can write in the first place. If they can't compose, well they shouldn't even be working. But some directors wouldn't know about that.

AF: Your own music is sometimes quite intricate. In particular I'm thinking of the way you tend to superimpose ideas on top of each other, moving at different rates but fitting together. I guess *The Mission* [Roland Joffé, 1986] is one of the most blatant examples of that. You can only achieve this level of complexity by writing it down.

EM: This is normal. Sometimes the elaboration is explicit, as in *The Mission*, where there are three fundamental elements in the film that, at the end, all flow together. It gives the sense of this community between the priests and the Indians, between the history of the music that had arrived with the priests, the music of the Renaissance, and of that moment in history in the 1700s – a flowering of instrumental music that came after the Council of Trent. This coming together is something that most people don't pick up, but as the composer I wanted to have these three elements that can be used in different combinations: one and three, one and two, two and three, and then one, two and three together. In this film it is rather explicit. In other cases, there are some aspects of the score that are private to the composer, and so these combinations of counterpoint don't come to light, but they are there. All this must be written down by the composer. You can't have someone else writing it. I insist on this, because I consider it one of the most unethical practices of these people.

AF: We should talk about Sergio Leone and your invention of the sound of his Westerns. Is it possible to say where that came from?

EM: It comes from the impression made by the film, from one's own studies and experiences. The composer's contribution is the sum of his experiences. When, in *The Good, the Bad and the Ugly*, there is the theme with the voice of the coyote, it means that the composer wants to add to the sound of the music, the sound of reality – of a possible reality. This retrieving of real sound was already there in *A Fistful of Dollars* [1964], and I also drew from real sounds in other films. But in this third Leone film it was more explicit than the others because those sounds of birds, animals – there was more than one, not only the coyote, there was also this bird – all these things are part of the written score. How did it come to my mind? Well these things are a bit strong, but they were suitable for Leone because his films are always so over the top. The stories that are being conveyed, and even more the protagonists, are always extremely quixotic and picaresque, and so in those films I could use unusual themes to convey the story to the audience. But you can't do this in every movie! You must usually be more measured. In Leone's films I was able to use these sounds, but in others you can't.

AF: I suppose there was a moment when you were working with Sergio Leone that people might have thought there was a certain type of Ennio Morricone film score, but since then you seem to have gone out of your way to prove exactly the opposite. I wonder whether you take a certain pride in your versatility as a film composer.

EM: In the other Westerns I worked on I didn't imitate the sounds I invented for Leone. Because of certain things that I had done in *A Fistful of Dollars*, Sergio Leone always wanted the same, because they had been successful before and so he wanted me to repeat them. And so we went on like that, with many variations, in *For a Few*

Dollars More [1965] and *The Good, the Bad and the Ugly*. But in *Once Upon a Time in the West* [1968] it was completely different. Everything changed, and also in our heads everything had changed. Leone, too, finally changed his mind and he understood that we had to move on, that we couldn't just stay the same. Because he used to say, 'No, no, you have to do it again! I want you to do the trumpets! In the duel you must have the trumpets! It went well before, so you have to continue like that!' Naturally, I discussed this with him, and I told him that he was wrong. He insisted, and then at some stage, even with many variations – because you have to be careful to have variations, and you must be able to perceive that they are variations – the approach was always similar. So if you compare the first and the third films, if you think of the musical symbols in the *The Good, the Bad and the Ugly* – the voices with the coyote theme for the 'Ugly', the sound of the *arghilofono* – a large, clay ocarina – for the 'Bad', and then the recorder for the 'Good' – these symbols, which are under the opening titles, are something completely different from the sound of that whistle in the first film, which Leone had wanted for the third time!

AF: I understand that you don't want to single out particular composers …

EM: I don't remember particular cases …

AF: Are there any moments in film where you regard the absence of music as a masterstroke?

EM: I remember a particular film where there is no music except for some trumpet sounds. *The Hill* [Sidney Lumet, 1965], starring Sean Connery, was a certain sort of film. It didn't need music, and it wasn't done. It all works very well. Music is not absolutely necessary. Sometimes music becomes a bad habit. Sometimes it has happened that I've been asked to compose the music that the director wanted, and I've told him if you do this film without, it will be much better. But he wanted the music and the result was just a big noise, so overwhelming that nothing emerged from it, because the music was covered by all the other essential elements, the noises in the film. And I told the director, 'You know, leave it. Leave the music out.' But he said, 'No, you must do it.' It was a film by Sergio Corbucci, he was the director. 'Let's not do the music,' I told him. 'No, no, you must do it, you must do it …' And then you couldn't hear anything! The music must be on its own. With Leone, the music seems to work better than with others, because the music is on its own. He had good intuition for when the music had to have a clear meaning, and when it has that meaning you must take away all the other elements of sound in the film – or else reduce their volume a lot and take some out completely. Because the brain – the hearing – isn't able to discern more than two elements of a different nature. We can't follow three conversations. We don't know what's happening. It's a matter of perception. The mixing process is where the director makes the decision to reduce the levels of some sound, or cut them, and to elevate sounds while excluding others. The final mixing produces the final musical result. In the mixing, the music also belongs to the director.

AF: Do you think sound effects in today's movies tend to be too loud?

EM: Sometimes directors want that. But it's not a trend, it depends on the individual case. But even with Leone, he multiplied the volume of the whip sounds and the punches; when someone was punched in the face it sounded like slamming the door. It was only a punch in the face, but he made the sound enormous. I remember in *Giù la testa – A Fistful of Dynamite* [1971] – he had the train crash done many times, but he said, 'It's not enough, it's not enough.' So then he put all these collisions together and finally made one big collision out of them. He multiplied the crashes! The audience sees only one crash and hears only one, but he had superimposed all the crashes to give it more strength. He was very sensitive to sound, but also good about isolating it from the music. And that's fundamental.

Richard Rodney Bennett

Although first and foremost a composer of music for the concert hall, and once a standard bearer of the avant-garde (he was Pierre Boulez's first pupil), Sir Richard Rodney Bennett is a remarkably flexible musician. Classical pianist, jazz pianist, jazz singer: he has been all these. This kind of facility is very useful in film work, and Bennett wrote his first score to a feature film when he was just twenty-one. We spoke in his New York apartment in April 2006.

ANDREW FORD: Can you think of a moment in films that has turned on its use of music?

RICHARD RODNEY BENNETT: When I was in Paris as a student, I saw a movie with Jeanne Moreau called *Ascenseur pour l'échafaud – The Lift to the Scaffold*. The music was by Miles Davis, and I don't know whether he wrote it especially, or whether it was adapted from things he'd done, but it was Jeanne Moreau tramping through the streets of Paris in a trench-coat, smoking Gauloises – in black and white – and on the soundtrack Miles Davis was breaking your heart. She wasn't doing anything. I mean, not that she's not a great actress, but the music was so important, because it was saying all of the things that she wasn't saying. That's what I loved.

AF: How did you end up in films yourself?

RRB: Well, like many of the things in my life, my early days were incredibly important to me. I was madly in love with composers;

I was in love with the idea of being a composer, and I always pretended to write music. I mean, before I could read music I was sort of scribbling away and giving it terrible titles. I was aware that people like Britten and Walton and John Ireland and Vaughan Williams and Arthur Bliss had written film music; it was just part of their life, so it wasn't anything exotic. It was the last days of the real composers doing film scores. The same thing happened, quite largely in France, less so in America for geographical reasons because of Hollywood being so far away. So those scores were coming out when I was a child – not that I went to see the films because I wouldn't have been allowed to – but they were part of daily life. When I was about sixteen, I was at school in Reading, a public school, and I went to the movies quite often to see movies that I thought would be sexy, like *A Streetcar Named Desire* [Elia Kazan, 1951]. Of course it had this marvellous score by Alex North and I sat there just transfixed. I mean the film was excellent, but the music was wonderful. And I'm talking about film music, I'm not talking about symphonies. Shortly after that I saw *On the Waterfront* [Kazan, 1954] – Leonard Bernstein – and while I was at the Royal Academy I remember seeing *East of Eden* [Kazan, 1955], which for all kinds of reasons knocked me dead. And *East of Eden* had a score by Leonard Rosenman, who was a student of Schoenberg. These scores were speaking a language that I understood, they were speaking a contemporary language, not avant-garde, but they were composed by people who had heard Stravinsky, and who had heard Bartók and who had heard Schoenberg. It was so important to me, and I suddenly thought, 'I can do that!' I don't mean I can be as good as them, but that's what I wanted to do. I knew I couldn't ever earn my living writing chamber music. So all the time I was in Paris as a student, and even before that at the Royal Academy, I was going to the movies. And I was listening to scores by those composers I've named, and people like Elmer Bernstein, and I was so aware of what was going on. So, one of my composition teachers in London, a lovely man called Howard

Ferguson, knew that I could write movie music, because he knew that I was facile, he knew that I was quick and he knew that I had a very good ear and responded to things, none of which are huge virtues – well, the good ear is a good thing … But, he knew I could do it. He put me in touch with a very, very nice man called John Hollingsworth, who was the assistant conductor at the Proms, but who was also in a way the second major musical director in England. The first of course was Muir Mathieson, who held movie music back for about fifty years. But John was interested in all kinds of things, all kinds of music. And he gave me my first film. It was a documentary about insurance, which is not quite as jokey as it sounds, because it was a documentary about why insurance happened, and it started with the Great Fire of London. Well, that's all right to write music for. I didn't see it until many, many years later, because it was put together from etchings and drawings and documents and so on from the various periods. I can remember that I was given 'lengths', which I thought was thrilling, and I wrote it, and it was recorded as it were next week, at Beaconsfield film studios, and my oboist was Léon Goossens, because he was doing studio work. I'd never heard music of mine played by an orchestra before. I remember standing there when the downbeat came on the main titles and practically bursting into tears, and I'm not being soppy, but it was just so fantastic. Anyway, there's one important name that I haven't mentioned and that's Elisabeth Lutyens, who was a giant influence on me in all kinds of ways, particularly because she was a twelve-tone composer, which was not two-a-penny in London, as you can imagine.

AF: This is still the early 1950s?

RRB: Well, I left school in 1953, and I would've met Liz in 1955 or so. She was a twelve-tone composer; she was on-and-off an alcoholic; she was a very dramatic lady indeed, and she did movie music. She was always scuffling wildly to get some score done to be played in two days, and she had this bass voice, and she would always say, 'I've got to write forty minutes in the next two-and-a-half days, and I don't know how I'm going to do it.' Well, of course, that was thrilling to me. Thrilling. Liz and I fell out a lot, and she never gave me work, but I was there when she was doing it, and I was in love with the idea of being a professional composer. I remember Stephen Kovacevich when he played my piano concerto said to me, 'What is your ambition as a composer? What is the one word …?' And I said, 'To be professional.' And he was rather shocked – I think he thought I would say something sort of poetic and dramatic; I said, 'No, to be professional.' That was what it was: I knew I was talented, but I wanted to be professional, I wanted to earn my living, I wanted to work. And I still do. I'm still in love with the idea of the phone ringing and someone saying, 'Can you write a piece for tuba and string quartet?' And I'll say, 'Well … hmmm … I wonder.' There is a little thrill that comes back.

AF: I think the earliest film of yours I know is *Billy Liar* [1963], which I like very much.

RRB: *Billy Liar* was the first time I ever worked with John Schlesinger, who, of all the directors I've ever worked with, was the single most musical, most infuriating and most exciting. And *Billy Liar* was the kind of film that was being made at that time – the new English film, you know, with Tom Courtenay and Julie Christie, who appeared, I think, for the first time. It was fun for me, because Billy was a fantasist. I mean, he imagined his own country, his own national anthem, and, you know, romantic scenes with impossible film stars, which of course involved music. The hardest directors to work with are the directors who think they know about music and can tell you about music. It's like me telling somebody how to construct a car – I know nothing about cars – but some directors try. John Schlesinger was truly musical, he came from a very musical family, he had been listening to music since he was born, and he could refer you to whatever. This is why he was so difficult to work with. In *Far from the Madding Crowd* [1967] we nearly killed one another we were so infuriated, because I could never get what he wanted. And of course it's very hard to put music into words, I mean, you tell me what the end of [Stravinsky's] *Symphonies of Wind Instruments* is about, right? In words, not at the piano. You might say, 'It's grand, hieratic, this fantastic, distorted ...' I don't know what you're talking about if I haven't heard it. So John and I would drive one another crazy. But he laid, of course, temp tracks – which means pieces of music that are mainly for the distributors, I think, to see what the scene would be like with music – and his taste was so excellent. At the end of his life I did a film for him which I loved, but it wasn't a success. It was a TV movie, *The Tale of Sweeney Todd* [1997]. It had Ben Kingsley and that wonderful actress Joanna Lumley as Mrs Whatever-Her-Name-Was. On the temp track John Schlesinger used the Poulenc *Concert champêtre*. Instead of blood-and-thunder and screams and bangs, he laid this elegant, sort of prickly music, which was so clever. And I said, 'Well, what you should've laid actually was Stravinsky's piano concerto,' which is one of those scary neoclassical things. But he was so right. So that was a perfect example of the director telling you what he wanted by choosing what he wanted, choosing the music.

AF: One of the musical moments I remember best from a film you scored was that extraordinary opening of *Far from the Madding Crowd*. Nicolas Roeg's camera is looking out to sea, then it turns around very slowly to show us the cliffs of Thomas Hardy's Wessex.

RRB: It was a very stark shot; it was practically colourless. It wasn't a riot of greenery. John had directed it like that so you saw Julie Christie on a horse, way off in the distance, and I had this good idea of using just a single instrument to begin that film. I had worked in some orchestra pit, I don't know where it was, with Jimmy Galway, and I heard him playing the piccolo in quite a low register and I thought, 'Oh my God, that's so beautiful.' I just had Jimmy Galway playing the piccolo, which was not as sumptuous as a flute, it was slightly more, how can I say, it was slightly more stark, and if you like, slightly more pagan. It was magic. But that was a very demanding film to do, and in a way, possibly it's one of my best three scores.

AF: What about *Nicholas and Alexandra* [Franklin J. Schaffner, 1971]? Where did that very Russian accent come from?

RRB: I've got two movies which I did slightly with my tongue in my cheek, not joking, but slightly too knowingly. One is *Nicholas and Alexandra* and the other is *Lady Caroline Lamb* [Robert Bolt, 1972]. I was asked to do this enormous epic, *Nicholas and Alexandra*, by Sam Spiegel, the producer, and I had to do it in quotes; it wasn't genuine, it didn't come from my heart. Whereas, *Far from the Madding Crowd*, in a funny way, did come from my heart. I spent a lot of weeks listening to minor late-nineteenth-century music – Lyapunov, you know, that sumptuous thing. It was like learning a little language to speak, because I knew that the music had to go from late-nineteenth-century gorgeous tunes to horror. I enjoyed it very much, but I can't say it was from my heart. There was one dreadful thing that happens in films I'm afraid. Of course Rasputin was a character in [*Nicholas and Alexandra*], and there was a ghastly sequence where they did everything to him to try and kill him. And I went to town. I did the full Ligeti, I mean the full horror music. Which is one of the nice things about doing movie music, you can try out these mad things. They were so anxious to get the groans and the chains, that they turned the music down to a sort of pianissimo, which was heartbreaking for me, because I thought everyone in the cinema would be reeling with horror, instead of which it was just a sort of mishmash.

AF: I guess apart from John Schlesinger, the other director I most associate you with is Sidney Lumet.

RRB: I loved working with Sidney Lumet. He got me to work on *Murder on the Orient Express* [1974] and on *Equus* [1977]. *Equus*, you know, had a very successful score on the stage, by Mark Wilkinson, who was a sort of avant-gardish composer. But when I saw the film, I realised you couldn't possibly do it like that on the screen and I decided the music ought to stand back and be very compassionate and grave and serious. So I scored it for ten violas, eight cellos and six double basses. Frederick Riddle was my lead viola, and every good viola player in the country was working for me. It's a sort of Henze/Stravinsky/neoclassical grave, beautiful score. I like it very much. But, as I've said, I'm very specific about where I put music, and I do not put it any old place, and so in the score, in fact, there was only about twenty minutes of music. When we came to do the LP, as it was in those days, unfortunately we had to have lots of bits of Richard Burton emoting on the soundtrack, which is *not* a good idea.

AF: I thought he was a terrible over-actor.

RRB: Terrible! And such a prick. But *Equus* is a score I liked very much. I took a very definite stance that I was going to do only this very grave, slow, serious music, I wasn't going to go along with that hysteria at all. And, bless them, they let me do it.

AF: Sidney Lumet also gave you your head on *Murder on the Orient Express*.

RRB: He was a lovely guy to work with. Unfortunately he came up with a movie later on which I looked at and I thought, 'Oh I can't do this.' He's not a comedy director and he attempted to direct a comedy and I got myself out of it and he was very offended and that's showbiz.

AF: But we must talk about *Murder on the Orient Express*. This is a good example of a composer bringing something to a film that wasn't there. How did you get to the point where you invented that music for the train?

RRB: My ambition, always, has been to add something that wasn't there before. I was talking to you earlier about scores that impressed me: *On the Waterfront*, *East of Eden*, and so on. But there was one other that I saw, I think when I was a student of Boulez in Paris, and it was called *The Bad Seed* [Mervyn LeRoy, 1956]. It was a very good second-rate movie, if you see what I mean. Very good. And it was about a child murderess, who was just doing horrifying things to people, and nobody knew. At the beginning of that film, there's a sequence where the mother and the next-door neighbour are getting this little girl ready to go off to a school picnic and it's all sunshine and her hair's in braids, you know. And it's just adorable. But the music is saying, 'Oh no, oh no, there's something terribly wrong going on here.' And I remember thinking – and I was probably twenty, twenty-one – *that's* what film music should be about. If one can do that, if one can add something that wasn't there before, that's the best thing for music. And in *Murder on the Orient Express* I did have the chance, particularly in that famous scene where the train takes off, to do something that wasn't there before. So, I'm not a train person. I like travelling by train actually, but I certainly didn't want to do chuff-chuff cheerful music. That was a glamorous train. There's a famous story of Bernard Herrmann seeing that sequence and saying to Elmer Bernstein, 'Bennett got that completely wrong. That was a train of death!' Elmer told me. It wasn't a train of death, it was a very good time for everybody, and it was extremely glamorous. So when I saw that thing, I realised I could make something incredibly glamorous out of that sequence, not a train of death at all, but a waltz, a ballet. And that's what I did. I was always in love with Ravel, notably the *Valses nobles et sentimentales* and *La valse*. Stephen Sondheim had also heard those things and borrowed from Ravel in the best way possible when he wrote *A Little Night Music*. It was just at that time, just after *A Little Night Music*, that I got that gig, and so I did a huge waltz, which was a sort of third-generation Ravel waltz. I did enjoy myself and on the first day of recording I started with that, just to give the producers a taste of what they were in for. It was very hard to get the orchestra playing with a real sexy swing that early in the morning. Then I saw the director, Sidney Lumet, and the producer sort of huddling in a corner of the recording both whispering, and I said, 'Have I screwed up?' And they said, 'No, it's absolutely marvellous.' It was a very moving moment in my life. I knew I'd gone out on a limb, doing a huge waltz for a train, and it worked.

AF: And you changed the film.

RRB: I don't know about changing the film. It did add something that wasn't there before, like Alex North's music for *The Bad Seed*.

AF: So you don't agree with Bernard Herrmann, then, that music is essential to a film?

RRB: I don't believe music is essential to a film. No. I mean it might need just a thread of music every now and again, but no, music is not essential. I admire directors who have the balls not to use music. What is so awful, what horrifies me so much in music in movies today, is how they think it's compulsory to have this trickle going on, so that when music does come forward it means nothing, because you've been dimly listening to it for the past forty-five minutes.

AF: Joseph Losey was, I think, a very interesting director, and your paths crossed a few times.

RRB: I worked several times with Joe Losey, who was a marvellous, silly, musical, crazy director, and he did an adaptation of *A Doll's House* [1973] with Delphine Seyrig and I can't remember who else. (There were two being made at the time, one had Jane Fonda, one had Delphine Seyrig.) I went to the viewing cinema, and I sat there, and apart from the fact that they talked incessantly from beginning to end, there was a lot of sort of waltzing music and folk song and everything. And I said, 'Joe, don't put music in this movie. Don't do it. You don't need it.' And he looked at me pityingly and got Michel Legrand ... who's a marvellous composer, he was a big influence on me. But that movie shouldn't have had music. Should not.

AF: Speaking of Losey and Michel Legrand, didn't you compose a score for *The Go-Between* [1970]?

RRB: Yes, in 1970 I did the music for *The Go-Between* for Joe, and Harold Pinter wrote it. Joe was very difficult to pin down, he wasn't a verbal person, and he had this idea that the score – the movie was set in Norfolk in 1900, beautiful, Julie Christie, you know – the score should be electronic jazz. I couldn't tell what the hell he was talking about. Now *The Go-Between* is a movie about a child who had been corrupted, because the child is being used as a go-between between two extremely unsuitable people, a rich girl and a poor farmer who are having an affair. And everything comes out and ... it's a very frightening book. But the surface is beautiful. It's summer 1900, and I thought the music could do something serious and worrying. And I wrote a serious and worrying score that they didn't like, so they threw it out. It happened that year that I was teaching in America and so they got Michel Legrand, who's a perfectly marvellous composer, to do it. And I didn't like what he did, but there it is.

Michel Legrand was one of my big influences for various reasons. I mean, his virtuosity, his technical command are breathtaking, but there was one thing that he did – I think he started doing it probably in the '60s – which impressed me enormously, which I did forever after. It was to use little, what used to be called 'germs' – not an attractive word – little phrases which were all that the music was about. So you can sum the theme up in one little group of notes, and that is incredibly useful when you're doing film music, which has to be enormously plastic and flexible. You don't have to go on for sixteen bars. [Sings the first eight notes of Legrand's music for *The Thomas Crown Affair* (Norman Jewison, 1968)]: that's the whole tune. Michel Legrand was a composer who influenced me more than anybody I think, except Leonard Rosenman. Unfortunately, at a certain point, Michel Legrand started writing music of an extraordinary vulgarity, and he started copying himself, which is the worst thing you can do. Finding something you do that works, and then doing it over and over and over, louder and louder and louder. But at one time, he was astonishing, he was amazing. His score for *The Thomas Crown Affair*: that was genius.

AF: Your name comes up on the screen at the beginning of *Four Weddings and a Funeral* [Mike Newell, 1994], but isn't that mostly old pop songs?

RRB: I did music for a TV movie which became inordinately successful called *Enchanted April* [1992]. It was one of those Sunday-night movies, you know, with a pretty landscape and six players, and I did some very nice music for it, and it was directed by Mike Newell. So they got in touch with me when they did *Four Weddings and a Funeral*. Now, they had no idea what that film was going to do. They thought I was going to do a tasteful little number, and that's what I started out to do. I liked the film, I thought it was genuinely funny, but it didn't occur to me it was going to be a huge, international success. They had a couple of test screenings. One was in Santa Monica, and one was in Secaucus, which is a suburb of New York, and I went to the one in Secaucus. There was a very young audience, and they were completely flabbergasted by the film. And from all the questions they asked afterwards, they found out that it was going to be a colossal success with men under thirty. Well you can imagine, they put in a lot of music that would appeal to men under thirty, and they took out any chance I had of doing a score. Which is fine. Listen, this is a commercial gig, it's not fine art. I got paid, but there's practically nothing of my music left, except one very pretty love scene. And, P.S., I got sued by a French composer who said that I had stolen his music for some thriller that played on French television one night in 1983. And unfortunately it starts with the same four notes. And there's no way you can prove that you didn't happen to hear this tune and think, 'What a good idea, I think I'll steal that.' I had a call from Elmer Bernstein, whose name I seem to be dropping a lot, and he said, 'There's nothing you can do, you just have to pay up. It's happened to everybody.' You cannot prove that you didn't steal it. They even asked for a photocopy of the page in my diary to prove that I wasn't in Paris the day when this God-awful thriller with this God-awful score was shown on French television. As a matter of fact I was rehearsing in New York City with an oboe player. But what can you do? So you can imagine that the idea of *Four Weddings and a Funeral* doesn't actually make my heart leap up.

AF: Have you stopped composing for films? These days, it seems to be all concert music – and painting.

RRB: I don't need to write for movies anymore for financial reasons, because I've a perfectly good income from all the movies I've been doing over the past … forty years? Maybe more …

AF: More like fifty …

RRB: It's more than that, is it? Thank you! Some awful B-picture I did in 1958 with Anita Ekberg and Victor Mature is probably playing in Paraguay, and I'm probably getting, you know, sixty cents for it. But that's why I did it. I wanted to insure my future, so I could write the music I wanted to without worrying. I don't really want to do movies anymore, because movie music has turned into something else these days, and it's something I don't want to be associated with.

AF: Why not?

RRB: I'm a member of the American Academy of Arts and Sciences. It's because I was nominated three times for an Oscar. It means that I get sent about sixty videos and DVDs every year. The thrill wears off, actually, but I do watch quite a lot of new movies, and more and more these days I am aware that there is always music going on. Now we're going out to dinner. There'll be music in the restaurant, probably. There'll be music in the subway, there'll be music in the elevator. And it's not serving anything, it's not serving any purpose. I remember years ago I was doing music for an ill-fated television adaptation of Eugene O'Neill's *Strange Interlude* [Herbert Wise, 1988]. The producer said, 'Now Richard, you need to give us music to take us from the dining room to the front door.' I said, 'What do you mean?' He said, 'We need music. We need you to take us there.' I said, 'I'm not a conveyor belt, what do you mean? There's no emotional affect in these scenes.' And that's how it is. I remember seeing a film adaptation of a Stephen King novel, I can't remember what it was called, and at the end, I suddenly became aware, to my horror, that there had been music going on for the past two hours and I hadn't heard a note of it, because it was sub-audible. There was just a trickle going on. It's television, I think, that does it. Also, producers and directors tend to be twenty-five years old and are used to this constant trickle of music. Well, all my life, in films, I've tried to find the perfect place to put music. The spotting sessions where you choose where the music's going to go are extraordinarily demanding for me, because I'm always looking for the perfect moment, the perfect word, the perfect silence. That's when the music sneaks in. And it's not when the door opens and the kiss happens or whatever. It's something much more subtle than that. I love it and it's fascinating to do. And yet nowadays there's just music all over the place. It's like you turn on a tap and the music pours out.

Dick Hyman

Dick Hyman is a jazz pianist and composer, best known in his film work for scoring Moonstruck *(Norman Jewison, 1987) and for being the music director on a dozen Woody Allen films. I recorded the following conversation with him at his townhouse in Hoboken, New Jersey, one evening in April 2006.*

ANDREW FORD: Perhaps you could tell me first how your involvement in film began.

DICK HYMAN: Oh, my involvement with film, as with so many other things, began with my being a piano player for hire in all kinds of recording orchestras. I had played piano in *The Wiz* [Sidney Lumet, 1978], for example, and *The Godfather* and so forth. I was one of a gang of recording musicians in New York and we did all kinds of miscellaneous work, and some of my work is evident in those and many other films.

AF: The work you've done in films seems to fall into four categories: composing, of course; arranging; playing; and also, to some extent, choosing music. Maybe we could take these one at a time.

DH: Well, 'choosing' I think we ought to qualify. People often give me credit for choosing the recordings that Woody Allen uses in his films. I do not do that. Woody does that. Sometimes I might express an opinion about what old songs we might use for certain scenes, but mostly that's Woody's very excellent choice of old recordings.

AF: But when you play a tune ... Let me see, at the end of *Hannah and Her Sisters* [1986], I think that's you playing Rodgers and Hart's 'Isn't It Romantic?'

DH: Well, actually we're getting to be involved in a number of exceptions here. There are four of us piano players in that film. I'm one of them. Derek Smith, I think, is the man who plays 'Isn't It Romantic?'; and there are others as well. That was not really a scoring job or anything where I had responsibility.

AF: But when you *do* play, you presumably have some sort of say in how fast, how ... intimate ...

DH: Oh, sure. And I did do exactly that sort of job for the last film I worked on with Woody Allen, and that was *Melinda and Melinda* [2004]. There are two piano-playing scenes, and I was pretty astonished that the scenes had been shot and we hadn't even discussed what music was going to be played. And so the actors were reacting in a neutral way, because they weren't hearing anything. The camera focused on the pianist, and then there was a little dialogue as he appeared to be playing, but really they weren't hearing anything because Woody hadn't even decided what we would do. Later on in one scene it got a bit complex. Woody said we should have something classical here, to indicate that the pianist has had a classical education, and then one of the actresses takes over and continues what he has been playing. So all of that had to be retro-timed and the piece – that I *did* select, in this case – was a Bach Invention, and it needed to be started from the preceding scene and to bleed over into the following scene in order to make sense of the whole piece. And Woody accepted that notion and we got it together, but it was a little more complex than just putting in a recording or whatever.

AF: Sticking with 'choosing', are there any other moments in Woody Allen films where you did select the music?

DH: Yes. There are times when the director doesn't really care what's to be played, and the issue is whether he and the film company wish to pay for the use of a piece or whether they would be happy if I were to compose a piece, which is much less costly. That's a situation that a pianist–composer might run into: is he going to be performing somebody else's song, or shall he supply something 'neutral' in that respect? Of course you do get paid as the composer in that case, but not as much as the very large fees that have to be paid if you're playing a Gershwin or Cole Porter piece.

AF: With a couple of Woody Allen films in which you've been involved – I'm thinking of *Zelig* [1983] and *Sweet and Lowdown* [1999] – there's been, as it were, 'fictional' music required. You've been responsible for this?

DH: Yes. In *Sweet and Lowdown* [1999], the given was that there was this crazy guitarist – fictional guitarist – who idolised Django Reinhardt, the great French Gypsy guitarist, and the whole film was a sort of biography of this fictional character. Woody wanted him to be playing some numbers that presumably he would have learned from his hero, but he didn't want to make this guitarist into just a carbon copy of Django Reinhardt. The man should not sound exactly like Django, but he should have an equal facility and should have been exposed to other influences. So Woody suggested a number of titles which Django had recorded, and I suggested a number of titles of around the same era that he *might* have recorded, and we came to an agreement on those things. But mostly with the titles it's Woody's selection. I might intercede if I happen to know that a song was out of the era altogether and we're talking about something historical, but Woody is a practical musician and generally there's no disagreement about that sort of thing.

AF: What about in *Zelig*? Were you responsible for the big musical numbers, the Charlestons and whatnot, that gave the pseudo-documentary its period flavour?

DH: Yes. *Zelig* was somewhat different. There was the opportunity to do period music, and Woody liked the idea of having it be my original music. He supplied me with titles of fictitious songs: for example, 'You May Be Six People, But I Love You' and 'You Have Such Reptile Eyes' and others, which were supposed to have been written for the wild flapper era that Zelig found himself in, which would have been the flaming 1920s. I came up with some of the other things, because I found they were needed dramatically, and Woody approved my having written songs such as 'Doin' the Chameleon' and 'Chameleon Days' and a number of others. But we did use songs of the period, too, and we recreated certain things by Fanny Brice and by Paul Whiteman and the Rhythm Boys in order to have appropriate lyrics referring to Zelig. I'm a student of that period, musically, and what's more I like the music. I'm too young to claim to have grown up with it but I have always been involved in a large collection of old records and I'm comfortable in doing pseudo-songs of that time.

AF: This also relates to your work on *The Purple Rose of Cairo* [1985].

DH: Yes, that famous film in which the leading man steps off the screen and into the audience and promptly falls in love with Mia Farrow. There is music in there, much of it original but in the style, in this film, of the early 1930s. And things had to be worked out that involved a *maître d'* who suddenly acknowledges that nothing is the way it used to be and in that case he will break into a tap dance: that kind of thing had to be carefully planned and I wrote appropriate music for that. There were a lot of things that were fun to do, just digging into those old clichés, and I think everybody had a similar enthusiasm for that film.

AF: Walking here to your home from Hoboken station this evening, I had the Manhattan skyline alongside me. This is not only the skyline of most of Woody Allen's films, but also of another film for which you provided the music, *Moonstruck*.

DH: Well, *Moonstruck* was another New York film, you're perfectly right, although the interiors were shot in Toronto – I don't know if that's generally known – and we recorded the music in Toronto, because it was being done under the terms of a Canadian regulation. Norman Jewison, the director, is Canadian. I don't know where the famous bakery was. I believe I've heard that that was in New York. That score represented a decision reached early on at a conference with Mr Jewison to base a large part of the music on Puccini's *La bohème*. There is a scene in which Cher's character is being taken to see her first opera, which is *La bohème*, and in the book itself there are a great [many references] to Italian opera. And I always thought that Norman Jewison's direction of the film was operatic: the characters are somewhat over the top, they are highly emotional and they do sudden, mad things, and it reminds me, at any rate, of the classic Italian operas with characters you can't quite believe but they're singing beautifully. So that was the basic notion, but one which we refined. These, after all, are Italian Americans and the film is set in New York in the recent past, and the music ought to be in a genre which you might as well call Italian-American – you know, old Italian folk songs, Italian songs translated into English which have often been on the hit parade, songs that would be sung by Italian Americans: there's a very big subset of the pop-music business of the 1950s and '60s …

AF: Broadly speaking, the Dean Martin songbook.

DH: Yeah, that's right. And when the film editor happened to hear that Dean Martin record of 'That's Amore', that solved a problem which needed to be solved: how to open the movie in such a way that people understood that it was going to be a comedy. Because I was told that at the first viewing of the movie in a public theatre, nobody laughed for a half hour. They didn't understand that it was going to be funny. I had certain other ideas about how it might be begun. One problem, trying to follow through on my idea of having references to *La bohème*, is that *La bohème* has no overture: that was a blow to my plan. And I wrote a song, which is done instrumentally later on, which I thought might be called 'Mr Moon' [and open the film with] a 1950s vocal-group, hit-parade, tarantella kind of a song. But that didn't go over too well. Finally the film editor happened to hear the Dean Martin record and everybody knew that that set the tone for the movie.

AF: Well, when a film's called *Moonstruck* and one of its central characters works in an Italian bakery, it must be pretty hard to pass up a song that mentions the moon and pizza in its first line.

DH: Absolutely! And it's perfect for the playful Italian-American stereotype.

AF: You talked about some music that you had composed not going over well in the context of *Moonstruck*. Presumably you have other pieces, many of which you're doubtless extremely fond of, that remain in your bottom drawer for that same reason.

DH: Well, every composer … Let's put it this way: it's a rare composition which is direct from heaven-sent inspiration to your score pad. In film there are all kinds of opinions that have to be sought.

Everybody has an opinion, so there are many things that I've tried and had to reject. With Woody, I must say proudly that almost everything worked, and if it didn't work we were able to fix it quickly.

AF: You've worked so many times with Woody Allen that I wonder whether you know almost instantaneously if something's right or wrong. His films have a house style, musically as well as visually.

DH: Well, I suppose so. It just seemed to me, on those films we've named and pretty much all the others that I've worked on with him, that we both thought in the same terms. I think we both had a similar background of growing up with old traditional jazz and pop music; we both loved this period that was immediately before our times. So we had a meeting of minds. I can think of one time when we didn't, though. There was a scene in [the musical] *Everyone Says I Love You* [1996] in which a wonderful idea of Woody's was to have two principals taking a cab from Kennedy Airport into Manhattan, and the cab driver is apparently a man from India and he is wearing a turban and he breaks into song. And it was Woody's idea that the song would be 'Cuddle Up a Little Closer'. The first thing that needed to be done was to find somebody who could do a reasonable translation of 'Cuddle Up a Little Closer' …

AF: Into Urdu!

DH: I suppose it was. And that was successfully done. We had the man who did the translation do the singing, rather than the actor playing the driver, and we captured a nice performance of that with piano accompaniment. And then, as we did with most of the other songs in that film, we dubbed in the orchestra: the technique is that you eliminate the piano track and then you conduct the orchestra in synchronisation with the singing. So it was up to me to orchestrate it in an appropriate way, and I decided to go with all the bells and whistles of what little I know about traditional Indian music, using a sitar and various percussion instruments. And as soon as Woody heard it, he said, 'That's not it at all.' And he was right. It was overloading the gag, and as a comedy writer Woody understood that, and as a non-comedy writer I didn't understand that. But in the next session I had re-orchestrated it, given it a conventional schmaltzy background with a lot of strings, and that was the right way to do it.

AF: And there's an awful lot of Bollywood music that sounds just like that.

DH: That's right! Though this was before I was exposed to Bollywood.

AF: You said that your music overloaded the gag in that scene, but are there any moments in Woody Allen's films in which your music actually conveys the humour? Are there any musical jokes?

DH: Yes ... but you have to be careful. Sometimes the only person who understands the joke is the composer or the arranger. Well, if nobody else gets it, it's like a tree falling in the forest. You can't point it out to everybody – look how funny I am there! – because nobody really knows what you're talking about. So you learn not to do that, or to do it in a very subtle way so that it doesn't matter if the other people get the joke or not. There was another scene in that same movie in which the bank robbers make their escape through gorgeous countryside in the fall, with beautiful leaves and great scenic effects. They're rushing to get away from the police and lots of guns are being fired and there's yelling and screaming of tyres. In the previous scene, 'My Baby Just Cares for Me' had been sung and it seemed the right thing to do some very funny old-time chase music using that same song. That worked very well.

AF: Do you have any general theories about film music?

DH: Well, the rule used to be that if film music called attention to itself it was not fulfilling its job; it should always be felt and not intellectually registered. I'm not sure that is correct any longer, not in every case – or even the majority of cases – because a lot of times film music is trying to get a hit record. Even in the case of John Williams's famous score for *Close Encounters of the Third Kind*, that music is so vivid and works so beautifully, but it does call attention to itself. That is music that is meant to be heard, like an operatic score by Richard Strauss. Of course I have a professional interest, so when I hear a John Williams score, everything he does stands out to me.

AF: Bernard Herrmann said that music was essential to films. Would you agree?

DH: Music *is* essential. I saw a film recently – re-saw it, I'd seen it several times before – *Rear Window* [Alfred Hitchcock, 1954]. The music is all heard in a great echo, as though across the back yard. At times it focuses on a party in one of the apartments that is visible from our point of view; at times it focuses on a composer, in that same apartment, who is writing a great concerto; at times it's a hurdy-gurdy; there is music from people's radios. I thought that it was the work of a wonderful composer, somehow. And I watched the credits recently and saw that they were all separate recordings: there was something by Leonard Bernstein in there, there was a hurdy-gurdy arrangement of something by Harry Warren; and there was a number of other things. And if it wasn't a composer who put all those things together it was a really expert audio person. I watched and I hoped to find out his name but I didn't see anything in the credit. [He was Loren L. Ryder, and indeed his name does not appear in the credits.] But the music and sound really powerfully affect that film.

AF: Yes, and the night-time scenes when the radios are switched off and the composer isn't composing his concerto and everything is quiet are all the more striking for that.

DH: It's very well put together.

AF: Can you think of moments in films where the music has changed the meaning of what we are seeing?

DH: Well, there's that Orson Welles film, *Touch of Evil* [1958], that takes place in a Mexican border town. It was only recently put together, long after Welles's death [the so-called 'director's cut' of 1998]. What they used there was the very grave sound of a player-piano playing a very jolly Mexican waltz. It was so opposed to the grim action that was taking place on the screen that it lent everything a very ironic cast. And sometimes composers and directors will spot an opportunity to do that. If you play happy music while somebody's getting his throat cut, that can be a very effective use of the medium. You can also mock things with the musical backgrounds, though that's almost too easy. I'm thinking, for instance, of Charlie Chaplin in *The Great Dictator* [1940] doing a mock ballet with appropriate music in the scene of Adolf Hitler playing with the globe: that's too easy.

AF: A lot of modern directors play their composers music to show them the sort of thing they want. They say, 'What we need here is something very like the Barber *Adagio*.' Do you have views on this?

DH: I haven't been bothered too much by that. But I know this is commonplace in the industry now. And these 'temporary tracks' aid the director when it comes to editing. If you already have something scored, it's a great asset. But the trouble with putting temporary music into something that's already been filmed is that [the director] falls in love with it. And this puts the composer into a difficult game in which he has to make his music sound sufficiently like the temp track that it will be acceptable, but with some measure of difference so that the film company won't be sued – getting down to the legal aspect of it – and also so that the composer has contributed something more than just making a carbon copy. But occasionally it needs to be done, and I've had my share of doing it. Sometimes you can duplicate something in terms of the instrumentation and the tempo and that will satisfy people's urge to hear the temp track.

AF: You said you've had this experience. Can you give an example of having to turn a temp track into something else?

DH: Yes, I *can* ... But I think I'd rather not.

Lalo Schifrin

It is not only actors who can be typecast; so can composers. Hollywood quickly came to believe that the Argentinian-born Lalo Schifrin was the man to turn to if you needed music for a fast-paced suspense movie. He scored all the 'Dirty Harry' films, for example, and was responsible for many TV themes, most famously Mission: Impossible *(1966–1973). But Schifrin is a far more versatile composer than this might suggest. His classical training and vast experience as a jazz player and composer took him to Sydney in 2006, where he worked with the Sydney Symphony Orchestra on one of his 'Jazz Meets the Symphony' programs. This interview was recorded during a rehearsal break.*

ANDREW FORD: It seems to me that everything you touch has some jazz in it. Your film music, your TV themes: there is a jazz sensibility behind all of your music. Is that a fair comment?

LALO SCHIFRIN: It is a little bit stereotyped, because when you embark on a movie, or a television show, it depends on how the public accepts it. So the coincidence is that some of my most successful movies like, from the beginning, *The Cincinnati Kid* [Norman Jewison, 1965] with Ray Charles singing my title song, and *Bullitt* [Peter Yates, 1968] and *Dirty Harry* [Don Siegel, 1971] and even *Mission: Impossible*, have a theme which is syncopated and could be in the periphery of jazz. They became popular, but I've done movies like *The Four Musketeers* [Richard Lester, 1974] where I was inspired by Renaissance music, and I did dramatic movies like *Voyage of the Damned* [Stuart Rosenberg, 1976], which has nothing to do with jazz. I've done a hundred movies, and you can't say the hundred movies I've done were touched by jazz. I've done many television shows, movies of the week, mini series: very few of them were jazz-oriented. But the themes became jazz-oriented; that's why I got typecast.

AF: You trained as a classical pianist first of all; did the interest in jazz come later? Did it come when you were in Paris, perhaps?

LS: No, no, it came in between. During primary school I was only into classical music; my father was a concert master with the Buenos Aires Philharmonic and my first piano teacher was his friend, with whom he played chamber music, Enrique Barenboim, Daniel's father. So I didn't have any idea about jazz at the time, it was completely esoteric, actually I didn't even know that jazz existed. When I went to secondary school, some friends started to bring records of jazz artists from the United States, and I became converted. It was almost like a religious conversion.

AF: Who were you listening to?

LS: I was listening to all jazz, like Louis Armstrong, Fats Waller, Bix Beiderbecke, and I liked them all. Then some other friends came with Charlie Parker, Thelonious Monk, Dizzy Gillespie, George Shearing. So I embraced modern jazz; I realised that it was musically more demanding and more challenging, and it helped a lot my studies of harmony, because I realised that modern jazz had some similarities with the developments at that time in contemporary music in the classical field. If you could say there is an equivalent in jazz of Bartók, I would say Monk. The equivalent of Stravinsky? I would say Dizzy Gillespie. He wrote a piece called 'Things to Come' which is short – it's not as long as *The Rite of Spring*, but it had many things in common with it.

AF: So you saw all of this as different aspects of musical modernity, then?

LS: Let's say that this curiosity was open to these new explorations or discoveries they were making, and it helped my studies of harmony, as I said, because by learning from records what all these jazz artists were doing, I would go to a class of harmony and it was almost naïve what they were teaching. I couldn't understand why for instance parallel fifths were forbidden, where in jazz they use it and they are beautiful. But Ravel also used it, and Debussy. Anyway it was a very important period of my life, because I wakened to the developments that made me what I am now.

AF: You said that jazz taught you a lot about harmony, but what about rhythm? Because so much jazz is before or after the beat, rhythmically speaking, and if you play, I don't know, a composer like Webern even, there's quite a bit of the same thing going on there, where bar lines are no longer providing a strong sense of pulse. Did you find that connection as well?

LS: Oh absolutely, absolutely. I got a scholarship to the Paris Conservatoire and one of my professors was Olivier Messiaen. I already was aware of him because the professor of composition I had in Argentina, Juan Carlos Paz, had studied with Schoenberg before the Second World War in Vienna and he is the one who brought to Argentina the whole message of twentieth-century music. With him I had studied music of Messiaen, Boulez, Luigi Nono, Berio. He was in the real avant garde. And of course Schoenberg and Webern and Berg: the second Viennese school. He composed himself in that style. All of a sudden I'm studying with Messiaen. He was very nice to me, and I was avid to learn from him. He opened new windows, new horizons to my perception of music. In those days I was earning my living by playing jazz at night. Actually I became a professional jazz musician in Paris; although I was playing in Argentina, it was amateur, and the difference between amateur and professional is amateur doesn't get paid. So I played jazz at night, and when Messiaen found out, he got mad at me. For the very reason of your question, but from a different angle. He saw the walking bass in jazz as an *ostinato*. He called it *'pedale rhythmique'* – rhythmic pedal – which is repetitious. He said, 'How can you do that?' And I said, 'Well, there is another problem …' This was, like you say, going above the bar lines, borrowing from one bar and giving back maybe three or four bars later. He would have one of my jazz records, so he would say, 'Play it for me.' And so in a bar of 4/4, he was beating *one*-two, *three*-four, *one*-two, *three*-four. And in jazz it's one-*two*, three-*four*, one-*two*, three-*four* – the weak beats in classical music become strong in jazz. And that applies to 6/8, to any kind of metre. So, he didn't get it, he couldn't appreciate jazz, period. He stopped talking to me, but he was sending messages that I was doing very good exercises, and I did very well in his class. And the sad epilogue to this story is that after he died, I went to give a kind of talk to the Paris equivalent of the Academy of Motion Pictures in Hollywood. I had just finished a movie called *Tango* [1998], with Carlos Saura. There's no jazz there! I gave a lecture and then there was a dinner, and a classmate of mine in the Paris Conservatoire, who also studied with Messiaen and became also a film composer, was there, and he said, 'Oh, it's so nice seeing you and I enjoyed your lecture so much, and above all, I want to tell you that Maître Messiaen spoke so well of you, and he was so proud of your career.' I said, 'Why didn't he tell me that when he was alive?'

AF: A compliment from the grave.

LS: Yes, exactly.

AF: What would you say is the primary function of music in film? What does it bring?

LS: I was very lucky that my father took me from an early age to see opera. There are two opera houses in the southern hemisphere that are magnificent. There's the Sydney Opera House and the Teatro Colón in Buenos Aires. At that time there was not an orchestra for opera and an orchestra for the symphony. As a member of the Buenos Aires Philharmonic, my father had to play everything; he was a municipal employee, paid by the city of Buenos Aires. They played in the pit when it was the opera, and they played on the stage when it was a symphony concert. So he took me to see a lot of operas and I got the feeling of drama and comedy and tragedy from seeing operas. So I never had to study how to write film music. As a matter of fact I have a theory that films are the operas of the twenty-first century. If Verdi were alive today, he would be one of the most successful film composers. You listen to *Otello*, and what's going on in the pit is really background music for a film. He's underlined all the emotions and everything that's going on: it's really fantastic. The same thing you can say about Bizet. The same thing you can say about Puccini. And most of the more modern operas like *Pelléas et Mélisande* of Debussy, and a comic opera like *L'Heure espagnol* of Ravel, and then the [dramatic opera that] influenced me a lot, even before I became a film composer, *Wozzeck* by Alban Berg. So that's where I got my influence and then I applied it. It was not difficult to do films. This you cannot learn, you either have it or you don't have it. I had the techniques of writing music, orchestrating – it was part of my background. And the reason I went to Hollywood … Many composers go to Hollywood, because, you know, they graduate from music school and they have to make a living and Hollywood pays very well. I didn't go for the money. I went because that was the place where jazz could meet the symphony. I heard scores of Henry Mancini and many other colleagues who were using jazz, and they had a jazz group surrounded by a symphony orchestra. So I would say that 'Jazz Meets the Symphony' started in Hollywood.

AF: I spoke to Richard Rodney Bennett about a week ago, and he singled out a scene with no dialogue in Louis Malle's film *Ascenseur pour l'échafaud* in which we follow Jeanne Moreau walking the streets of Paris while Miles Davis's trumpet on the soundtrack is, in Richard's words, 'breaking your heart'.

LS: Well, this is a very accurate analysis. However, Miles Davis was not really a film composer. What happened in that situation – and I know that situation very well because I was told – was that the director liked Miles Davis and he already had it in mind to use his music. So he told him more or less what he wanted, but Miles Davis didn't have to work like we do – to the film, to timings – he didn't care about how long the scene is or if there's a cut. The director helped him a lot by saying, 'Record a piece like that, and then I'll edit it.' So Miles did what he always did; he was not really writing music for a film.

AF: So it's an example of the use of music.

LS: The use of music, yes. And it's happening more and more. Because of the media and the cross-fertilisation that's going on in the record world and on radio and the internet and in many areas, some filmmakers know music a lot. They are very well trained and they know how to communicate with a composer. Some of them know. But they go out and buy records and then they tell the composer, 'Write something like that', which is kind of parasitic. I don't like that. I tell them, 'I can make a contribution. Look, you're hiring me as an expert in music, like you hire a director of photography who is an expert in cinematography, so why don't you let me see the film without music and see what I can do? And if you like it …' It should be a collaboration, not a conflict. The director understands that I'm trying to help, but in some cases the director is brainwashed by living for nine months with the same edit of the movie with the same [temporary] music. It's difficult to get out of that, it's a habit. But sometimes he's open to my suggestions. The temp track is a new development. When I came to Hollywood, it didn't happen. But it's just a way for the director to show the movie to the producers and the studio executives, and for the film to have some kind of life. Music does give life to a film: even from the time of silent movies there was always a pianist in the room.

AF: Can you think of any places in films where the music does the opposite of what is happening on screen, where it tells you something quite different to what you're seeing?

LS: Oh, I like that. That's what we call audio-visual counterpoint. I've never done cartoons and I was maybe lucky. There's a lot of work in it and it is not always pleasurable work – although there were some fantastic composers doing cartoons and I admire them. But in a cartoon, if the mouse runs up stairs, the xylophone goes [sings an ascending scale], and if the mouse runs downstairs the xylophone goes [sings a descending scale]. So it is really parallel motion. What I like to do is counterpoint. I did a movie called *Rollercoaster* [James Goldstone, 1977] which was a kind of horror movie where an extortionist portrayed by Timothy Bottoms threatens to put bombs in rollercoasters in amusement parks, and people will die unless he gets money. And there were horrible scenes, really horrible scenes, and instead of doing all the time the tension and the horror and the fear, I told the director why don't we use children's rhymes and calliopes [fairground organs], in opposition to what is going on on the screen: innocent music for this evil, Machiavellian mind. And the director accepted this and we did it and it worked out all right. That's what we call in the trade 'playing against' and I like to do that a lot.

AF: Who are the film composers you've admired?

LS: Well, there are so many ... but Bernard Herrmann for his work with the movies of Hitchcock. I knew him personally and, as a matter of fact, he used to say there's no such thing as film composers. There are composers, period. And he was right, he was absolutely right. I think *Psycho* is his most brilliant score, but everything he wrote was really daring and original, right from the first score he wrote, for *Citizen Kane*. He was very aware and he had also that sense of drama. But there are film scores by Alfred Newman, by Franz Waxman. Very great films scores. But I must say something, without wishing to sound like a snob. The biggest influences on film music for me, as I said before, were Alban Berg, Debussy and Verdi. Of course when I went to see films and when I saw how well the music worked, I admired these amazing examples, but my main source was from the classical composers.

AF: What about directors? Who have been the directors you have most enjoyed working with? The ones you'd work with again, say, because they respected what you do and allowed you to be creative?

LS: Unfortunately one of them is dead and that's Don Siegel, with whom I did many films including *Dirty Harry*. And Stuart Rosenberg, who's alive [he died in 2007] but retired. For him I did *Cool Hand Luke* [1967], with Paul Newman. But I've worked with a lot of directors. I worked with John Sturges [on *The Great Escape*, 1963]. I worked with René Clément, who was the Hitchcock of France.

AF: Can you talk about working with Don Siegel on *Dirty Harry*?

LS: Yes. One thing that comes to my mind is that I told him I was going to use human voices, female voices. Not a big chorus, but in some cases three voices, in some cases just one. And he had never done a movie where the score had voices, he was used to instrumental scores. He said, 'Why do you want to use voices?' And I said,

'Well, it's because of you. You set me up.' He said, 'What do you mean?' So I explained that the villain of the movie, Scorpio, is a mass murderer, but he is an incongruous figure. The movie was done during the war in Vietnam, and Scorpio wears a belt buckle with a peace symbol. The guy is crazy. So I said to Don Siegel, 'Look, I think that he hears voices.' And he said, 'Oh, you have a point.' And I used a very haunting … not a song with lyrics, but just using the voice as an instrument. And that brought a chill … in combination with electronically sustained instruments, it brought a chill to the audience. Every time you hear that sound, even if you don't see Scorpio, you feel his presence. Don Siegel liked that, and it worked and it proved to be a success.

AF: And it's very operatic, isn't it?

LS: Exactly. Exactly. Well, it always comes back to the opera.

Howard Shore

Although his name is closely associated with the directors David Cronenberg and Martin Scorsese, the Canadian Howard Shore has written music for a wide variety of films, from The Silence of the Lambs *[Jonathan Demme, 1991] to* Mrs Doubtfire *[Chris Columbus, 1993]. But he is best known today, and will probably be best remembered, for the massive score he composed for Peter Jackson's trilogy* The Lord of the Rings. *He spoke to me on the phone from New York in February 2010.*

ANDREW FORD: I understand you have been attending 'Live to Projection' performances of the music for *The Lord of the Rings*. How do they work?

HOWARD SHORE: In the 'Live to Projection' concerts we play the entire score to *The Lord of the Rings* – the three films, with a symphony orchestra, chorus and soloists. Ludwig Wicki conducts them. And it's really a unique theatrical type of concert where you're hearing the music performed, which is thrilling, and you have the synchronisation to the film as well. I have a special print of the film with the dialogue and the sound effects separated, but principally you're at a symphonic concert with the imagery of the film. And the two are incredibly enhanced: the music could never sound better – it's like an enhanced type of reality, it's almost tactile – and then the images of the film and the storytelling are also very heightened.

AF: I'm interested that you speak of storytelling. Is that music's main function in a film?

HS: Well, I think that it's one function. It's not necessarily the main function. There are so many ways to use music in film, and none of them are wrong. Particularly in the case of *The Lord of the Rings*, music is used in a storytelling way for a very specific reason. The trilogy by J.R.R. Tolkien is considered one of the most complex fantasy works ever created, so the music was used for clarity of storytelling. It was something that the director, Peter Jackson, and I discussed very early on. So for an audience that is coming to the films without having read the book, it might help them to understand characters and cultures. Even in the first film, *The Fellowship of the Ring* [2001], you have two elf cultures at Rivendell and Lothlórien and you need to understand the difference between them. Rivendell is sophisticated and learned, and Lothlórien is more mystical and nature-oriented. But there's not that much time in the film to go into great detail, so through the different thematic material and details of orchestration, I hoped to give those cultures shape and a voice in music that would resonate with the audience. This is a more traditional use of music in film. You don't find it used so much in contemporary films, and it's really only one way to do movies.

AF: But when it comes to something as big as *The Lord of the Rings*, that way of working – the big orchestra, the use of the *leitmotif* – has never really gone out of fashion, has it?

HS: It comes and it goes. But of course this use of *leitmotifs* goes back to Wagner in the middle of the nineteenth century, and when sound came into films and scores were starting to be written in the 1930s it worked its way into the movies because the early Hollywood composers were themselves European.

AF: Can you describe how you found the right sounds for Lothlórien or the Orcs – or the Hobbits, for that matter?

HS: I broke down the cultures into north, east, south and west. Tolkien devised a complete world and you can't write north without understanding south and east and west. All of those things mean something to composers. All composers have certain relationships with those directions. Glenn Gould would talk about 'the idea of north'; Tōru Takemitsu would express the world of the east. The symphony orchestra was the basis of the sound in the film – it was a choral piece with symphony orchestra – but I used folk instruments from all over the world. By orchestrating the score myself, I was able to control the sound throughout – from film to film.

AF: How much music is there, all up?

HS: Close to eleven hours. It took four years to write and to orchestrate, and I was also recording it at the same time. Also the detail of the synchronisation was very precise. Because I was recording and editing, and I wanted the best recording that I could have, I worked out all of the expression in the composition in terms of *ritards* and *accelerandos*, all the tempos, all worked out so specifically, so that if I did multiple takes in the recording studio, I could edit a *ritard* and it would always have the exact same quality to it.

AF: I assume you generally provided music after the films were shot, but still you must have scored the first film before the last one was finished. So Peter Jackson would have had some of your sounds in his mind as he worked. Do you think it affected the way he worked on *The Two Towers* [2002] or *The Return of the King* [2003]?

HS: Peter and I worked very closely together for four years. Themes were always created first and then developed and we spoke in terms of these motifs and how they should be used in the films. You don't create something like those scores without a very close working relationship with the director and you need complete trust in each other. Peter was at all the recording sessions.

AF: And you were at all the spotting sessions?

HS: A spotting session is a meeting between the composer and the director. And the editor is usually involved in that too. And you're just asking questions like how and why and where there should be music.

AF: And perhaps where there *shouldn't* be music?

HS: Yes, of course. Silence is very important in films. You have to respect it. And we would also discuss the 'size' of the music. I had a rather large palette to work with – you know, 225 musicians – but we would discuss using one single voice for making a particular statement in a scene.

AF: In the lighting of the beacons scene in *The Return of the King*, I wondered whether the film was actually cut to the music, because the music seems to drive that scene.

HS: No, it wasn't. I scored that scene to the cut.

AF: When you're working on a film that already has a lot of music it must be a very different sort of job. *High Fidelity* [Stephen Frears, 2000] would be a good example, I suppose, because in a way it's a film about people listening to music.

HS: Yes. Well, source music is quite often part of a film, but the audience isn't thinking specifically that this is score and this is source, and you don't want the audience to think that. You want them to be immersed in the world of the film. A good example of that is the music to Martin Scorsese's film *The Departed* [2006], where there's a lot of source music and also a lot of score – it's probably about equal – and we tried very hard to make these things work well together.

AF: Yes, I remember the Rolling Stones' 'Gimme Shelter' at the beginning of that film.

HS: Coming out of 'Gimme Shelter' I wrote into 'The Departed Tango', a major theme of the film. I would use some of the guitar sounds of the Stones and match the two, one from the other, using similar recording sounds for the guitars.

AF: You've worked on a lot of suspenseful films – I suppose most recently *Edge of Darkness* [Martin Campbell, 2010] – where part of the composer's remit, or so it seems to me, is to control the tempo of the picture. Is that something you do quite consciously?

HS: Yes, it's an important function of the music. Sometimes it's discussed with the director and sometimes you just get a feel for the pace of the film and how you can help it. You feel it needs this kind of tempo or this kind of rhythm. Films are really about rhythm. It comes from the editing of the film and the way the actors move. So music is just another element of that.

AF: Have you ever set the pace with your music? Have scenes been edited to music you've already composed?

HS: That's happened. Yes, of course. There have been instances where the music has been put into the film as it was being edited and it was helping to shape the scenes. It's a good way to make films, actually, but it doesn't happen all that often. In the same way that a director takes a song and cuts the film to it, why not cut it to an existing piece of composition?

AF: What's your view of directors who use temporary scores?

HS: Well, Martin Scorsese never uses temp scores. He doesn't understand why you would watch a new film that you're making with music from another film. When he watches his film he never wants to see or hear anything that is only there temporarily; he only wants things that are part of the film, even if it's not complete. He builds the movie step by step, and he never puts things in temporarily just to take them out later.

AF: That must be quite rare these days.

HS: But he's a great filmmaker. He's one of the greatest filmmakers alive, and that's part of his technique. And frankly other good directors do that as well. David Cronenberg doesn't put temp music in his films. I write my pieces and I'll put them into the film in demos if we want to watch it. At least we know precisely what's in the film and what the composition is for the film. Those are good ways to work.

AF: Are there film scores by others that you particularly admire?

HS: Well, I think the music of Takemitsu in *Ran* [Akira Kurosawa, 1985]. Have you ever seen it?

AF: Yes. This is the *King Lear* movie.

HS: Yes. And do you recall the music?

AF: Well, it's been a while, but I'm remembering a big, powerful orchestral sound.

HS: Yes, there are a few large pieces for orchestra. But it's a very long film – three hours – and there is very little music. The first hour is mostly just very small percussion sounds and then later on it grows to these really beautiful symphonic pieces. But even though there's so little music in the film you always remember *Ran* as having this beautiful, epic, Mahler-type score. So it's interesting to analyse it and see how little music is used in the film. I learned a lot from watching it. I learned about the use of silence. I learned about the very minimal types of orchestration and also about the grand symphonic gesture.

AF: One of the things that is striking in Kurosawa's work, if you're used to watching Hollywood movies, is that often the music and the action don't line up. There isn't that sense of cause and effect.

HS: Yes! I love that. My interest was always in music. I mean I went into movies and writing film music because I wanted to spend time in the recording studio. I wanted to experiment with a lot of techniques that I was interested in. My interest in film music was always international. I loved watching Italian movies and seeing how Italian composers scored scenes. Or how the music was used in Japanese or French or English films. And of course American films as well. I was interested in how different cultures used music to tell their stories. I still am.

AF: Music can bring an extra dimension to a film. It can hint at things that are not on the screen …

HS: Yes, that's great. Subtext. You know in the work I've done with Cronenberg, we always work around what we call the edges, the fringes of the frame. We use music to add depth and subtext to the stories.

AF: What about sound effects? Often an elaborate score is barely audible because of the screams and explosions piled on top of it. Do you have any say in how sound effects are used in conjunction with your music?

HS: Depends on the film. On *The Silence of the Lambs*, I worked with the sound designer Skip Lievsay. We were friends in New York and we would visit each other in the studio, and I would see what he'd been creating and he'd hear my demos before we recorded anything. And once I had done my recording with the orchestra – and I was using electronics in the score as well – we put all our tracks together on a 48-track machine and pre-mixed the music and the effects before we even went into the dub. It's very good to hear how sound is being used in the film, because it'll affect the way you write the music.

AF: You mentioned using electronics in the score …

HS: I've used a lot of electronics in my writing over the years. In scores that I did like *The Silence of the Lambs* and certainly *Se7en* [David Fincher, 1995], they have a lot of electronics that are mixed in with the orchestra. I would use these techniques that I developed in the 1970s with ambient sound and with loops, and I would use the score as a guide. I would write the score the way I normally do in pencil and ink, and then I'd program the computer – in the '70s we had some very early digital computers like the synclavier – I'd program the synclavier to play the score and I'd assign it abstract sounds or industrial sounds or environmental sounds. I would mix that in with the orchestra and create a sense of unease and uncertainty to the harmonic sound of the orchestra, and I would vary it to different degrees depending on the subject. So when you hear scores like *The Silence of the Lambs* and *Se7en*, they sound symphonic, but if you listen carefully you'll notice a lot more going on in the depths of the recording.

AF: In 1986 you composed the music for David Cronenberg's film *The Fly*. In 2008, Cronenberg directed your opera *The Fly*. Some people say that cinema is the new opera, but the fact that we speak of Cronenberg's film but Shore's opera suggests they are quite different art forms. What are the main differences?

HS: When I started doing films, it was in the late '70s. Then in the early '80s I started going to the opera regularly – the Metropolitan Opera in New York. And I started making connections between the opera house and films, obvious connections with the proscenium arch, the stage, the lighting, the orchestra in the pit. I started setting up my orchestra in the same way as the pit orchestra from the Met with the violins split left and right. I used to set up my sound recordings, imagining the opera house and the podium, and the conductor being in the pit with the screen up above, and the relationship of the screen or the stage to the opera conductor. The first film I scored using this technique was *The Fly*, and then I developed it in other films like *Dead Ringers* [Cronenberg, 1988] and *M. Butterfly* [Cronenberg, 1993] and *Se7en*, right up to *The Lord of the Rings*. So I've always felt a strong connection between the opera house and film. And then a couple of years ago I wrote the opera, based on *The Fly*, with a libretto by David Henry Hwang, directed by Cronenberg, and I was reversing the techniques. It was a completely new piece and I was going right into the stage, using some of my compositional techniques from film, but taking them much further.

AF: Can you give an example?

HS: I think what I'd done in film music at the time was about as far as I could go compositionally in the medium, without going into experimental film. I've done, I don't know, seventy films? And in the seventy films I've used a lot of different techniques, everything I was interested in and everything I knew. Going into the opera house,

I just took the compositional language further. Harmonic ideas, the use of the voice, and contrapuntal techniques that I only hinted at in movies that I had done.

AF: And did the experience of writing the opera change you as a film composer?

HS: Yes, absolutely. I was able to do and try a lot of things that I always wanted to do. Also for the year I worked on the opera I didn't do any films, so after that year I came back to doing films with a nice sense of energy and openness to it. It really refreshed me.

LISTENING TO THE MOVIES

Classical Music in Films

In *Schindler's List* (Steven Spielberg, 1993), following the sweep of the Krakow ghetto, the German soldiers seeking to complete the liquidation return at night to search for Jews who are still in hiding. One man is inside an upright piano. As he climbs out under cover of darkness, unaware that there are soldiers listening downstairs, he steps lightly on the keyboard. The resulting cluster of notes alerts the soldiers, who rush upstairs and start shooting. The next thing we see is a German officer sitting at the piano playing Bach while the shooting continues in other rooms. It is a chilling moment, not least because it reminds us – if we needed reminding – that the Nazis were not monsters, but human beings behaving like monsters, and that some of them were accomplished and cultivated in other areas of their lives. Spielberg can't let them be too cultivated, however. In the doorway, as the officer plays, two soldiers watch in surprised admiration. One asks the other, 'Is it Bach?' The second assures him that it's Mozart. How much better, how much more horrifying, had the second soldier given the correct answer: 'It's Bach. The prelude from the English Suite in A minor.'

The use of classical music to denote culture – even in Nazis – has become a cinematic commonplace. In *Lifeboat*, as far back as 1944, Hitchcock has his young Nazi sing Schubert, and in *The Pianist* (Roman Polanski, 2002) it is Chopin's music that helps sustain the central character, Wladyslaw Szpilman (Adrien Brody), in the Warsaw ghetto, and ultimately charms the Nazi captain who discovers him.

Polanski's film opens with Szpilman playing Chopin in a radio studio during a German bombing raid, but after that it is two hours before we see him play again. There is, however, a scene in which we hear music. Szpilman arrives at a safe house. He is in poor shape, sick and malnourished, but left alone in the apartment, he seems restored by the presence of a piano. The last thing he is told by the people hiding him is to make no noise, so when he approaches the piano and his face relaxes into a half smile, we worry that he will give himself away. Immediately there is the sound of an orchestra. It plays the introductory bars of Chopin's *Grande Polonaise Brillante*, as Szpilman, heart-stoppingly, raises his hands in the air and launches into the solo part. But then another camera angle shows us these hands hovering just above the keys, miming out the music that he is playing only in his imagination. The scene is actually more touching than the famous scene with the German captain. Szpilman plays him Chopin's G-minor *Ballade* (or at least highlights of it) and persuades him, through his playing, not to shoot him or report his presence. On the contrary, the officer now brings him food, gives him his coat and tells him to hold tight for a couple more weeks because the Russians are coming. Over the closing credits, Szpilman, on stage with an orchestra, plays the *Grande Polonaise Brillante* for real.

In spite of the fact that *The Pianist* tells a true story, based on the memoir of the real-life Szpilman, the film would quickly lapse into sentimentality did it contain too much piano playing. One of the strengths of the film – and presumably this was also based on fact – is that the eponymous hero is unable to do the thing the title implies, which is why the scene in which he mimes out his performance is affecting. By giving us so little of it, Polanski ensures that the music seems significant. We may never knowingly have heard a note of Chopin before, but we feel the power of his work and, indeed, its humanity. The sound of this rather flamboyant music, where previously there had been none, is all the more dramatic.

In modern Hollywood, classical music rarely has so noble a role to play. In the minds of mainstream American filmmakers, this art of 'old Europe' is associated with intellectuals. And intellectuals are, at best, untrustworthy. Just as Hollywood villains now generally speak with English or European accents, so they like opera or play the piano. In *The Silence of the Lambs*, Hannibal Lecter (Anthony Hopkins) bloodily kills two guards and escapes his cell, all while listening to a recording of Glenn Gould playing Bach's *Goldberg* variations. In the sequel, *Hannibal* (Ridley Scott, 2001), we discover Lecter himself playing the same piece on the piano in his well-appointed Florence apartment. This ability to play presumably makes him extra villainous. It's as though eating people were not enough.

It wasn't always so. In Hitchcock's *Saboteur* (1942), Barry Kane (Robert Cummings), on the run for an act of wartime sabotage he did not commit, stumbles, handcuffed, into the house of a blind man, Phillip Martin (Vaughan Glaser). Phillip's grand piano is not the sign of danger it might be in a recent American film. On the contrary, it is comforting and reassuring; it denotes civilisation. The man plays a few bars from Delius's *Summer Night on the River*, explaining to Barry that, like himself, Delius was blind. The scene reminds us of the blind man who befriends Frankenstein's monster in Mary Shelley's novel. Because he cannot see the creature's startling appearance, he treats him kindly. By the same token, Phillip cannot see Barry's handcuffs, though we later learn he had heard them the moment Barry entered his house and decided his visitor was harmless.

The tendency of classical music to elevate a character in this way was quite common in the 1940s, just as common, in fact, as today's tendency for classical music to incriminate. Abraham Polonsky's *Force of Evil* (1948) has a subtly calibrated score by David Raksin, but also uses the late string quartet in C sharp minor by Beethoven, arranged for string orchestra. This is unusual musical territory for a *film noir*, though the Coen brothers in their *noir*-ish comedy-thriller

The Man Who Wasn't There (2001) had Scarlett Johansson as a not-quite-good-enough child pianist work her way through several of Beethoven's sonatas.

Force of Evil is the story of two brothers, Joe and Leo Morse. Joe (John Garfield) is a lawyer working for a gangster. Their aim is to wipe out all the small-time banks in the illegal numbers racket and take over their business. Leo (Thomas Gomez) is one of these small-time bankers, but while his business might be illegal, he's a decent enough fellow with an old-fashioned boss's attitude to the welfare of his staff, whom he treats as family, especially his secretary, Doris (Beatrice Pearson). The Beethoven quartet plays during the tense, climactic scene in a restaurant in which Bauer, Leo's bookkeeper, is shot and Leo himself abducted. Straightaway we cut to a piano playing a slow boogie-woogie bass in the bar in which Joe is chatting up Doris. The jazz piano is a cliché, but the Beethoven isn't. This is not easy music, even in the concert hall, and it certainly isn't reassuring. It is the first movement of the quartet that we hear, with slow, stark and rather chromatic melodic lines yielding a kind of gentle, tortured lyricism. It's certainly no one's idea of restaurant music, and its very oddness is why it is so effective.

Robert Eroica Dupea (Jack Nicholson) is the central character of Bob Rafelson's film *Five Easy Pieces* (1970). Once a piano-playing prodigy, he now works on an oil rig. The film has no score, only classical piano music and country songs, and the main title features Tammy Wynette singing 'Stand By Your Man'. It becomes clear that Bobby is opposed to this song both in terms of its sentiments and its music.

'It's a question of musical integrity,' he explains.

Five Easy Pieces follows Bobby back to his childhood home when he learns that his father is dying. After checking his pregnant girlfriend Rayette (Karen Black) into a nearby motel, Bobby visits his musical but highly dysfunctional family, including his brother Carl Fidelio Dupea and his sister Partita. He spars with Carl's girlfriend Catherine (Susan Anspach), another pianist, but they end up having sex anyway.

There are not many films that give their music details in the opening credits, but this one does, listing four Tammy Wynette songs and five classical pieces, four of them hardly so very easy: Chopin's Prelude in E minor and Fantasy in F minor, Mozart's Piano Concerto K 271 and the D-minor Fantasia, and Bach's 'Chromatic' Fantasy and Fugue.

It is the simplest of these pieces – the Chopin prelude – that Bobby chooses to play to Catherine, telling her it is the 'easiest piece' he knows. But it is a flat performance. Bobby himself admits that he felt nothing and played it better when he was eight years old. It might not be obvious to Bobby, and the film doesn't spell it out to its audience, but Rayette sings her country songs with more feeling and musical insight than he plays Chopin. *Five Easy Pieces* is not musically judgmental at any level and neither does it invite us to judge. But as Bobby finally abandons Rayette at a truck stop, we are certainly able to make the connection between an ability to behave well, or at least with regard for others, and the 'musical integrity' that Bobby spoke of at the start of the picture but only Rayette demonstrated.

If modern Hollywood views classical music – and classical music lovers – with suspicion, it is not true of the independent sector. The Canadian film *Away from Her* (Sarah Polley, 2006) makes use of the C-major prelude from the first book of Bach's *Well-Tempered Clavier* and it also draws the composer into Jonathan Goldsmith's score (such as it is) by making one of Bach's lute preludes the basis of a section of music using electric instruments. This comes with the opening credits as the two main characters, Grant (Gordon Pinsent) and Fiona (Julie Christie), walk away from the camera across a wide expanse of snow. This can only be a conscious reference to an earlier Canadian film which uses rather more Bach, François Girard's *Thirty-two Short Films About Glenn Gould* (1993).

In *The Young Victoria* (Jean-Marc Vallée, 2009), Prince Albert is associated with Schubert's 'Ständchen' (Serenade). It is one of the composer's best-known songs and eventually we will hear it played as a piano solo by Albert (Rupert Friend) to Victoria (Emily Blunt). But, long before that, the song begins turning up in the score whenever she thinks of him. It is subtly done, too. We do not hear Schubert's melodic line in Ilan Eshkeri's score, merely the distinctive accompaniment. This is a reversal of the usual approach to musical quotation in films, in which a song or other piece of music is heard and then its significance underlined by its remaining in the score, quoted wistfully or triumphantly at some later key moment. In *The Young Victoria*, the score anticipates the song. If we recognise the accompaniment, it lets us a little further into the story. If we don't, at least it primes us for the song when it comes.

Martin McDonagh's very different film, *In Bruges* (2008), does something remarkably similar with 'Der Leiermann', the final song in Schubert's cycle *Winterreise* – a winter's journey. Carter Burwell's score makes much use of the harmonic structure of this song and the melodic line, especially the opening phrase, but this time we hardly notice until the song is sung on the soundtrack, encapsulating the sense of melancholy verging on madness in this otherwise very funny film about two assassins.

Pascale Ferran based his French-language film *Lady Chatterley* (2006) on *John Thomas and Lady Jane*, D.H. Lawrence's second go at writing *Lady Chatterley's Lover*. (Lawrence wrote his novel three times, and the third version is the familiar one.) The story is the same in all essentials: Constance Chatterley, married to the crippled and impotent Sir Clifford, finds sexual fulfilment with his gamekeeper, called Parkin in this version. The main difference in the telling is one of tone, the second writing of the novel more poetic and less wilfully coarse than the final version. So this is a correspondingly tender film, and musically – indeed sonically – of considerable interest and detail.

The film begins with Sibelius's *Valse triste*, which establishes the early twentieth century and the melancholic mood of the Chatterleys' house, if not its English (or even French) location. Thereafter, music of any sort is sparingly used. But we do hear Constance (Marina Hands) playing Bach on the piano, and we notice that she plays tolerably well. Off screen, she launches into the tricky, chromatic D-minor fugue from Book II of the *Well-Tempered Clavier*, giving up after a couple of bars, before opting for the easier C-minor fugue from Book I. After another false start, she plays on to the end. So the music is part of the household, but it is also a symbol of her gradual sexual awakening. As the sound of Connie's playing drifts in from the other room, Sir Clifford's nurse, Mrs Bolton (Hélène Alexandridis) comments to her employer that she didn't know 'my Lady played the piano', to which Sir Clifford (Hippolyte Girardot) replies, 'We'd all forgotten.'

Shortly after, when we see Connie walking happily and purposefully to the hut in which her affair with Parkin (Jean-Louis Coullo'ch) will take place, there's another burst of Bach on the soundtrack – just a few seconds of perky music from the *Partita* in C minor. It's a brief and simple moment, but it tells the audience a lot. The music is quite gratuitous, like a sudden happy thought that strikes her as she walks along. She is very clearly a changed woman, and she is about to change more.

Sudden bursts of baroque music have enlivened other films, particularly from France. In *L'Enfant sauvage* (François Truffaut, 1970), the music of Vivaldi stands for enlightenment. The wild child of the title (Jean-Pierre Cargol) has been living in the forest like an animal, it would seem since birth. At the start of the film he is hunted down and captured by men with dogs. There is no music and no dialogue here, only the dogs' excited barking, the hunters' exhortations and the heightened sounds of the forest. As soon as we meet Dr Jean Itard (played by Truffaut himself), we enter the civilised world of Vivaldi – the gentle 6/8 *Siciliano* from his concerto in C for *flautino* and strings.

The story is essentially true. Truffaut based his film on the real doctor's own account of the events, which occurred at the end of the eighteenth century (so the music is almost of the right period, Vivaldi having died some fifty years before). Itard becomes convinced he can educate the boy, whom he names Victor, and save him from a future in a Paris freak show by taking him home. Home, musically speaking, is another concerto by Vivaldi – also in C, but for mandolin and strings. Victor's steps towards civilisation – having his face washed, learning what a mirror is – are always marked by music, sometimes no more than a few notes. All three movements of the mandolin concerto are used and because they have thematic similarities – strong similarities in the case of the fast outer movements – there is a sense of musical unity. The music always comes in bursts, the fast movements associated with achievement – Victor walking upright – the slow movements for setbacks. So it serves as both punctuation and illustration, presented in a simple, storybook manner. But then that is true of the whole film and, one might argue, of Truffaut's work in general.

Robert Bresson's films, in contrast, have some of the qualities of classical painting, and his use of music is even cooler than Truffaut's. Bresson's music is less tied to the action of his pictures, more to their philosophical, perhaps even spiritual, content. In *Pickpocket* (1959), the music is from the opera *Atys*, by the seventeenth-century composer Jean-Baptiste Lully. There is no obvious connection between the story of the opera (a love triangle gone wrong) and the film, so the question arises why a filmmaker in the mid-twentieth century would want to use music from 300 years before. What does the film gain?

Well, style for one thing. This is the story of Michel (Martin La Salle), who picks pockets for kicks, giving himself something between a sexual and an intellectual thrill. He is also the film's occasional narrator and in his detached manner resembles Camus's 'outsider', Meursault. Like Meursault, he has a dying mother.

Although his thieving disgusts his friends, to Michel it is almost a calling, and Lully's orchestral overture (we hear no singing), with its slow, stately, dotted rhythms in the French baroque manner, brings something like nobility to the enterprise. In one scene, in which Michel is given a masterclass in picking pockets by a nameless accomplice played by the illusionist Kassagi (who was also the technical adviser to the film), Lully's music transforms the demonstration of lifting wallets from coat pockets into something sensuous, the hand movements appearing almost balletic.

Mozart was another composer whose music Bresson used, more than once and quite memorably in his 1956 film, *A Man Escaped*. The French Resistance fighter Fontaine (François Leterrier), captured by the Nazis, is trying to break out of Montluc prison. Bresson employs the music as sparingly as in his other films, which is to say that mostly there is none at all, and then, without warning, a short passage from a baroque or classical piece, often the same excerpt repeated. In *A Man Escaped*, it is the *Kyrie* from Mozart's C-minor Mass, and it works very much like the Lully in *Pickpocket*, the music bringing some dignity to Fontaine's plight, taking him out of his surroundings and onto a higher plane.

One wonders whether Neil Armfield had Bresson's film in mind when he made *Candy* (2006) and used Mozart's *Ave Verum Corpus* for those scenes in which Candy (Abbie Cornish) and Dan (Heath Ledger) drift into a heroin-induced haze. Perhaps the words that Mozart set – 'Hail, the true body' – were also significant. Certainly we can assume that Bresson's use of Mozart's *Kyrie* was not an arbitrary choice. Even if the primary function of the music is specifically musical, those opening words of the Mass, 'Lord have mercy upon us', are a commentary on the story. They might be Fontaine's prayer.

Ten years after *A Man Escaped*, Bresson was still using music in much the same way. *Mouchette* (1967) starts with the *Magnificat* from Monteverdi's *Vespers for the Blessed Virgin* of 1610, another anachronistic choice, but again with a specific point to make. Mouchette (Nadine Nortier) is the thirteen-year-old daughter of a dying mother and a violent, alcoholic father. One night on her way home she is raped, and at the end of the film takes her own life. The words of the *Magnificat* – 'my soul doth magnify the Lord' – come from Luke's gospel, where they are spoken by the young Mary. For Bresson, raised a Catholic, to begin and end his film about the destruction of a young girl with Monteverdi's musical setting of the Blessed Virgin's words is bleak irony.

Bresson liked to work with non-professional actors and it is partly this that gives his films their cool, classical-painting look. Because non-professionals do less, their faces generally stiller than those of trained actors, we look harder. Because they tend to speak their lines with less artifice, we listen harder. Pier Paolo Pasolini worked similarly, both he and Bresson having been influenced by the Italian neo-realist films such as Rossellini's *Rome, Open City* (1945) and de Sica's *Bicycle Thieves* (1948). The neo-realists set their films either in poor urban locations or in the countryside, and their stories were of working people and the out-of-work. They tended to engage non-professional actors and to shoot in a simple, quasi-documentary style that encouraged audiences to imagine they might be voyeurs. Pasolini did all this too, but dramatically he was drawn not to the working people of post-Mussolini Rome, so much as to the peasantry of the Middle Ages and mythical times. Perhaps his masterpiece was *The Gospel According to St Matthew* (1964). Musically, it is certainly his most interesting.

On paper, the film's music is a mishmash of styles, ranging from the blues of Blind Willie Johnson to an African Mass to Bach and Mozart and the music Prokofiev composed for *Alexander Nevsky*. In the context of the film, however, it doesn't seem so varied. Like Matthew's gospel, the film is episodic, but visually it has an impressive unity and perhaps that is why the music too seems remarkably of a piece. Another non-professional cast brings an array of striking faces to the screen, among the most memorable a staring (female) Angel of the Lord and a dark, angry Jesus (Enrique Irazoqui). Pasolini was interested in Jesus the revolutionary, the one who sends not 'peace, but a sword' and who sets 'a man at variance against his father, and the daughter against her mother'. Accordingly he draws from Irazoqui a moody and often dynamic performance in which prayers and parables turn into political diatribes. In the fervour of its delivery, the Sermon on the Mount is only a couple of notches below Castro. Somehow it helps that Pasolini was such a devotee of post-synching his dialogue. Many of the voices we hear (including Jesus's) do not even belong to the actors we are watching, and this gives them a disarming quality that veers from detached belligerence to otherworldliness. The way the framing of the photography resembles classical paintings helps here too: Jesus himself might have walked straight out of El Greco's *The Purification of the Temple*, but the backgrounds and buildings and many of the minor characters – the Magi and the Pharisees, for example – are from Piero della Francesca and other painters of the early Renaissance.

So is it a religious film? Pasolini seems to have been having an each-way bet. The director was a communist, certainly, and had previously lampooned the Church. The film's Italian title leaves out any mention of sainthood – the author of the gospel is just plain 'Matteo' – and the director was annoyed when the English-language version put the 'Saint' back in again. But when all is said and done, the film is dedicated to the memory of Pope John XXIII and it won the Church's approval. And there is also the matter of the musical choices. It is not that music necessarily spells spirituality. On the contrary, this film keeps its feet pretty firmly on the ground in that respect. But the music does regularly conjure pathos, which feels somewhat at odds with the revolutionary figure Pasolini sought to create. Bach's is the prevailing musical contribution: concerto movements, 'Dona nobis pacem' from the B-minor Mass, as well as two sections of the *St Matthew Passion*, the final chorus and the violin obbligato from the aria 'Erbarme dich'. This last is the one musical moment in the film that is tied to its scriptural inspiration, Peter's denial, although it also crops up in other scenes. Odetta's singing of 'Sometimes I Feel Like a Motherless Child' accompanies the scene of the Magi visiting the baby Jesus, and it comes back in the first scene featuring John the Baptist; Blind Willie Johnson's 'Dark Was the Night, Cold Was the Ground' is heard as the lame man walks towards Jesus, the song returning at the moment of Judas's suicide. Mozart's *Masonic Funeral Music* is always associated with the crucifixion.

The two most striking uses of music in the film, however, are also the two least likely: the recycling of music from *Alexander Nevsky* and the inclusion of *Missa Luba*. Prokofiev's severely ominous motif of winds and strings an octave apart are heard at the opening of Eisentein's film, returning as the troops wait for the start of the battle on the ice. In *The Gospel According to St Matthew* it sounds just as ominous heard as different soldiers await the command to swoop down from the hills and slaughter the innocents. But the actual opening of Pasolini's film is as impressive in its way as Eisenstein's. *Missa Luba* was an arrangement of the Mass by a Belgian friar working in the Congo in the 1950s. He drew on traditional Congolese songs and dances but also left room for the singers and drummers to add embellishments of their own. It is not quite as obscure a choice as it might seem. A recording was released in 1963 – the year before Pasolini's film – and a single even entered the British pop chart, so it was hardly unfamiliar. And yet, of course, to Western ears, the music of this Mass still sounds authentically African, authentically 'other'. The 'Gloria', in particular, is bursting with energy and very much at odds with all the other music in the film, and the director's use of it, not only to open and close his film, but especially at moments of revelation – the appearance of the angel, the curing of the leper – is bold.

Stanley Kubrick's films, perhaps more than those of any other film director, are known for their bold use of music. Some of Kubrick's choices were so bold, indeed, that it is difficult to disentangle quite well-known pieces from the images to which Kubrick fitted them. You might think that the 'Blue Danube Waltz' of Johann Strauss II would, for all time, conjure up the ballrooms of imperial Vienna, but to anyone who has seen *2001: A Space Odyssey* (1968), the strains of the waltz are just as redolent of the docking operations of space craft. To those who lived through the Second World War, Vera Lynn singing 'We'll Meet Again' probably brings back memories of the home front, but for those of us who didn't, it's just as likely to be the images of nuclear explosions at the end of *Dr Strangelove* (1964). The march-like *Andante con moto* from Schubert's Piano Trio in E flat recalls the long, nearly wordless seduction scene in *Barry Lyndon*. The slow movement of Bartók's Music for Strings, Percussion and Celesta evokes the eerie quiet of the snowed-in hotel in *The Shining* (1980). And Richard Strauss's *Also sprach Zarathustra* unfailingly conjures images from *2001*. Has any other classical piece – at least its first minute – ever achieved greater popular fame through its use in a film?

Kubrick's films always tended to be long, and the scenes within them were often correspondingly long. Perhaps this is why he also used long stretches of music. Certainly if one compares his work with Ingmar Bergman's, there is a marked difference. Bergman also used classical music, but typically in short bursts. Sometimes you just hear a few notes. Kubrick was the opposite. While we may seldom hear complete movements – even the Schubert in *Barry Lyndon*, which runs through a number of scenes, fades before it reaches its end – nevertheless he used music lavishly.

But there is also the matter of musical choices. Bergman was rather conservative here. Bach was a favourite, but he also used Mozart, Chopin and Schumann well. And Bergman tended to tie his musical choices to character. In *Fanny and Alexander* (1982), for example, the Bishop (Jan Malmsjö) plays Bach on his flute. Bach is generally a benign ingredient in a Bergman film but this Bishop is one of the director's most loathsome creations. So why Bach? In fact what the Bishop is playing is only half a piece. It is a sonata for flute and harpsichord, but the Bishop plays it without the accompaniment. This man's hateful nature – Bergman seems to be saying – means he must always be alone and incomplete.

Kubrick's musical choices were seldom obviously linked to individual characters and were always unpredictable. The 'Blue Danube' in *2001* is probably the most surprising selection, but it works well, and this may be because we hear so much of it. The sense of incongruity quickly slips away and it is not long before we imagine the docking space craft are waltzing. The music of the contemporary Hungarian composer György Ligeti was also a surprising choice in this film, not least to the composer himself, who had no idea three of his works were being used. The other composer who was surprised by the use of Ligeti's music was Alex North, who was suddenly told his own specially composed score was no longer needed.

A Clockwork Orange (1971) is full of incongruous musical choices, most of them classical. Of course the principal musical decision was made for Kubrick by Anthony Burgess, the author of the short novel on which the film is based. Alex (Malcolm McDowell) lives in a Britain of the future. He speaks Nadsat – the argot of his age-group and class – and is addicted to 'the old ultraviolence', 'the old in-out' (sex) and the music of 'the old Ludwig van' (Beethoven). In particular, he is obsessed by Beethoven's Symphony No. 9 in D minor, of which we hear plenty, specifically the *Scherzo* and the *Finale*. On the surface, Kubrick's film seems to use classical music to ameliorate the discomfort involved in watching some fairly violent acts: we see a brutal fight between two gangs (one of them Alex's) while we listen to the overture to Rossini's *Thieving Magpie*, the latter distancing us from the former. At the time of its release, and since, the film was both praised and criticised for this.

But the use of music in *A Clockwork Orange* goes deeper. Alex seems only properly alive when he is beating someone up or running other people's cars off the road, or when he is alone and listening to music. So the music in these scenes tends to be real and unadulterated. We hear orchestras, we even see which Deutsche Grammophon recording of Beethoven's ninth he is listening to. Elsewhere – in the milk bar with his 'droogs' (friends), or visiting the record store or having sped-up sex with two girls at once – the music, while it might still be classical, is synthesised.

Following Alex's arrest, imprisonment and subjection to the Ludovico method (aversion therapy), he cuts a pathetic figure, turned off both violence and good music, unwilling to defend himself against physical attack and happy listening to plastic pop. Beethoven's ninth symphony encourages suicidal thoughts, and it is after such an attempt that he finds himself back in hospital. At the end of the film, with the treatment reversed, Beethoven's ninth again seems the very stuff of life and Alex is his old violent self.

So *A Clockwork Orange* is not a film with an especially uplifting message, and it was greeted by a predictable wave of moral outrage. But amid the warnings that the film would produce legions of violent gangs roaming our city streets, no one seems ever to have wondered whether it might also encourage young men to listen to Beethoven. Probably it did neither. The life-changing effects of cinema are always overstated.

Bold music is integral to the experience of a Stanley Kubrick film. We notice it, and are meant to notice it. And because many of Kubrick's scenes are steeped in music, we also sometimes notice when it's not there. The silent space walk of *2001* is famous, but the domestic sterility of Alex's parents' home in *A Clockwork Orange* is also partly created by the absence of the music that dominates the rest of the film.

The use of Sergei Rakhmaninov's Piano Concerto No. 2 in *Brief Encounter* (David Lean, 1945) may also be counted as bold. It was the express choice of the film's producer, Noël Coward, on whose one-act play *Still Life* the screenplay was based. Apart from a running joke about the music in a café, Rakhmaninov's concerto is the only music heard in the film and it plays an important role, helping to elevate a provincial, middle-class affair to great romantic heights. So famous is the combination of film and music that it quickly became a cinematic touchstone for the emotional pain of marital infidelity and, for much the same reason, the butt of a few good jokes. In Billy Wilder's *The Seven Year Itch* (1957), Tom Ewell, wearing Coward's trademark smoking jacket and speaking with his clipped patrician vowels, sits on a piano stool beside Marilyn Monroe and attempts to seduce her with Rakhmaninov's concerto. In *A Touch of Class* (Melvin Frank, 1973), Glenda Jackson watches the film on television, identifying with its story and weeping copiously. In *Truly Madly Deeply* (Anthony Minghella, 1990), the ghosts that come to stay with Juliet Stevenson watch the video and recite the closing dialogue in synch with the film.

Brief Encounter is the story of an illicit affair between Laura Jesson (Celia Johnson) and Alec Harvey (Trevor Howard). Both are middle-aged and seemingly happily married with families. She does her shopping every Thursday in Milford, a fictional English country town. He is a GP who visits Milford Hospital once a week, also on Thursdays. They meet in the tearoom of Milford Junction railway station where Alec removes a piece of grit from Laura's eye, then they bump into each other the following week outside the hospital. At lunchtime on the same day Alec walks into the crowded Kardomah café where the only available seat is at Laura's table. From then on there is no looking back. Or rather there is nothing but looking back, because the story is narrated as a series of flashbacks.

The structure of the film is rather intricate and the use of the music reflects this. In the first scene, we see Laura and Alec together in the tearoom. We do not yet know it, but they are saying goodbye for the last time, a parting that is interrupted by the arrival of 'poor, well-meaning, irritating Dolly Messiter'. When Laura gets home to her family, she sits with her husband and imagines telling him about the whole affair. So she becomes the film's narrator as we watch the events unfold from the beginning (with regular present-tense interruptions), concluding with that opening scene, but this time with Laura's commentary.

On the surface, Rakhmaninov's second piano concerto is a standard three-movement work – fast/slow/fast – and Lean's film starts, obviously enough, with the main title over the beginning of the first movement. But the structure of the concerto is less conventional than it seems. Like the Vivaldi mandolin concerto in *L'Enfant sauvage*, the themes in Rakhmaninov's piano concerto have shared characteristics, common intervals and rhythmic figures that bring a strong sense of unity to the music of all three movements. It would be possible to cut up the concerto and reorder its parts without doing it too much damage, which is precisely what Lean and his editor did, echoing the cut-up structure of the film. Music from all three movements is presented quite out of order and very much in the manner of a specially composed score, which, by the time Lean had finished with it, the concerto became. It is worth comparing and contrasting this use of a single piece with Luchino Visconti's use of Mahler's fifth symphony in *Death in Venice* (1971). Visconti uses the Mahler a lot, but it is always the same movement – the *Adagietto* – and each time it starts from the beginning.

There is far less Rakhmaninov in *Brief Encounter* than one remembers, but it is totally integrated with the film. In the scene in which a flustered and disappointed Laura looks for Alec on the railway-station platform, a restless orchestral passage from just before the end of Rakhmaninov's concerto accompanies her darting glances. As the solo piano enters, so does Alec, running towards Laura, accompanied by the piano's skittering figuration. As the musical climax breaks it largely obliterates Alec and Laura's hurried greeting and farewell as he rushes to catch his train. It is a perfect match between action and music and, since the piano concerto already existed, this scene can only have been edited to fit it.

In 1945, the two lead actors were relative newcomers to the screen, but everyone in the audience would have known the Rakhmaninov concerto. Today, we might think of this music as somehow highbrow – especially if we accept the contemporary Hollywood attitude to classical music – but in the 1940s it was nothing of the sort. *Brief Encounter* was made at a time when popular classics were still a staple of radio schedules, and Rakhmaninov's concerto was very popular indeed. Lean's use of the Rakhmaninov, then, is not unlike the way many modern films employ pop music to comment on characters and their actions, but in its constant reference to this one concerto throughout the entire length of the picture, *Brief Encounter* remains one of the most extreme examples of musical borrowing in the history of cinema.

Pop Goes the Score

'All I knew was I didn't want to have a score,' says David Chase, creator of the HBO series *The Sopranos* (1999–2007), in a short interview feature accompanying the DVD release of the final series. One of his producers, Martin Bruestle, goes further, explaining that Chase 'didn't want to hire a composer because he didn't want to tell the audience how to feel'.

Of course this is nonsense. They might have ditched the score, but in its place Chase and his team put dozens of songs. Mostly these were well-known songs, occasionally they were dug out from an obscure back catalogue, but in virtually every case they reflected some aspect of the story on the screen. More often than not, as Chase admits, they were songs with lyrics, so they functioned like 'a Greek chorus'. And he adds that even he can still 'get choked up' when he watches the scenes from an episode in the second series, in which Christopher Moltisanti (Michael Imperioli) lies in hospital having been shot, and Otis Redding sings 'My Lover's Prayer' on the soundtrack. So much for not telling the audience how to feel.

In the theatre of Ancient Greece, the chorus consisted of more or less disinterested bystanders to the action who spoke directly to the audience, filling in details of the story, clarifying events and proposing a response to the characters and their actions. This is usually how songs function in films. When they are heard only on the soundtrack, they have an authorial quality: it might as well be the filmmaker speaking directly to us. We hear the songs, but the characters don't. The songs address our emotions, our memories (if we already know the song) and our interpretative faculties. They colour the way we respond to the film. Even if the song is heard by one or more of the film's characters – because it's playing on a radio or coming from a car stereo – it is still separate from the action, because mostly we regard the music (from a dramatic point of view) as a random act. Sometimes a song has been specially commissioned for a film, in effect becoming a theme song. Sometimes, as with *The Sopranos*, an existing song is found that seems to fit a particular scene or mood. And then there is the phenomenon of the pop soundtrack that resembles a compilation tape of the director's favourite songs. In some cases, these songs co-exist with a composed score and even find their way into those scores.

One of the earliest and best examples of a film with a theme song is *High Noon* (Fred Zinnemann, 1952). The ballad 'High Noon' was written by the film's composer, Dimitri Tiomkin, who won Academy Awards for both his song and his score. The lyrics of the song were by Ned Washington, among whose hits to date were 'The Nearness of You' (with Hoagy Carmichael) and 'My Foolish Heart' (with Victor Young). This was Washington's first collaboration with Tiomkin, although more would follow, including the theme to the television series *Rawhide* (1959–65). By the time *High Noon* was released, the song, known variously as 'High Noon', 'The Ballad of High Noon' and 'Do Not Forsake Me', was already a hit. Indeed there were three recordings, the most successful of which, from a commercial point of view, was by Frankie Laine. On his record Laine affected a stylised crooning and there was a choir providing backing vocals. All in all, it's a rather lush affair. But on the soundtrack of the film, the accompaniment is sparse and the world-weary voice that of the 'singing cowboy', Tex Ritter.

The song starts the film and it functions to a remarkable degree like a Greek chorus. First the lyrics set up the basic dilemma: 'Do not forsake me, oh my darlin' / On this our wedding day / . . . / The noonday train will bring Frank Miller / . . . / And I must face that deadly killer.' It only lasts two-and-a-half minutes, but the song manages to fill us in on the back story ('He made a vow while in State's Prison / That it would be my life or his'n') and hint strongly at the final outcome ('I can't be leavin' / Until I shoot Frank Miller dead'). As Ritter sings his précis of the story on the soundtrack, the action slowly begins to unfold in pictures. We watch as three men meet up and then together ride towards the town of Hadleyville. They are Colby (Lee Van Cleef), Pierce (Robert J. Wilke) and Frank Miller's brother, Ben (Sheb Wooley), and they are on their way to the rail depot to await the arrival, at 'high noon', of the train carrying the vengeful Frank (Ian MacDonald).

Now the film cuts to the office of the Justice of the Peace, where a judge (Otto Kruger) is presiding over the marriage of the town's marshal, Will Kane (Gary Cooper), to his Quaker bride Amy Fowler (Grace Kelly). As of this moment, indeed, Kane is no longer marshal. He and Amy will be leaving town straight after the wedding. But the new marshal is not arriving until tomorrow, and meanwhile Frank Miller is coming at noon. The clock on the wall in the judge's office shows 10.35: this will be a film that takes place, more or less, in real time.

The opening 'ballad' returns during the film, but never in its entirety. On the contrary, underlining its choric function, relevant lines from the song crop up at key moments in the story. After Kane has decided to stay and face his nemesis, Amy drives off to the train depot in her trap, accompanied by the opening of the song ('Do not forsake me, oh my darlin' ...'). Later, when Kane walks through the empty town, having tried and failed to recruit deputies, we hear the song's middle section ('Oh to be torn 'twixt love and duty / ... / ... my life or his'n'). But more commonly it is Tiomkin's orchestral score that draws extensively on elements of the song, there being scarcely any music on the soundtrack that does not in some way make reference to the ballad. At the wedding in the judge's office, a harmonium in the background is playing the opening part of the song ('Do not forsake me') and these notes continue to appear in the score throughout the film, acting as a *leitmotif* for Amy or for Kane thinking about Amy. Similarly, the music of the middle section ('Oh to be torn 'twixt love and duty'), with its steady march rhythm, represents the coming threat of the train carrying Miller. Often enough this element in the score begins with pulse alone, set in motion by a clock pendulum – everywhere you look in *High Noon*, there is a clock on the wall, ticking ominously – then transformed into the 'Oh to be torn' rhythmic motif.

High Noon is heavily scored. The only extended scene with no music is the debate in the church. Because the score makes continual reference to a song that has already spelt out the story, the connection between the music and the action is particularly close, but Tiomkin's score does more than recall Washington's lyrics. The very *sound* of the score also refuses to let go of the song. Tex Ritter's singing was accompanied by guitar, accordion and a friction drum, which is rubbed, not struck. Tiomkin's orchestra uses these instruments too, often pairing the accordion with a high, muted trumpet to produce the effect of a mouth organ. A piano, used percussively, is also prominent in the orchestral mix. Tiomkin was always an innovator in terms of instrumental colour. In his music for *Red River* (Howard Hawks, 1948), he had used the banjo, not so much as a solo instrument, but as part of the overall sonority of the orchestra. But in *High Noon*, the instruments in the orchestra forge a direct link with the action. In one scene we see Colby waiting at the depot playing a mouth organ, and whenever we enter the saloon a mechanical player-piano is hammering out 'Buffalo Gals Won't You Come Out Tonight'.

High Noon was not the first film to feature a song so prominently – it wasn't even the first Western to do so – but it established a trend that continued with, for example, *The Man from Laramie* (Anthony Mann, 1955), *Gunfight at the O.K. Corral* (John Sturges, 1957) and *3:10 to Yuma* (Delmer Daves, 1957), all of which had songs that bore the same title as the picture, all with lyrics by Ned Washington. In no case were the lyrics of these songs quite as explicit as in *High Noon*, but each song became a major element in its film's score. In *3:10 to Yuma*, based on an Elmore Leonard story with pronounced similarities to *High Noon* (a bad man, a train timetable and a worrying shortage of deputies), there is a rather dreary song by Washington and George Duning that opens the movie. Almost immediately, however, it is transformed in the score (also by Duning). The song featured a Spanish-sounding guitar, and in the scene between the robber Ben Wade (Glenn Ford) and the barmaid Emmy (Felicia Farr), the guitar continues its prominence. Much of the time it plays alone, but even when the orchestra creeps in to take over the theme, the guitar interjects strummed chords. Something about the plangency of this strumming and the languorous pace of the dialogue – which is a seduction by Ben of Emmy – creates a gentle, dreamlike, yet quite intense atmosphere. At the end of the scene, when the music stops, Wade whistles the beginning of the tune, the melody having completed its journey from song to score to character. Much later, in the hotel room in Contention City, a female voice is heard in the distance singing the song. Wade comments to his guard, Dan Evans (Van Hefflin), that he likes the sound of a girl's singing.

The tradition of cowboy movies with songs survived into the 1960s, and lies behind one of the most famous film songs of all, 'Raindrops Keep Fallin' On My Head' in *Butch Cassidy and the Sundance Kid* (George Roy Hill, 1969). In this film the song could hardly be further from its role as a commentator, and neither does it get caught up in the score, because there is no score. In fact there is hardly any music at all in *Butch Cassidy and the Sundance Kid*, so that when the eponymous heroes turn up at the home of Etta Place (Katharine Ross) and Butch (Paul Newman) takes Etta bicycling, the scene and the song bring a complete change of pace. Possibly inspired by the bicycling scene in Truffaut's *Jules et Jim* (1962), which is a musical highlight of that film, the three-minute scene in *Butch Cassidy* has scarcely anything to do with the rest of the movie, and the song by Burt Bacharach and Hal David has even less. Is this why it lodges so firmly in the memory? Standing apart from the action, part interlude, part video clip, the scene was shown a good deal on television in support of the song (sung by B.J. Thomas), which was a major hit. Just as Tiomkin and Washington's ballad promoted *High Noon*, so 'Raindrops' helped to sell *Butch Cassidy and the Sundance Kid*, and this was a part of their function – a function firmly established by the 1960s. One thinks of 'Moon River' in *Breakfast at Tiffany's* (1961), 'The Look of Love' in *Casino Royale* and 'Windmills of Your Mind' in *The Thomas Crown Affair* – all songs with lyrics that have no very obvious connection with the films, all giving rise to memorable scenes and all major international hits.

In cinema, the best-known instance of specially commissioned songs is the James Bond films. From the second film in the series, *From Russia with Love* (Terence Young, 1963), the songs were always an important part of the Bond franchise, their commercial success linked to the commercial success of the movie, which is why no one can remember the songs to *On Her Majesty's Secret Service* (Peter R. Hunt, 1969) or *Moonraker* (Lewis Gilbert, 1979) or any of the films from the past twenty-five years. But when Bond was new, the success of the films helped to make big opening songs fashionable, and in the 1960s, hit films and hit songs (or cult films and cult songs) went together – *The Graduate* (Mike Nichols, 1967), *Midnight Cowboy* (John Schlesinger, 1969) and *Easy Rider* (Dennis Hopper, 1969) are only three of the more obvious examples of movies with hit songs over their main titles. In fact, none of these three begins with its titles. Just like the Bond films, *Midnight Cowboy* and *Easy Rider* plunge us directly into the action, so that it is several minutes before the credits roll and the song is heard.

More recently, opening credits themselves seem to have become unfashionable, pushed further and further into the film. In *The Departed*, the titles appear seventeen minutes into the picture, and it is not unknown for a film to delay showing its title until the closing credits. Parallel to this trend has been the tendency to leave the big song for the finish. Rather than establishing the tone of the film, then, as Steppenwolf's 'Born to Be Wild' certainly did in *Easy Rider*, a song can come along at the end and provide a twist or a comment on what has gone before or simply prime the cash register. In *Titanic* (1997), Celine Dion sings 'My Heart Will Go On' to a tune that the composer James Horner has already introduced in the body of the film. If we're still awake, we will be ready to sing along. But sometimes the final song can seem plain incongruous. It is hard, for instance, to guess what the producers of *The Young Victoria* imagined they were achieving by putting Sinéad O'Connor's 'Only You' over its closing credits. This song doesn't just change the mood of what has gone before, it mocks it. The tune and words are banal, and in her performance the singer would appear to be channelling the old queen on her death bed.

In the late 1990s, songs over the closing credits – a different song each week – became the norm with HBO-style television series such as *The Sopranos*. Typically, these were not specially written, but songs the audience would already know, and this meant that an extra layer of meaning was available to the filmmaker. The song comes to the soundtrack with associations. It might make the viewer feel nostalgic; it might bring sad or happy memories; it is even possible that the song will be one the viewer never liked in the first place. It doesn't matter. The point is that the song re-engages the viewer with the episode.

The most obvious advantage of using pop songs on a soundtrack is that it locates the film in time and possibly place. In 1955, Richard Brooks started *The Blackboard Jungle* with Bill Haley and the Comets playing 'Rock Around the Clock'. The record had been released the previous year, to small acclaim, and now the film helped make it a hit. But from the first bars of the song in the cinema, the 1950s audience was bang in the middle of youth culture and it knew it. George Lucas's *American Graffiti* (1973) also has 'Rock Around the Clock' at the start, but this time it told filmgoers they were watching a film set in the past. In fact, *American Graffiti* is not set as far back at *The Blackboard Jungle*, and there are more than forty songs following Bill Haley that span the eight years from 'Rock Around the Clock' to 1962, the year of the film's setting.

American Graffiti has one of the most celebrated soundtracks in cinema history, and it consists of much more than the songs. The sound designer Walter Murch constructed an elaborate montage in which we hear the voice of (real-life) disc jockey Wolfman Jack introducing songs and filling in with foolish DJ-chatter ('Sneakin' around with the Wolfman, baby'). There are advertisements, hoax phone calls, the standard noise that cluttered commercial radio in the 1960s and clutters it still. The radio sound fades in and out of earshot as sources (mostly car radios) come and go. Very occasionally a radio is switched off, but in general, one car radio fades and another replaces it. The songs themselves serve two purposes beyond locating the film in time and place. The first and most important is to regulate the pace of the film, speeding up the action, slowing it down, helping the film to turn dramatic corners. The second is at the more local level of interaction with the story. The young people on the screen seldom seem to be actively listening to the sounds from their radios, but occasionally they pass judgment.

'Rock-and-roll's been going down hill ever since Buddy Holly died,' complains Milner (Paul Le Mat) as he gives the Beach Boys' 'Surfin' Safari' the flick. The radio shuts off, but only briefly before another radio takes over. And so it goes throughout the film. When Toad (Charles Martin Smith) and Debbie (Candy Clark) leave their car to make out in a field, their brief attempt at intimacy distracts us from noticing that the music has stopped.

'The radio's gone,' Toad says suddenly.

'Yeah?'

'That means the car is gone!'

It is, of course, the ephemeral nature of pop music that makes it so useful for situating a film and so good at provoking a wistful response. Pop music is of its time. This is possibly truer of disco than of any other music in history, and both *Boogie Nights* (Paul Thomas Anderson, 1997) and *The Last Days of Disco* (Whit Stillman, 1998), in their different ways, managed to take the likes of the Commodores' 'Machine Gun' and Alicia Bridges' 'I Love the Nightlife' and give them a kind of nobility. Stillman even managed to create a genuine sense of regret for the passing of an era. That these films should achieve such feats when both are essentially comedies and when the music itself was, in its day, roundly despised by people who didn't go to discos (the vast majority of us) says something about the passing of time and the way it is capable of bestowing, if not gravitas, then at least nostalgia. *Boogie Nights* and *The Last Days of Disco* were films that looked back only two decades. The more years that have passed between the music and the film, the more respectable the nostalgia.

Woody Allen's *Radio Days* (1987) is a paean to the music and personalities on American radio in the early 1940s. In particular, it celebrates the way in which one family listened intently to everything from 'The Flight of the Bumble Bee' to Carmen Miranda, via sports reports and quiz shows. The radio helped define their lives and give it structure. A decade later in Terence Davies's Liverpool, the BBC of the 1950s was the purveyor of an equally eclectic mix of words and music. *Distant Voices, Still Lives* (1988) includes Ella Fitzgerald and Eddie Calvert, Kenneth Williams and Kenneth Horn, but also *A Hymn to the Virgin* by Benjamin Britten and Vaughan Williams's *A Pastoral Symphony*. Perhaps most evocative to anyone acquainted with British radio from the period (and later) was the BBC Shipping Forecast, its list of magical names – 'Humber, Heligoland, East Dogger …' – read at dictation speed and in a tone of mild regret by a male voice with an upper-middle-class accent. Both Woody Allen and Terence Davies have returned to the music of their childhoods, especially when they are making films about their home towns. Where the Manhattan skyline will summon the ghost of Benny Goodman to a Woody Allen soundtrack, for Davies the freshly scrubbed doorstep of a Liverpool terrace evokes Kathleen Ferrier singing 'Blow the Wind Southerly'.

In *Children of Men* (Alfonso Cuarón, 2006), set in a future when 'the world has collapsed' and 'only Britain soldiers on', the filmmakers use music to conjure a fictional past. A recording of Dietrich Fischer-Dieskau singing one of Mahler's *Kindertotenlieder* plays in the house where the elderly hippie Jasper (Michael Caine) lives, and alongside it we hear the Rolling Stones' 'Ruby Tuesday', but in Franco Battiato's sweetly spooky version. The subtle implication is that in this dystopian future the Stones are classical music. Meanwhile, on Radio Avalon, a DJ plays 'Wait' by the Kills, telling us it is 'a blast from the past, all the way back in 2003'. This is contemporary pop being used in order to create a sense of history.

Martin Scorsese was always good at using pop music to evoke period and much else. Like everything in his films, pop generally packs a punch. In particular, the director is a master of the opening song. The beginning of *Mean Streets* (1973), a film which is something of a touchstone for its use of pop music, has little to do with image, but everything to do with sound. It opens on a black screen with the director's voice speaking to his audience quickly, quietly, bluntly: 'You don't make up for your sins in church. You do it in the streets; you do it at home. The rest is bullshit, and you know it.' Then Charlie (Harvey Keitel) opens his eyes, as if from a bad dream, gets off his bed and walks to the mirror. There is the sound of traffic and police sirens. Still looking disorientated he gets back into bed, and as his head hits the pillow we hear – suddenly, marvellously – the Ronettes singing 'Be My Baby'. The song plays in full under the credits, while we watch home-movie footage of Charlie in a suit and tie, doing deals with businessmen, shaking hands with a priest, attending a christening. Two minutes later, at the end of the song and the credits, and without another word being spoken, we already know that the confident, outwardly successful man we have seen in the scratchy, hand-held clips is not the true Charlie. It is partly the nervous look in his eyes, partly the way those handshakes go on too long, and partly the pleading voices of the Ronettes.

Scorsese devised a similar trick for the opening of *Goodfellas* (1990). This time the black screen has Saul Bass's titles sliding across it (they resemble the titles he designed for Hitchcock's *Psycho*), and the first thing we hear is the traffic, fast traffic on a busy freeway. Now we see the back of a car travelling quickly down this road at night, and then we cut straight to its interior. Henry Hill (Ray Liotta) is driving, Jimmy Conway (Robert De Niro) is asleep beside him in the passenger seat, Tommy DeVito (Joe Pesci) is in the back. No one speaks, but in addition to the traffic noise, we begin to hear knocking or banging.

'Is it a flat?' asks Tommy. They pull over. It is not a flat tyre; it's a not-quite-dead body in the boot. Tommy pulls out a very long knife and begins stabbing the man, who is already wrapped in blood-stained sheets, and then Jimmy finishes him off with a few gun shots.

It is the sounds that make this scene: the traffic, the mysterious banging, the knife repeatedly entering the man's body, the gun fired at point-blank range. Then it stops and Henry speaks to the audience in voice-over: 'As far back as I can remember, I always wanted to be a gangster.' Under the last words, Percy Faith and his orchestra begin the brassy, big-band introduction to Tony Bennett singing 'Rags to Riches'. The music is ironic in view of what has happened in the first 100 seconds of the film, but it quickly seduces us, and by the end of the opening credits we believe, in spite of ourselves, that perhaps the life of a gangster really is glamorous. Then Scorsese spends the rest of the film showing us why we're wrong.

*

In *High Fidelity* (Stepher Frears, 2000), the central character, Rob Gordon (John Cusack), explains that in making a compilation tape for someone, you are 'using somebody else's poetry to express your feelings'. Well, the same goes for films that adopt this approach, and *High Fidelity* itself is an interesting example, because it is partly about men who are obsessed with popular music and its associated trivia and live their lives through 'somebody else's poetry'. Rob manages a record shop, Championship Vinyl, and employs two part-time workers who come to work every day because all they do is think about music. Nick Hornby's 1995 novel, on which the film is based, is set in north London and many of the musical references were changed when the location of the film was moved from Crouch End to Chicago. Certainly jokes about Richard and Linda Thompson albums would have seemed out of place. But it's also true that the film makes less of the music than does the book. Songs dominate the novel; the narrator, Rob, vividly describes their sound and their power (Hornby is as good a music writer as he is a novelist). Rob and his co-workers endlessly make 'top five' lists of their favourite songs in various categories, building an overall picture of the characters, and of Rob in particular. In the film, songs have far less prominence, for the most part providing only the background to scenes and reinforcing on-screen situations and emotions.

The film that established the compilation-tape approach to pop music in films was *The Big Chill* (Lawrence Kasdan, 1983). The songs are certainly of pivotal importance and they provide many of the film's best moments, but they also offer an early masterclass in the ways in which this music can be used. First, they establish time and place. This is not the time and place in which the film is set, but from which the characters and their relationships arise. So while we are looking at a peaceful winter house in present-day South Carolina (the present day being 1983), we are listening to the music that resounded on an American college campus in the late 1960s. This is where these friendships were forged, and the musical scene-setting is not only historical and geographical, but political and social. Beyond this, there are inevitable correspondences between the songs and the events of the film, although not as many as it might seem. (If any song is placed on top of any film, the audience will immediately begin to make connections, even where none but the connection of proximity was intended.)

The Big Chill has no score and, as though to emphasise this, the film begins with the Columbia Pictures logo still on the screen, as we eavesdrop on a child's bath-time. The affectionately inane father/child chatter continues over the film's title on a black screen, until finally we see them. The father, Harold Cooper, turns out to be Kevin Kline.

A phone rings and through the open bathroom door we watch Harold's wife, Sarah (Glenn Close), answer it, while Harold continues the childish banter with his son. She replaces the receiver, a meaningful look is exchanged between the parents, and music starts up, familiar music. It is Marvin Gaye singing 'I Heard It Through the Grapevine'. The song plays complete as the rest of the credits roll and we meet, one by one, the film's other main characters. The grapevine has brought them all the same news, that their old friend Alex has killed himself, and now they are on their individual ways to his funeral. The song ends as cars arrive in the car park of a white clapboard church.

Inside the church, another of the friends, Karen (JoBeth Williams), is invited to play 'one of Alex's favourite songs' on the organ. She plays the introduction to the Rolling Stones' 'You Can't Always Get What You Want', her performance cross-fading with the Stones' record as the congregation leaves the church. This plays on through the car ride to the cemetery, fading in and out behind snippets of conversation, and through the burial, finally fading away completely as the mourners gather at Harold and Sarah's home for the reception.

'I saw her today at the reception' is the first line of the Stones' song, and it is small correspondences such as these that helped to give the film its reputation for the use of music. Some have found it heavy-handed. But the songs in general have quite a light touch, with a phrase here and there connecting with the film, or a beat providing an apt counterpoint to the pace of a scene. We remember the film as having a lot of music, but there are ten-minute stretches with none at all and when songs do come along, they come in little clumps. Sometimes the characters on the screen can hear them, sometimes not. When 'A Whiter Shade of Pale' plays, Michael (Jeff Goldblum), a journalist the same age as the others, but trying to seem younger and cooler, asks, 'Harold, don't you have any other music? Like from this century?' A modern audience must remind itself at this point that the present in which the film is set is only fifteen years after Procol Harum's song was a hit.

Later in the film, the songs seem chosen more for their capacity to comment on the story or reflect aspects of it. Meg (Mary Kay Place), a single woman who wants a baby, is speaking to one of Sarah and Harold's children on the phone, while Sarah glances from Meg to her husband and back, an idea forming to Spooner Oldham's sultry organ-playing in 'When a Man Loves a Woman'. This device is repeated when Sarah puts to her husband the suggestion that he might be willing to father Meg's child.

'It's about Meg,' she begins, and this time we hear the gentle piano chords at the start of Aretha Franklin's '(You Make Me Feel Like) A Natural Woman'.

Occasionally the music of *The Big Chill* teeters on the brink of sentimentality (both those examples come close), but it regularly undercuts that possibility with other choices. For example, when Karen and Sam (Tom Berenger) go out into the garden at night, ripping at each other's parkers, to have sex on the cold ground, Sam's first grunt coincides with the first heavy beat of Wilson Pickett's 'In the Midnight Hour'.

The Big Chill was enormously influential in its day. The famous scene in which the characters sing and dance as they clean up the kitchen spawned similar singing/dancing scenes in other movies and TV advertisments. The TV series *thirtysomething* (1987–91) was more or less a direct act of homage to the film and as recently as 2007, the first episode of the TV series *Californication* (2007–) began with an unlikely scene in a church. This time is wasn't a funeral, but they still played 'You Can't Always Get What You Want'. The song also surfaces momentarily in *High Fidelity* when the denizens of Championship Vinyl attempt to come up with their top five songs about death. 'You Can't Always Get What You Want' is proposed but immediately disqualified 'because of its involvement with *The Big Chill*'.

What remains fresh about *The Big Chill*, in spite of the imitations and occasional mockery, is not the closeness of the music to the story, but the looseness of that association. In many cases the precise tracks had not been decided upon when the film was shot, let alone when the script was written, and perhaps it is this that allows room for the viewer to create – and recreate – a relatively personal response to the characters and their stories, unhampered, for the most part, by songs that tell us 'how to feel'.

*

Two directors with idiosyncratic attitudes to pop music are Wes Anderson and Quentin Tarantino. The latter and his musical choices have been much written about. Clive James once wrote that, with Orson Welles, filmmaking became self-conscious. With Tarantino, it goes beyond self-consciousness. It's self-absorption, bordering on self-abuse. At any rate, the director is always the real star of any Tarantino film, and the obscurity of his musical choices serves to remind us of this. His films frequently employ music from other films, thus making links with forgotten pictures from Italy and Hong Kong, all at the cheaper and more splattery end of the canon. In the two *Kill Bill* movies and *Inglourious Basterds* (2009) much of the music came from Spaghetti Westerns. The whistling tune that accompanies Elle Driver (Daryl Hannah) down the hospital corridor in *Kill Bill: Vol. 1* (2003) is by Bernard Herrmann, from the Boulting Brothers B-grade shocker *Twisted Nerve* (1968), a film controversial in its day – and surely unscreenable now – for its association of Down syndrome with murderous intent. You can see why Tarantino would like it.

So while this director certainly avoids using music to underline a plot point, let alone evoke feeling, his choices are nonetheless pointed. For his more assiduous fans, there are connections to be made with old surf-music records and kung-fu films. There's no doubt about it: Tarantino is the quintessential postmodernist filmmaker, his work a tacky labyrinth of intertextuality.

Wes Anderson's films, on the other hand, demonstrate a far looser approach to the choice and placing of pop songs. Some of his selections are as obscure as Tarantino's, but one doesn't feel obliged to admire the director's cleverness in choosing them. Anderson displays an unlikely affinity with some of the forgotten corners of 1960s British pop – unlikely, because he was born in Texas in 1969 – and this is perhaps the signature sound of his movies. Certainly one finds oneself unusually grateful to hear a song such as 'Concrete and Clay' by Unit 4 Plus 2, which was number one in the UK for a single brief week in 1965. It turns up, for no very good reason, in *Rushmore* (1998). But that is why it is refreshing: that very lack of a reason. There is plenty of forgotten pop music in Anderson's films – the Faces, the Kinks, Nick Drake – and it is used for musical reasons, not because its lyrics have messages for us, and generally not because the director is drawing a connection with a film we're unlikely to have seen.

That said, in *Hotel Chevalier* (2007), Anderson's short film that serves as the upbeat to *The Darjeeling Limited* (2007), Peter Sarstedt's 'Where Do You Go To My Lovely' plays in its entirety. The pretentious French ambiance of the song – the accordion introduction, the references to Zizi Jeanmaire and Sacha Distel – fit with the

Parisian hotel room. Jack (Jason Schwartzman), whose room this is, sports a droopy, late-1960s moustache à la Sarstedt himself. It might be a coincidence, but probably isn't. Before Jack's (ex-)girlfriend (Natalie Portman) arrives at the hotel room, he has already cued the music. And after their attempt at sex, the song having finished, it plays once more. This time it starts up all on its own, and ends prematurely. Altogether, it plays for half the length of the thirteen-minute short, which in turn comes to resemble a music video. In the main feature, there's further use of the Ray Davies back catalogue, but the principal musical contributions come from the soundtracks of a dozen different films by Satyajit Ray – from *Pather Panchali* (1955) to *Joi Baba Felunath* (1979), much of the music composed by the director himself – and from a handful of James Ivory's Indian pictures. The three American brothers whom we follow in the film are tourists in India, so there is a certain rightness in Anderson choosing his Indian music from a little stack of soundtrack CDs.

The music in Wes Anderson's films is a lot like his writing, and therefore his characters. The audience is kept guessing. There is nothing predictable about any of them. We are drawn to the characters without necessarily approving of them. On the contrary, most of Anderson's characters behave rather badly – scarcely anyone in the *Royal Tenenbaums* (2001) is less than reprehensible – but it is the sort of bad behaviour that's easy to identify with. Selfishness, in a nutshell. And while the characters are often outwardly jejune, this tends to disguise deep feeling and even passion. What is completely missing from Anderson's work is sentimentality.

In Richard Curtis's writing, from his TV series *The Vicar of Dibley* (1994–2007) to his feature films, there is always a streak of sentimentality. It masquerades as something a bit risky, a bit quirky, a bit dark. But make no mistake, it is sentimental. It is also cute: the 'actually' in *Love Actually* (2003) tells you all you need to know. Curtis not only wrote but directed this film, and so sentimentality and cuteness are greatly to the fore. For one thing, it's Christmas;

there's a little boy coping with the death of his mother; there's a lonely woman whose love life is wrecked by calls from her mentally ill brother; there's a man in love with his Portuguese housekeeper; there's a prime minister in love with his tea lady (much of it is a peculiarly British brand of class-cuteness, come to think of it). And there is sentimentality and cuteness in the music, too. The surprise choir singing 'All You Need Is Love' in the wedding scene is a good example, with instruments suddenly popping up all over the church. And there's Hugh Grant's dance. Grant plays the British prime minister, and when a song on the radio is dedicated to him and the Pointer Sisters' 'Jump' starts up, you know instantly, because he's such a cute prime minister, that he is going to dance. To sentimentality and cuteness, we may add predictability.

Pop music in these films tends to replace dialogue. This is not in itself a bad thing. But it is difficult to believe the songs weren't chosen in advance and the script fitted to explain them, a bit like a music video. Of course, there are effective moments. Among the multiple story strands, the least cute and sentimental involves Karen (Emma Thompson) and her husband Harry (Alan Rickman). It has already been established that Karen likes Joni Mitchell, regarding her as something of an emotional role model. In a very small intertextual joke, Rickman's character says, 'I can't believe you still listen to Joni Mitchell.' (It's funny if you recall the scene in *Truly Madly Deeply*, where Rickman and Juliet Stevenson sang Mitchell's 'A Case of You'.) For Christmas, Harry has bought Karen not the necklace she has already stumbled across in his pocket, but a Joni Mitchell CD – so the necklace must be for someone else – and we watch her break down as she listens to 'Both Sides Now'. This isn't the original 1960s version of the song. This is Mitchell's worldly wise remake from 2000 (the assiduous product placement of the CD cover leaves us in no doubt), the tired maturity of her voice part of its power in the context of this story.

But the fact remains Curtis is a big rationaliser: when a song turns up in one of his movies, you generally hear the clunk. In *The Boat That Rocked* (2009), the writer/director found what ought to have been his ideal subject, one in which there is a blanket reason to include a lot of old pop music. After all, as the caption at the start of the film has it, the year is '1966, the greatest era for British Rock & Roll', and we are aboard a pirate radio ship broadcasting to the British Isles from the North Sea. The writing still seems lazy and the characters are more than ever cyphers, but at least now the inevitable songs have a built-in rationale. However, even a boatful of disc jockeys isn't enough justification for Curtis. Stories are invented to accommodate songs. A girl called Marianne (Talulah Riley) comes on board, mostly so that Carl (Tom Sturridge) can fancy her, then lose her to Dave (Nick Frost), then sit around moping as we all listen to Leonard Cohen singing 'So Long, Marianne'. Scarcely have we recovered from having this pointless rationalisation foisted on us, but we learn that another of the floating DJs is to marry a woman called Elenore (January Jones). Anybody who has even a nodding acquaintance with 1960s pop music is now waiting impatiently for the Turtles. And sure enough, a few minutes later there they are on the soundtrack, even though their hit record 'Elenore', which the whole crew seems to know and sings along to, wasn't released until late 1968. This film is very specific about dates, but only when it suits its purpose. In the film's single most meretricious scene, Cat Stevens's 'Father and Son', first released in 1970 and mawkishly sentimental even before Curtis got his hands on it, is provided with extra layers of cuteness as we watch Carl and his newfound father (Ralph Brown) enact an underwater ballet while the boat sinks. This cannot happen soon enough.

As a corrective to sentimentality, it is always worth watching *Withnail and I* (Bruce Robinson, 1987), which contains a good example of music used not for its meaning or implications or associations, but simply for its sound. Jimi Hendrix's version of 'All Along the Watchtower' runs behind the drunken road trip made by

Marwood (Paul McGann) and Withnail (Richard E. Grant). There is no conceivable connection between Withnail's affronted dignity and his shouted taunts at the passing schoolgirls ('Scrubbers! … Little tarts, they love it!') and Hendrix's ecstatic elevation of one of Bob Dylan's more mystical lyrics, but as the scene goes on and Hendrix digs into his solo, the music seems made for the scene. There's danger in the music and danger in the driving. The first might be serious, the other comic, but that contradiction is why the scene is so strong. Had both the driving and the music been comic in tone, we'd have ended up with Benny Hill.

A musical road trip lies at the very heart of *Broken Flowers* (Jim Jarmusch, 2005) as Don Johnston attempts to find the mother of his son. Johnston (Bill Murray) is constantly amusing people because his name sounds like that of the star of *Miami Vice*, but the writer/director has a more mythological namesake in mind. This Don Johnston is an ageing Don Juan and the first time we meet him, he is sitting in front of his television set watching *The Private Life of Don Juan* (Alexander Korda, 1934) while his latest girlfriend is busy leaving him. Simultaneously, the mail brings a pink envelope containing an anonymous letter purporting to be written by one of Don's ex-lovers, telling him that he has a nineteen-year-old son. Don makes a list of possible names, his neighbour Winston (Jeffrey Wright) discovers their addresses and off Don goes to visit them. Before he leaves, Winston hands him a compilation CD he has made for him to listen to in his car. This is where things could go so badly wrong – imagine what Richard Curtis would do – but this is a Jarmusch film with the ever-taciturn Murray, and anyway Winston's CD turns out to be all instrumentals. In the ensuing driving scenes, as Don goes on his odyssey of rediscovery, the jazz of Mulatu Astatke offers a flowing contrast to the stilted, pause-choked conversations Don finds himself having with his former girlfriends.

Contrast is also the point of most of the musical choices in Sofia Coppola's *Marie Antoinette* (2006). Where a director such as Bresson used baroque and classical music in wholly modern settings, and did so without apology or explanation, Coppola's anachronisms are all the other way. Just as *A Knight's Tale* (Brian Helgeland, 2001) made stunningly effective use of Queen's 'We Will Rock You' in the opening joust – music from the 1970s in the dramatic context of the 1370s – Coppola also employs music that is incongruous to the historical setting, but utterly appropriate to her film.

In *Marie Antoinette*, alongside music from the mid-eighteenth century – Rameau at the wedding, Vivaldi in the bedchamber – Coppola chose pop music from 200 years later for the court of Louis XVI and his Austrian queen. Specifically, she used a lot of songs of the so-called New Romantics, bands that brought a sudden burst of retro-glamour to British pop in the early 1980s, following the garbage bags and safety pins of punk. Adam and the Ants and Bow Wow Wow even liked to dress in eighteenth-century fashions, so the connection is not forced. More to the point, the songs enliven the movie. In the context of eighteenth-century excess, this aggressively joyous music is simultaneously apt and jarring, bringing humour to the proceedings, as well as a touch of theatrical alienation that insists we think critically about the characters rather than simply becoming absorbed in their story. At a Parisian masked ball, Siouxsie & the Banshees' 'Hong Kong Garden' plays in an arrangement for amplified strings and hyperactive harpsichord that gradually morphs into the original. A home-shopping party at Versailles is given to the accompaniment of Bow Wow Wow's 'I Want Candy'. Finally, Marie-Antoinette (Kirsten Dunst) succumbs to her Swedish stalker Count Fersen (Jamie Dornan) in a two-stage encounter involving a stark musical jump-cut. On the couch she puts up token resistance to the strains of Couperin's 'Les barricades mystérieuses'. But the pounding drums of Adam Ant's 'Wild Frontier' arrive to tell us the barricades are down, as we see the two of them going hard at it in bed. Besides the eighteenth-century baroque sounds and the anachronistic 1980s pop, there is a third strand of music. The cool, spare, repetitive pieces by composers Dustin O'Halloran and Aphex Twin conjure the contemporary world of chill-out music, a necessary antidote to the exuberance and exorbitance that fill the rest of the film.

Coppola's picture ends before the royal pair are guillotined. Had we seen their heads roll, we probably wouldn't have cared much anyway. They are not very likable people in the film, and we suspect they weren't in real life. Still, by stopping short of the executions, which would have anchored the final reel in historical reality, Coppola, with the music of three centuries, each tied to its time and place, leaves us feeling that we might just have watched a movie about spoilt, rich kids being obnoxious at any time and in any place.

Pictures of Sound

The first time we see the *Washington Globe* reporter Cal McAffrey (Russell Crowe) in Kevin Macdonald's film *State of Play* (2009) he is driving to a crime scene. We are about to learn a lot about him in a short time. The interior of his car is a mess. He drives recklessly and far too fast. He listens to Irish music with the volume up high, the music somehow underscoring the style of his driving. And he knows all the words to 'The Night Pat Murphy Died'. We learn this last fact because as Great Big Sea sing the song on McAffrey's car stereo, the journalist is joining in at the top of his voice. By the time he gets out of his car, we already like him, and it's mostly because of his passionate attitude to music.

Philip Seymour Hoffman's Jon Savage, also driving his car, though more sedately, sings 'Solomon Song' from Bertolt Brecht and Kurt Weill's *Threepenny Opera*. He is singing along in German with Lotte Lenya in *The Savages* (Tamara Jenkins, 2007). Jon is writing a book about Brecht, which goes someway to explaining the scene, but more immediately Weill's regretful music underlines his introspection and, even if we don't understand the German, we might guess that the words also apply to him. Jon's relationship with a Polish woman is dying from his own neglect, he is discovering he doesn't know his sister, and his father (whom he neither really knows nor likes) has dementia. 'Solomon Song' is an ironic hymn of praise to those who lack wisdom (after all, look what happened to Solomon), beauty, courage and passion, so Brecht's lyrics certainly fit. But it's Weill's forlorn waltz tune and Hoffman's singing that do the work here. It's a heartbreaking scene.

Aaron Altman (Albert Brooks) can also sing in a foreign language, rather brilliantly as it turns out, Francis Cabrel's 'L'edition spéciale' containing a lot of tongue-twisting words to be delivered at breakneck speed. In *Broadcast News* (James L. Brooks, 1987), Aaron is an experienced television journalist who has just been snubbed and humiliated by his network, passed over for a special news broadcast in favour of Tom Grunick (William Hurt). Grunick is inexperienced and none-too-bright, but he has the authentic square jaw of a news anchor and looks serious in a suit. Aaron is hurt and angry but feigning insouciance. Since he is at home alone in this scene, the insouciance is purely for his own benefit, and he listens to Cabrel to reassure himself. Cabrel's song is, at least partly, a satire about current affairs in the mass media, but that is not the point of the scene, which is to make Aaron look impressive – in his own eyes as well as ours – by rattling off a lot of fast French lyrics.

These are perhaps relatively simple examples of the ways in which, without actually turning into a musical, a film can be enhanced by song. Characters who are not singers find reason to sing (and sometimes dance) and, in the process, something about them is revealed. Singing brings a new dimension to a role, and scenes such as those described above are capable of changing or enhancing the audience's view of a character and moving the story forward. So in *The Deer Hunter* (Michael Cimino, 1978), there is the celebrated bar-room scene in which the jukebox plays Frankie Valli singing 'Can't Take My Eyes Off You' and all the main characters join in. The scene demonstrates their friendship, their ease in each other's company, and it invites the audience to feel a part of it. Something similar happens in the best-remembered scene in *The Big Chill*. Clearing up after dinner, the principal cast members dance around the kitchen while singing along with the Temptations' 'Ain't Too Proud to Beg'. Some of this film's late-1960s pop hits are heard by and commented on by the characters, but mostly they are just on the soundtrack. So the music, in a way, belongs to the audience more than to the people on the screen, and particularly to an audience of baby-boomers. Consequently this scene, at the exact centre of *The Big Chill*, in which we watch the characters identifying with and participating in the music – *our* music – brings them closer to us and lets the audience into the action. We feel we have joined their party; we are all in this weekend together.

The dichotomy between music that is just on the soundtrack and music that is in the film (heard by the characters) can be stark or blurred, and often one sort of music is transformed into the other. For instance, in the final reel of *Amarcord* (Federico Fellini, 1973), as everything turns to sepia, we are at the outdoor reception for Gradisca's wedding. The gorgeous Nino Rota theme that has dominated the film is now heard played just on an accordion. We see the accordionist – he is at the reception – and occasionally his playing is interrupted. The music has slipped right off the soundtrack and into the picture. Similarly, the Shostakovich waltz that plays over the opening credits of *Eyes Wide Shut* (Stanley Kubrick, 1999) ends mid-phrase when Bill Harford (Tom Cruise) turns the radio off at the start of the first scene.

In *Brief Encounter*, Rakhmaninov's second piano concerto also goes from the soundtrack to the radio. At the end of the scene in which Laura Jesson and Alec Harvey admit their love for each other, the concerto instantly wells up, doing what a romantic score is expected to do in a romantic film. But simultaneously we hear the voice of Laura's dull husband, Fred (Cyril Raymond), trying to make himself heard.

'Do you think we might have that down a bit, darling?' Fred is saying, and abruptly we are jolted from flashback into the present. We are in the Jessons' living room, where the Rakhmaninov – which by this point in the film is strongly identified with Laura and Alec's affair – is blaring out of the radio.

'It really is quite deafening,' says poor Fred as he walks over to the radio. I wonder are there any other movies in which one of the characters asks for the soundtrack to be turned down. Certainly it seems a bracingly postmodern conceit for a film made at the end of the Second World War.

The producer, Val Lewton, must have had a thing about unaccompanied singing, because it turns up in most of his films. In the famous sequence of horror flicks he made for RKO Pictures in the 1940s, these singing women are everywhere. In *The Seventh Victim* (Mark Robson, 1943), Mrs Romari sings Giordani's 'Caro mio ben'; in *The Body Snatcher* (Robert Wise, 1945) the blind ballad singer sings traditional Scottish songs right up to the moment of her murder, which occurs mid-phrase. Lewton's first film for RKO was *Cat People* (Jacques Tourneur, 1942), in which the main character, Irena Dubrovna (Simone Simon), sings a song that is also heard on a radio and features prominently in the score. This is the lullaby 'Dodo, l'enfant do', very well known in France, and possibly it was suggested by the French actress who sang it, because there is no apparent connection with her character, who is meant to be Croatian. There is also no obvious reason for her to be singing a lullaby. It might be that the composer, Roy Webb, simply liked the idea of working into his score a song that had already been appropriated by Debussy (in 'Jardins sous la pluie') and Fauré. He certainly made full use of it, and two years later it was back in *The Curse of the Cat People* (Gunther von Fritsch and Robert Wise, 1944). Irena had died at the end of *Cat People*, and in the sequel her husband Oliver (Kent Smith) has a new wife and a daughter, Amy (the eight-year-old Ann Carter, supplying the best acting in the film). Amy wishes for a friend and the ghost of Irena appears. She is still Simone Simon and she sings 'Dodo l'enfant do' to the child, which now at least makes some sense. In another, rather magical scene, as carollers round the family piano sing 'Shepherds Shake Off Your Drowsy Sleep', Irena's ghost, standing outside in the snow-covered garden, gives a spirited rendition of another French song, the Christmas carol 'Il est né le divin enfant'. Roy Webb, who again wrote the score, would have us believe that Irena's carol fits exactly on top of the one being sung in the house, but the effect is only managed by virtue of adjustments to the latter. Webb's score, however, again makes good use of 'Dodo, l'enfant do' right from the first notes of the main title.

Since talking pictures began, it has been a standard technique of the film composer to take a song that is on the soundtrack or is sung or played on-screen and make it a principal theme in the score. *Some Like It Hot* (Billy Wilder, 1959) provides a brilliant example. When Sweet Sue's all-'girl' band arrives in Florida with its new saxophonist Joe/Josephine (Tony Curtis) and bass player Jerry/Daphne (Jack Lemon), it is to the sound of a female chorus line singing Abe Olman's 'Down Among the Sheltering Palms'. But we don't see dancing girls; instead there is a line of elderly millionaire bachelors in rocking chairs. Shortly after, on the bandstand, Sugar Kane Kowalczyk (Marilyn Monroe) sings Kalmar and Ruby's 'I Want to Be Loved by You'. Following the show, Sugar has a date with Joe/Josephine, whom she believes to be Junior, the heir to the Shell Oil fortune. They are rushing to meet each other before having dinner aboard his yacht. The yacht actually belongs to Osgood Fielding III (Joe E. Brown), who has taken a shine to Jerry/Daphne, and come ashore so they can go tangoing at the local roadhouse. The film now cuts back and forth between the two couples rushing to meet each other (in Joe/Josephine's case this involves a quick change into nautical leisurewear and a bike ride) while Adolph Deutsch's score provides an elaborate musical fantasy. Closely matched to the pictures, the music oscillates between 'I Want to Be Loved by You' for Sugar and Junior and 'Down Among the Sheltering Pines' for Daphne and Osgood, with several strong hints of 'La Cumparsita', the tango still to come.

Deutsch dazzles us with his scoring for this scene, but the basic idea is certainly commonplace. Considerably less standard are soundtracks that become visible. A small if particularly vivid instance of this – the soundtrack almost literally walking on to the screen –

occurs in *Two Hands* (Gregor Jordan, 1999), when Les (Kiri Paramour) is chasing Jimmy (Heath Ledger) and Alex (Rose Byrne) through Sydney's Chinatown at night. Les is trying to report their whereabouts to Acko (David Field) but his mobile phone is out of juice and bleeping at him. He runs to a public phone but finds he has no loose change. Cezary Skubiszewski's tense, jazz-tinged score underpins this action, and a solo saxophone joins the other instruments to add to the almost *noir*-ish character of the music. But then the other sounds drop away to leave the saxophone playing on its own. Suddenly we see the sax player in the distance, busking in the street, just as Les, in the foreground, discovers that he has no coins for the phone. Cursing loudly, Les turns around, strides over to the sax player and reaches into his takings. When the busker asks him what he thinks he's doing, Les takes his sax off him and hurls it at the ground, then races back to the phone. We watch the busker bend down to pick up his instrument, parts of which fall off and clatter on the pavement, then slowly walk over to the phone and whack Les over the head with it.

In Bertrand Tavernier's *Ça commence aujourd'hui* (1999), Louis Sclavis's little band, which has been heard on the soundtrack throughout the film, comes marching onto the screen for the celebration in the final scene. In *Leatherheads* (George Clooney, 2008), which has a score by Randy Newman, the composer is also the piano player in the barroom where a fight breaks out. Newman goes on playing but is required to duck a bit. Duke Ellington, whose music, new and old, is heard on the score of *Anatomy of a Murder* (Otto Preminger, 1959), also happens to play piano in the bar frequented by the lawyer Paul Biegler (James Stewart). In one scene, Paul and Pie Eye (Ellington) play a duet. All these instances depend for their full effect upon the audience recognising the musicians. In a sense, a more straightforward use of music on-screen is when one of a film's characters is a musician, for example Hoagy Carmichael's Cricket in *To Have and Have Not* (Howard Hawks, 1944). Unlike

Ellington, Carmichael was not the composer on the film, but his character is the bandleader and he performs a few of his own (Hoagy Carmichael) songs, including 'How Little We Know' with the female lead, Lauren Bacall.

We come closer to the genre of film musical when the songs in the film begin to refer to the action. In George Clooney's *Good Night, and Good Luck* (2005), which has no score, musical interludes are provided by Dianne Reeves singing songs of the 1950s. The picture is set in a studio of CBS television where news reporter Edward R. Murrow (David Strathairn) and his producer Fred Friendly (Clooney) are intent on exposing Joseph McCarthy's anti-communist campaign for the paranoid witch-hunt it was. The film is shot in crisp black and white, with scenes between the journalists interspersed with archival footage of McCarthy (who at no point is represented by an actor). Dianne Reeves performs her songs in an adjoining music studio with a small quartet of sax, piano, bass and drums, other characters from the film occasionally walking past and peering in through the window. In the context of this story, it is hard not to read a song such as Cole Porter's 'I've Got My Eyes on You' as an oblique commentary on the era's grubby politics. Reeves's character doesn't have a name. She is there simply to sing and to offer what we might think of as a musical or poetic perspective. In other words, we are back with the Greek chorus.

In Robert Altman's *Short Cuts* (1993), Annie Ross fulfils a similar function. Typical of Altman's movies, *Short Cuts* has a large cast of characters whose lives intersect and overlap. In this case, they come from nine unrelated short stories and a poem by Raymond Carver. There are also two characters that are inventions of the director: the jazz singer Tess Trainer (Ross) and her daughter Zoe (Lori Singer), a classical cellist. Tess – her name borrowed from Carver's widow, the poet Tess Gallagher – is considerably more fleshed out than Reeves's jazz singer in *Good Night, and Good Luck*. She's a selfish lush, more concerned about her broken pool filter than her suicidal daughter. At the Low Note club, she sings about the condition of humankind – or at least the people who live in Altman's Los Angeles – and about her own (doubtless embellished) life.

'Here's a song I want to sing for myself,' she tells her audience, before launching into 'Conversation on a Barstool', specially written for the film by Bono and the Edge, and approaching, one imagines, musical autobiography for Tess: 'It isn't as if I was just anybody / On Broadway I danced for that senator …'

Ross's delivery is jaded and very slightly amused, which is apt for the three numbers by Doc Pomus and Mac Rebennack (Dr John) that form the bulk of the vocal material. 'Prisoner of Life', which might almost be the motto of *Short Cuts*, opens and closes the film; 'I Don't Know You' sums up the manner in which most of these characters, even members of the same family, relate and respond to one another. Mark Isham is the named composer on the film, but the songs dominate, and not only in Annie Ross's performances. Altman 'unmixed' her voice from the recordings, leaving behind just her small backing combo, then layered these purely instrumental tracks under many of the scenes. In some cases the voiceless recordings precede Ross's performances (giving the songs an oddly familiar feel when she sings them); in other cases we hear the instrumental versions after her songs, which consequently echo on through the film. In this way, Tess's detached commentary permeates *Short Cuts*.

Michelangelo Antonioni's *Blow-Up* (1966) represents swinging London, musically, with a jazz score from Herbie Hancock. American jazz had not yet been eclipsed by British pop as the lingua franca of the 1960s; indeed it had been only four years since Hancock's 'Watermelon Man' was itself in the pop charts. Even so, near the end of the film, the photographer Thomas (David Hemmings) finds himself visiting a club where the Yardbirds are playing. As we watch the boyish faces of Jeff Beck and Jimmy Page and listen to their music, which is certainly not jazz, a statement is being made. Films of the 1960s set in London often used the pop music of the day to convey the zeitgeist, and *Blow-Up* was not the only film to put these sounds on the screen, showing us the musicians. The Zombies had appeared in *Bunny Lake Is Missing* (Otto Preminger, 1965), not singing their hit song 'She's Not There', which would certainly have been apt, but 'Just Out of Reach' – and the Spencer Davis Group would feature in *Here We Go Round the Mulberry Bush* (Clive Donner, 1968). And this is to say nothing of films made as vehicles for the pop groups themselves, most obviously Richard Lester's *A Hard Day's Night* (1964) and *Help!* (1965) for the Beatles, and John Boorman's *Catch Us If You Can* (1965) for the Dave Clark Five.

So Antonioni was positively swimming in the zeitgeist putting the Yardbirds in *Blow-Up*. Even post-Eric Clapton, this band's brand of r&b represents something altogether darker and more dangerous – and by extension more modern – than the music in Hancock's score. The Yardbirds' largely unsmiling poses certainly help, not to mention the demeanour of the audience, which is clustered around the small stage. Riveted and reverential, the audience stares intently at the band, the only occasional movement an appreciative nod of a head. When one of the loudspeakers starts emitting short bursts of static, guitarist Jeff Beck first pokes, then bashes it with his instrument, before throwing the guitar down, jumping on it a few times and finally flinging the fretboard into the crowd. The mood of the room now changes from solemn to chaotic, the audience scrambling for the piece of the guitar as though they were starving beggars thrown food. Thomas ends up with the prize and after a bit of a scuffle runs off with it into the night. When he is a safe distance from the club, he takes a look at the fretboard and chucks it away. Undoubtedly there is a message here, but as with so much in *Blow-Up* – and, one is tempted to add, Antonioni's work in general – it is not completely obvious what the message might be.

Michael Winterbottom's *9 Songs* (2004) also suffers from self-importance. Like *Blow-Up*, the film contains live rock performances, but on a far grander scale. Matt (Kieran O'Brien) and Lisa (Margo Stilley) meet at a Black Rebel Motorcycle Club concert, then go back to his place and have energetic sex. Already a pattern has emerged, the remainder of the film consisting of on-screen screwing interrupted by trips to live shows by the likes of Franz Ferdinand, Elbow and Primal Scream. Perhaps if the sex scenes were not so serious and the general tone of the film so doom-laden, the music wouldn't seem weighed down with significance. In truth, the choice of songs has little obvious relevance to the plot; but then there is little obvious plot, just the feeling that it will end badly (which we've known from the start, because Matt told us) and that somehow this is important (which, in the great scheme of things, it certainly isn't). So in spite of some good music, the film lurches from pretension to unintentional humour. The decision to follow the 'money shot' with footage from Michael Nyman's sixtieth-birthday concert falls into the second category, although it is hard to say which aspect of the unfortunate juxtaposition makes it so funny.

Lindsay Anderson was a vital figure in British cinema, as a director and a critic. Although he directed a great deal for the stage, both in London and New York, he made only a handful of feature films, all of them worth seeing. His filmmaking tended to have a strong theatricality to it; he encouraged an acting style that was not always or even often naturalistic, and that gave his work something of a knowing quality. This was particularly true of the films featuring Malcolm McDowell as Mick Travis, *if…* (1968), *O Lucky Man!* (1973) and *Britannia Hospital* (1982), the first two of which are musically interesting. McDowell made his film debut in *if…*, a black comedy about a bloody revolution at an English public school. It has a score by Marc Wilkinson, but the most memorable music consists of the singing of hymns. Anderson uses these ironically, especially the not-terribly-committed singing of Bunyan's 'To Be a Pilgrim' in the school chapel. In one ironic, though rather touching scene, the house master of College House, Mr Kemp (Arthur Lowe) sits on his bed singing Purcell's secular hymn to Britain, 'Fairest Isle', while Mrs Kemp (Mary MacLeod) accompanies him on the recorder from the neighbouring bed. Interestingly, the soundtrack to this film also contains parts of the *Missa Luba*, at one point coming out of a jukebox. (Anderson would certainly have known Pasolini's *Gospel According to St Matthew*, which had made such memorable use of the same music.)

O Lucky Man!, Anderson's next film, is yet more theatrical in tone, with most of the large cast – even McDowell, the star – playing multiple roles and Anderson himself playing the film director. While it is not, like Fellini's *8½* (1963) or Truffaut's *Day for Night* (1973), a film about making a film, it nevertheless delights in 'breaking the frame', particularly with its music. Mick Travis, part rake, part pilgrim, makes his progress through this three-hour movie to the accompaniment of songs by Alan Price, performed by Price himself on screen. But instead of putting the singer in a club, say, like Annie Ross in *Short Cuts*, or in some other way making him part of the story, Anderson shows us Price and his band performing the songs in a studio, as though they were recording the soundtrack album. Indeed, the first time we see Price is in the opening credits, and moreover we see Anderson, too, sitting in on the session, listening closely and advising. So, here's that Greek chorus again, its role as commentator evident in songs such as 'Poor People', 'Sell Sell' (Travis begins the film as a travelling salesman) and the title track, 'O Lucky Man!': 'Smile while you're making it / Laugh while you're taking it / Even though you're faking it …'

But then comes a nice twist, because at around the halfway mark, Price suddenly does enter the story. Travis has been forcibly kept in a hospital until he discovers the doctors there are experimenting on patients (he finds a man's head on a sheep's body), whereupon he panics and escapes. On a lonely stretch of road at night, he hitches a ride in a van that turns out to contain Price and his band, with whom he goes to stay in London. Right at the end of the film, Travis attends an audition for a role in a film called *O Lucky Man!*, directed by Lindsay Anderson, who smacks him across the side of his head with the script when he can't smile on cue. And then the entire cast has a party at which they dance to Alan Price's music.

There is a Dickensian spirit at work in *O Lucky Man!*, from the picaresque story and grotesque minor characters, to the concerns with social justice, crime, punishment, poverty, great wealth, corruption and religion. As in *if…*, hymn tunes also turn up, and Price's final number neatly closes the gap with this other strand of music, taking the tune of 'What a Friend We Have in Jesus' and putting to it his own lyrics: 'Everyone is going through changes / No one knows what's going on …' As Price sings the song, the words come up on the screen in seven different languages, inviting the audience to join in.

Lindsay Anderson's influence may be felt in *Bad Boy Bubby* (Rolf de Heer, 1993). Thirty years old and having sex with his mother, Flo (Claire Benito), Bubby has never seen the world outside the dingy basement the two of them share with an unfortunate cat. Because he is mentally a small child, Bubby is the centre of his own very limited universe and we tend to see things from his point of view, especially in the first part of the film. For example, when he places clingwrap over his face to see if he can breathe, we find ourselves inside the clingwrap. And we also have his viewpoint when his father, Pop (Ralph Cotterill), suddenly turns up. All the conversations between Pop and Flo are heard from Bubby's perspective, the voices tending to come and go, occasionally fading from our hearing when Bubby is no longer paying attention.

As a child in a man's body, Bubby has little ability to communicate beyond imitating what others say, but he is rather gifted at this. After he uses the clingwrap to dispose of his parents, he reaches the outside world equipped only with phrases learned from them, delivered in uncannily lifelike imitations of their voices. The phrases include 'Christ, kid, you're a weirdo' and 'You're a sexy woman, Flo'.

This essentially musical ability to hear and repeat sounds, regardless of meaning, lands Bubby in trouble, but it also becomes the key to his survival. Throughout the film, Bubby accumulates phrases, mimics voices, and then turns his random repertoire into songs as the frontman of a rock band. And Bubby's ability to maintain his own point of view is oddly sustained by his memory of Handel's 'Largo', which he uses to blot out anything he doesn't like, including an argument among members of his band and the kicking he earns from a women's group whose members he unsuccessfully attempts to grope. *Bad Boy Bubby* – like *O Lucky Man!* – is a comedy with music, and as Bubby's life is celebrated in songs that evolve from what is said on the screen, performed to a pub full of dedicated fans who show their enthusiasm by dressing and talking like Bubby, he completes his journey to a happy suburban ending with a wife and two children. It is the film's most surreal moment.

Three more recent films with specially written songs sung on screen are *Magnolia* (Paul Thomas Anderson, 1999), *Once* (Jim Carney, 2006) and *Shortbus* (John Cameron Mitchell, 2006). The last, though groundbreaking in other respects, is musically the most conventional in that it establishes a performance space as part of the story – the Shortbus club, where the characters meet to overcome (or indulge) their sexual hang-ups. In its general attitude to music, then, it is not so different to *Short Cuts*. As in Altman's film, the club atmosphere even allows conversations to continue while the songs are being performed, and the musicians in *Shortbus* are characters in the film, though not fully developed in the manner of Tess Trainer. The songs, written and performed by Yo La Tengo and Scott Matthew, among others, are mostly genial, sometimes whimsical in tone, rather giving the lie to the much-quoted line from the film that Shortbus is 'just like the '60s only with less hope'. In fact the film has 'plenty of hope', and the music sees to that. The final candlelit scene is especially memorable. Scott Matthew's song 'In the End' begins as a gentle instrumental (the composer on guitar) before Justin Bond sings the lyrics, and finally the Hungry March Band arrives for a spirited full-cast sing-along, assuring us that 'your demon's your best friend / And we all get it in the end'.

In their unobtrusive, folksy manner, Aimee Mann's songs for *Magnolia* resemble the songs in *Shortbus*, but the use of music in Paul Thomas Anderson's film is generally far more complex and multilayered. Like *Short Cuts* and *O Lucky Man!*, *Magnolia* is a sprawling three-hour epic with a great many characters and with music playing a vital and prominent role in holding it all together. Indeed, Anderson was originally inspired by Mann's songwriting, so the tone of *Magnolia* might be said to arise from her music and lyrics. Following the elaborate soundscape created for the opening sequence depicting multiple coincidences, a simple two-note chord begins to pulse away. This forms the introduction to Harry Nilsson's 'One (is the loneliest number)', sung by Mann, and sets the sonic pattern for rest of the film, which alternates between unusually long musical cues (by composer Jon Brion) and soundscapes rich in detail, and simple songs by Mann and others. A little over two thirds of the way through the film, most of the characters have reached some crisis point. Earl Partridge (Jason Robards) is dying, his daughter Linda (Julianne Moore) is attempting suicide, the cop (John C. Reilly) is paralysed by religious doubt. Claudia (Melora Walters) looks up from snorting a line of cocaine as Aimee Mann's 'Wise Up' begins on the soundtrack. In what seems like a small miracle, she begins to sing along, before passing the tune to the other principal characters, each alone in his or her own place – house, apartment, car – first to Reilly, then Philip Baker Hall, then William H. Macy, then Philip Seymour Hoffman nursing Robards, then to Moore, then Tom Cruise and finally Jeremy Blackman, who plays the embarrassed child quiz contender and completes the song, his piping treble voice blending perfectly with Aimee Mann's. 'It's not going to stop / Till you wise up' is the chorus. Dramatically this song does a lot of work, allowing each of the characters – within the space of just a few notes and words – to reach an acceptance of their situation, and either a sense of equilibrium or of purpose. As the characters 'wise up', not only does the song stop, but so does the rain for the first time in a hundred minutes of film.

In *Once*, the songs are composed and sung by the stars of the film, Glen Hansard and Markéta Irglová, playing characters whose names we never learn. He is a busker who assists his widowed father repairing vacuum cleaners, she is the mother of a small girl and makes her living selling single roses and the *Big Issue* in the centre of Dublin. By day, he plays Van Morrison songs for money, but 'after hours' he plays his own material. She makes regular visits to a music shop where she is allowed to play the piano – one of Mendelssohn's *Songs Without Words* on the occasion we hear her. They are both shy, both separated from others – his ex-girlfriend is in London, her husband in Prague – but they begin to inspire each other musically. *Once* is a simple film with simple songs, although one of them won Hansard an Oscar. Charming, touching, if ultimately unimportant, *Once* also turns out to be a genre film. Unlike the pictures already discussed, it is a genuine musical, and not just any kind of musical. With its homespun music-making, starry-eyed enthusiasm and obstacles overcome by sheer self-belief, the film belongs to the 'let's-do-the-show-right-here' sub-genre of musicals that starred Mickey Rooney and Judy Garland.

Of course, Mickey and Judy only pretended to write their own material in *Babes in Arms* (Busby Berkeley, 1939) – their ghost-writers included Rodgers and Hart, Harold Arlen and Nacio Herb Brown, who, together with the producer, Arthur Freed, wrote 'Good Morning' for the film. That song would later feature in *Singin' in the Rain* (Stanley Donen & Gene Kelly, 1952), also produced by Freed. The 1930s and '40s were the heyday of film musicals, and unlike *Babes in Arms*, they didn't always start on Broadway. Some of the most famous, for example *42nd Street* (Lloyd Bacon, 1933) and the Fred Astaire and Ginger Rogers musicals, were 100 per cent the creations of Hollywood. The same was true of *Singin' in the Rain*, a film about the film industry that didn't reach the stage until 1983.

Although comparatively rare, film musicals persist today. Generally, they are inspired by a body of existing music (*Once* was very much the exception with its specially composed songs), weaving a story around songs that are occasionally forced to fit. This isn't new. *Singin' in the Rain* did precisely the same with Freed and Brown's songs from the first decade of talking pictures (the period in which the film is set), and still it is generally regarded as the greatest film musical of them all. This goes to show that the quality of the songs is not necessarily the most important feature of a musical, and two recent films offer further evidence for this.

Julie Taymor's *Across the Universe* (2007) is inspired by the songs of the Beatles, and Phyllida Lloyd's *Mamma Mia!* (2008) is a film version of the successful stage musical based on Abba songs. There may be those who believe that Abba's music is of greater significance than that of the Beatles, but there can hardly be very many, so it is interesting that *Mamma Mia!* should turn out to be by far the more successful of the two films. In a way, the problem with *Across the Universe* is the same as the problem with *9 Songs*, only in reverse. The self-important narrative (such as it is) in Winterbottom's film rendered the musical interludes pompous, but Taymor seems to have been overawed by the Beatles' songs. The quality of the Beatles' music and lyrics is generally very high – the lyrics in particular, if your point of comparison is Abba. But it is more than that. The rather precise imagery in the Beatles' songs makes them difficult to fit into a new narrative. It is surely no coincidence that Cirque du Soleil's successful stage show, *Love*, took a generally abstract approach. Even with such veterans as Dick Clement and Ian La Frenais writing the screenplay for *Across the Universe*, a project in which the characters are called ('Hey') Jude, Lucy ('in the Sky'), Max('well's Silver Hammer'), ('Sexy') Sadie, ('Dear') Prudence and Jo-Jo is going to be so tied to the lyrics of the songs that it will find it difficult to break free. As in *The Boat That*

Rocked, we can hear the songs coming a mile off. But what is worse, *Across the Universe* attributes such gravitas to the Beatles' music that it buckles under the burden of its own pretensions.

The makers of *Mamma Mia!* had no such problems. It is almost impossible to take Abba's songs seriously, they are so light they seem to want to float away. And if it ever occurred to the writers to create a character called Fernando who hears drums, they sensibly abandoned the plan. Having nothing much to live up to in terms of the lyrics, the writers of *Mamma Mia!* were able to take their story anywhere they wanted. And, remarkably, the mostly silly song lyrics fit the mostly silly plot very closely. It's a million miles from pretension, and the energy that comes off the screen sustains the film very well. Occasionally one even finds oneself listening to patently ridiculous lyrics, such as those in 'The Winner Takes It All' (an orgy of clichés, melodrama and forced rhymes), and finding that as Meryl Streep acts her way through the song, it turns into something quite powerful. The line 'the winner takes it all' still may not make sense, but if we've got this far into the film we're past caring.

The choice of songs can transform a film, whether or not we see them being sung. Sometimes the transformations that occur over the course of a film are brought about or underscored by musical transformations. In *The Bodyguard* (Mick Jackson, 1992), Frank Farmer (Kevin Costner) is guarding the hugely successful singer and actress Rachel Marron (Whitney Houston). Since she is unable to go out on a date without him, she proposes that he be her date, and they end up at a small bar. They dance to the music playing on the jukebox, Dolly Parton's song, 'I Will Always Love You', sung by John Doe (formerly of the punk band *X*) very much as a country and western tune. Rachel, who sings soul and r&b, is amused by the music ('This is kind of a cowboy song, huh?') and is struck, in particular, by how depressing it is ('Have you listened to the words?'). Farmer has to agree, though it is clear enough from the scene that the song represents his musical preference.

Rachel's attitude to Farmer alters considerably during the remainder of the film. Minutes after the scene with the jukebox, they are in bed together; then he insists their relationship return to a purely professional footing; then she is angry, distant, uncooperative; then she is threatened, afraid; then angry again. Finally, at the climax of the film, Farmer takes a bullet for her, just as she is receiving her Academy Award. The last time we see the two of them together, it is for a relatively formal and chaste farewell on the tarmac at an airport (shades of *Casablanca*, here). As Rachel boards the aeroplane, her voice is heard, stripped bare, unaccompanied, singing the Dolly Parton song. At first, it blends with the sounds of the aircraft engines. A few instruments join in, then a big orchestra and by the time the chorus comes round the song has miraculously turned into a soul anthem (and, in real life, one of the biggest-selling records ever made). The song reaching its climax, Rachel cannot control her emotions. She comes racing down the steps for one last big embrace with Farmer, the camera spinning around them. So Bergman and Bogart they avowedly are not, but the transformation of the song – from country to soul, from his to hers – means that while she may still have to reboard the plane and fly away from him, at least she's acknowledged there's nothing wrong with his musical taste that can't be fixed up with a big, brash orchestration and some well-struck high notes.

The transformation of a song in the course of a film can convey the passing of time or deliver a commentary on the action or the characters. *The Bodyguard* sets out to achieve all of these with 'I Will Always Love You'. And often, of course, this is precisely how a film score works: a simple theme is ennobled, a grand theme is gradually trashed. In *Darling* (John Schlesinger, 1965), the actress Diana Scott (Julie Christie) moves from partner to partner, from mentor to Svengali to dupe, the emotional high point coming during a sojourn on the island of Capri. Marriage has been proposed by Prince Cesare (José Luis de Villalonga) and Diana cannot sleep as she considers the offer. It is at this point that we first hear the Neapolitan song 'Santa Lucia', sung rather splendidly by a tenor with chorus and orchestra. The song starts on the soundtrack but it quickly becomes apparent that Diana can hear it, too. When she goes to the window, the song seems to be drifting up from the town square below. It is a powerful moment, not least because it is really the only point in the film at which Diana seems to display some qualms about her actions and some genuine emotion. The following day she turns the prince down, and then marries him anyway.

Half an hour later, the film ends with a very different performance of the same song. The camera gives us a close up of Diana's face on the cover of a magazine. Throughout the film, Diana's voice-over had been in the form of an interview and now we realise that this magazine contains the interview to which we have been listening. The camera pulls back to show us a news-stand and as it does so we hear 'Santa Lucia' sung unaccompanied by a female voice. The camera pulls back further and we see that the news-stand is in Piccadilly Circus and that the song is being sung by a beggar woman in late middle age standing beneath the winged statue of Eros.

At one level, of course, this is a 'sic-transit-gloria-mundi' moment and undeniably a bit heavy-handed. But it's also more than that. This time there's no orchestra to join in and nothing obviously triumphant about the song. At Piccadilly Circus, there's no one even listening. Yet while this woman might be a beggar, her rendition of 'Santa Lucia' is far from pathetic. It is spirited, full of gusto. She sings with a radiant smile on her toothless face and we recognise in her performance a candour that has been signally absent from the life of Diana Scott. In this very unconventional, downbeat ending to *Darling*, the beggar's singing transforms the song, in the process shining a bright and revealing light on Diana's story.

Listening for Clues in Hitchcock

The composer Barrington Pheloung has scored several feature films, including *Truly, Madly, Deeply* and *Hilary and Jackie* (Anand Tucker, 1998), but he is best known as the provider of music for all thirty-three episodes of the British television series *Inspector Morse* (1987–2000), and for a unique approach that went well beyond the setting of scenes and conjuring of moods. As Morse (John Thaw) solved the murders on our screens, Pheloung amused himself by devising rhythmic motifs for his incidental music that would reveal – in Morse code – the name of the murderer. Viewers who knew their dots and dashes could therefore solve the crime half an hour before the chief inspector.

Musical clues abound in films, even if they are not so precise as Pheloung's coded spoilers. The mere sound of music can alert us to something that has happened or is about to happen. Sometimes, if we recognise the music we are hearing, it will contain a clue in its title or lyrics. On a pop soundtrack, as already discussed, individual songs can do half the work for a lazy writer or director, telling us what the characters think and feel and what they are going to do about it.

In pre-pop cinema, the film director who most consistently used music to further the plot of his films and, in many cases, to provide clues was Alfred Hitchcock (1899–1980). It is no coincidence that Hitchcock's name should crop up in this book more than that of any other filmmaker. He had a particular sensitivity to sound and music, and he employed both with skill and flair. The director's career began with silent, black and white films in the United Kingdom and ended with Technicolor in Hollywood. He directed his first feature, the unfinished *Number 13*, in 1922, and made his last, *Family Plot*, in 1976, with a score by John Williams (one year after Williams had become extremely famous for his music in *Jaws*).

Hitchcock's keen ear was evident even before his first talking picture. In *The Lodger* (1927), a serial killer is on the loose and bumping off blondes. A mysterious man (Ivor Novello) comes to lodge with a family, whose daughter Daisy (June – just June) is herself fair-haired. No sooner has he gone upstairs than the family has suspicions about him, as does Daisy's detective boyfriend Joe (Malcolm Keen). They hear the lodger's ominous footsteps coming from the room above. Hitchcock would like us to hear them too, but because it is a silent picture, he must contrive to show us the sound. Daisy, Joe and Daisy's mother (Marie Ault) look up at the ceiling where the chandelier is swinging slightly, and then the ceiling promptly dissolves into transparent glass allowing us to see the lodger's feet pacing back and forth. In later scenes, the actors only have to glance up for us to hear the footsteps again.

Blackmail (1929) was originally planned as a silent movie, then as a film with partial sound, all but the final reel remaining silent. But Hitchcock was able to persuade his studio to allow him to reshoot some of the earlier scenes with sound. In the event, only the opening minutes remained silent, and *Blackmail* is generally regarded as the first British talkie. Immediately we find the director not only using a modest score, but also putting music on screen as part of the story and experimenting with sound. Following an argument with her detective boyfriend (John Longden), Alice (Anny Ondra) has gone home with an artist, Crewe (Cyril Richard). Crewe shows her around his studio while whistling Billy Mayerl's 'Miss Up-to-Date'. Then he sits at a piano and sings the song as Alice changes into a tutu so that he can sketch her. Crewe's psychopathic nature becomes suddenly evident in a second performance of the tune as an increasingly out-of-control piano solo, ending with violent banging on the keyboard.

Alice is now alarmed and when Crewe attempts to rape her she stabs him with a bread knife.

After wandering the streets of London for the rest of the night, Alice creeps home just after dawn and climbs into her bed fully dressed. Her mother (Sarah Allgood) comes in with a morning cup of tea and takes the cover off the bird cage hanging in the window. The bird immediately begins to trill as Alice's mother tells her there's been a murder. At first the bird's whistling recalls Crewe's, then when Alice looks up at the picture of her boyfriend dressed as a London bobby, the bird seems to become a police whistle. Then Alice begins to undress, Hitchcock's camera giving us a close-up of Ondra's legs as she removes her stockings, and the bird's whistling takes on an entirely different connotation. Suspense and humour were never far apart in a Hitchcock film.

In the following scene, round the breakfast table, a neighbour (Phyllis Konstam in a nice comic turn) stands in the doorway riffing on the subject of murder and particularly murders involving knives. The sound editor increasingly blurs her speech so that the only word we hear clearly, again and again, is 'knife'. Meanwhile the camera gives us a close-up of Alice's face, transfixed with fear. Her father's voice overrides the neighbour's prattle ('Alice, cut us a bit of bread would you?') and the camera remains on Alice as she slowly looks down at the table and takes up the bread knife, which might as well be the murder weapon itself. The neighbour's repeated 'knife' continues until, quite suddenly, the word is shouted – by the neighbour? by Alice herself? – and the knife jumps from Alice's hand and falls to the floor. It is the first example of Hitchcock's great sound shocks.

Hitchcock's devotion to music in his films might be divined from some of his on-screen appearances. In *Spellbound* he walks out of a lift carrying a violin case, in *The Paradine Case* (1947) he gets off a train with a cello, and in *Strangers on a Train* he boards a train struggling with a double bass. In his appearance in *Vertigo* it looks like a trumpet case he's carrying down the street and in *Rear Window* he is standing behind a composer who is seated at a piano, working on his new song. Among Hitchcock's lead characters, Michael Redgrave in *The Lady Vanishes* (1938) is an ethnomusicologist who plays the clarinet and Farley Granger in *Rope* (1948) is a pianist with a fondness for the music of Poulenc. Effectively playing herself, Marlene Dietrich in *Stage Fright* (1950) is a music-hall entertainer, while Doris Day in *The Man Who Knew Too Much* (1956) is a retired popular singer. Henry Fonda in *The Wrong Man* (1956) plays double bass in a jazz combo at the Stork Club. Even when not professionals, the main characters are sometimes musical. In *The Paradine Case*, Mrs Paradine (Alida Valli) reprises Franz Waxman's main title music on the piano as she waits for the police to come and arrest her; in *The Birds*, Melanie Daniels (Tippi Hedren) plays Debussy's early 'Arabesque' on the piano – Hitchcock made her learn it, just as he had made Fonda learn the bass. And then there are the minor characters ...

The musical clues in Hitchcock's films fall into three categories. First there are clues for the audience alone: second, there are clues for the main character(s) and for the audience; finally, there are actual pieces of music that are meant to represent or contain clues, for example the secret information embodied in the tune hummed by Miss Froy (May Whitty) in *The Lady Vanishes*.

One of the most celebrated musical sequences in a Hitchcock film – celebrated primarily for its impressive tracking shot – comes near the end of *Young and Innocent* (1937). A woman has been strangled by a man with a nervous twitch that takes the form of uncontrollable blinking. The young writer Robert Tisdall (Derrick de Marney), wrongly accused, is on the run with Erica Burgoyne (Nova Pilbeam), who happens to be the daughter of the chief constable who is searching for Robert. They meet a tramp, Old Will (Edward Rigby), who has acquired the killer's overcoat but knows only that the culprit is prone to twitch under pressure. In the pocket of the coat is a box of matches from the Grand Hotel. So at the climax of the film there they are, Erica and Old Will, in the foyer of the hotel and as they enter the ballroom, the band strikes up a tune of some significance.

Unfortunately, the significance is lost on them. Seated at their table, they discuss the unlikelihood of finding a man with blinking eyes at a tea dance in a crowded hotel. Meanwhile the conductor/vocalist begins singing the verse of that song: 'Who's the fellow you seldom think of / When you think of a band?'

'He must be here somewhere,' says Erica, and as though on cue Hitchcock's camera sets off to look for him. The famous crane shot starts high up at one end of the ballroom then sweeps elegantly down and across the heads of the dancers. The conductor/vocalist continues: 'When it comes to doing tricks / With a pair of hickory sticks / I'm right here to tell you, Sister, / No one can like the drummer man.'

The camera now moves in on the band, who are all, save the conductor, in black face. This is a nice touch: as though finding one man in this crowd were not hard enough, we realise that he is also going to be in disguise. The camera moves past the conductor, through the band, finally giving us a close-up of the 'drummer man'. But it is not yet close enough. The camera inches nearer and nearer until it is right in front of the man's face and the screen is filled with his eyes peering through the black make-up. And of course they start to twitch. Hitchcock could seldom resist a joke, and here the joke is that not only has the camera found our man but it has caused him to blink.

So the murderer has been revealed, not to Erica and Old Will (they're still sitting at their table, looking a little bored), but to everyone watching the film. The song has identified the villain and the camera has tracked him down, literally. The song was a clue for us, the audience, and had we only known to listen for it we might have heard it right at the start of the movie: 'No One Can Like the Drummer Man' by Sammy Lerner, Al Goodhart and Al Hoffman had furnished the principal theme in Jack Beaver's musical score under the main title.

There are often such retrospective elements in Hitchcock. Sometimes they are lines that you can't possibly understand unless you have already seen the film. When, in *Psycho*, Norman Bates tells Marion Crane that 'Mother ... isn't quite herself today', it isn't obviously funny. Not the first time. The second time round it's a brilliant piece of black humour. There are also musical clues that work like this. Bernard Herrmann's score for *Psycho* begins the film with a syncopated stabbing figure, alerting us to the forthcoming violence, well ahead of the high-pitched slashing strings in the shower scene. It is also worth pointing out that it is not just the music, but also the editing of the shower scene that matches the murder and the murder weapon: the famous scene runs for only one-and-a-half minutes of film, but Hitchcock makes more than fifty cuts. This is in contrast to *Rope*, a film that names its murder weapon in the title. Here there is no cutting of the film at all. On the contrary, like the rope itself, Hitchcock gives us a seamless, uninterrupted stretch of film in which even the ends of reels are disguised. All is continuous in *Rope*. Even the piece played on the piano by one of the murderers is Poulenc's 'Mouvement perpétuel', music that goes on and on with no end in sight.

Another clue for the audience, albeit a small one and far more subtle than the 'drummer man' song, comes in *Rear Window*. Among the plethora of musical sounds that reach us up in 'Jeff' Jefferies's apartment is a distant barrel organ in the street outside the courtyard. As we watch a little dog sniffing around the flowerbed, the organ is playing 'Carnival of Venice'. This time the clue hinges on our knowing and remembering the children's rhyme popularly sung to the tune. A couple of years later Samuel Beckett would have Vladimir sing it at the start of Act II of *Waiting for Godot*: 'A dog came in the kitchen / And stole a crust of bread / Then cook up with a ladle / And beat him till he was dead ...' If you recognise the tune and remember the words, you fear for the animal's welfare.

In *Suspicion* (1941), Hitchcock provides a musical clue for both Lina (Joan Fontaine) and for the filmgoer. But it turns out to be a false clue. From the ball scene early in the picture, when she and Johnny (Cary Grant) first dance together, the Strauss waltz *Vienna Blood* is associated with their happy times. It plays behind scenes of their honeymoon in Europe, and when they return to their extravagant new house in England it is playing on a gramophone. As the film continues, Lina grows wary of her husband's fecklessness, and suspicious of his actions, especially where money is concerned. Finally, she is prepared to believe that Johnny might have murdered his bumbling friend Beaky (Nigel Bruce) by pushing him off a cliff. When she arrives home, full of apprehension, she hears Johnny whistling *Vienna Blood*. The whistling is fragmented, off-key and somehow sinister, the effect made still more chilling because it is all we can hear. We see Lina come into the house, we see her close the front door behind her and then walk through the hallway, but we hear none of those sounds, only the tuneless whistling. She looks through the open door of the living room and there is her husband bent over the gramophone. When he calls out, 'This ought to do it, put in the plug now' and Beaky's head comes peering round the door, we share Lina's relief. At once the recording of *Vienna Blood* starts up, more joyous than ever.

There's another waltz in *Shadow of a Doubt* (1943), and this time it dominates the film and Dimitri Tiomkin's score. It is the famous waltz from Franz Lehár's operetta *The Merry Widow*, and to appreciate how the film works, it is important to understand just how popular this tune was. The operetta had its premiere in Vienna in 1905 and quickly became a great success all round the world. Today, when the work is performed, it will be by an opera company, but really, like most operettas, *The Merry Widow* is closer in nature to a musical. Certainly the level of success it enjoyed in the first half of the twentieth century can only be compared to a hit musical. In London's West End, the English-language version of *The Merry*

Widow ran for 778 performances and on Broadway for more than 400. The point is that just about anyone who went to see Hitchcock's film when it opened would have immediately recognised the waltz and most of them would have known what it was called. As they watched family members around a dinner table attempt to remember its name ('I can't get that tune out of my head. Maybe if somebody tells me what it is, I'll forget it') and make wild stabs at its identity ('It's Victor Herbert', 'It's "The Blue Danube"'), audience members would have been prompting them: 'It's "The Merry Widow Waltz"!'

The significance of the waltz isn't explained until a little over halfway through the film. It turns out that a man known as the 'Merry Widow Murderer' has killed three rich widows and is on the run somewhere in America. The police have two suspects, one in Santa Rosa, California, where *Shadow of a Doubt* is set, the other 'back East'. Young Charlie (Teresa Wright) has somewhat more than a shadow of a doubt that her Uncle Charlie Oakley (Joseph Cotten), currently visiting her family and borrowing her bedroom, is the man they're after. After all, at the climax of that dinner scene, she had finally hit on the name of the waltz ('I know. It's "The M—"'), at which point Uncle Charlie had knocked over his glass of wine and the subject was dropped. Her uncle also cuts reports out of newspapers before others have had a chance to read them. And that emerald ring he gave her has someone else's initials engraved inside it.

As it turns out Charlie is correct in her suspicion, and so are we. (For that matter, Joan Fontaine in *Suspicion* was correct to have doubts about Cary Grant until the studio intervened to remind the director that this particular leading man was not allowed to be a murderer and Hitchcock was obliged to change his ending.) In *Shadow of a Doubt*, Hitchcock doles out clues from the start, as he had done in *Young and Innocent*. We knew nothing about a 'drummer man' when we heard the song over the opening credits of the earlier film, and in *Shadow of a Doubt* we have no idea why we are hearing 'The Merry Widow Waltz' and watching dancers waltzing round a ballroom. These entirely symbolic waltzers will return to the screen whenever young Charlie's suspicions are raised and Lehár's melody wells up in the score.

So while we realise there's something afoot before we know what that is, it is only in hindsight, when we are aware of Uncle Charlie's guilt and of his association with the waltz, that we are able to spot the film's very first clue. After the picture's main titles, 'The Merry Widow Waltz' plays on over shots of the back streets of Philadelphia, until we come to focus on one particular window (the same basic set-up that would be repeated at the start of *Rope* and again in *Psycho*). In the boarding-house room on the other side of this window, relaxing on a bed, is Uncle Charlie. He is fully clothed and between the fingers of his right hand is a cigar which is twitching very slightly, as though Charlie were conducting the final bars of the Lehár. Well it is, after all, his tune. As the music stops, so the cigar comes to rest, and the landlady enters to tell him there are two men looking for him. The next time we see him in the context of the waltz is on the station platform in Santa Rosa. As Uncle Charlie walks towards young Charlie, the score gives us a hint of the waltz – no more than a memory jogger – but instantly we see him reach for the cigar in the top pocket of his jacket. Later, following the dinner-table debate over the identity of the tune, young Charlie is lying in bed in her sister's room, still humming the waltz. We cut straight to Uncle Charlie, lying on the bed in his niece's room, smoking his cigar. The shot reprises the opening scene, but this time the 'Merry Widow Murderer' is blowing an ostentatious smoke ring.

The ability of an audience in the 1940s to recognise and name Lehár's waltz is no different from a modern audience's knowledge of pop music. To all intents and purposes, 'The Merry Widow Waltz' *was* pop music. Popular classics played on the radio in the 1930s and '40s alongside hits of the day, so we can reasonably believe, for instance, that many of the people who went to see *Scarface* (Howard

Hawks, 1932) would have been familiar with one of the hit tunes of Donizetti's opera *Lucia di Lammermoor*, the great sextet 'Chi mi frena'. This is the tune that Tony Camonte (Paul Muni) whistles on his way to assassinate Big Louis at the start of the film. We hear him whistling it before we even see him. He whistles it again in the bowling-alley scene and once more before he has Guino (George Raft) shoot Johnny Lovo (Osgood Perkins). It is as ominous a sound as Peter Lorre's whistling in *M* (Fritz Lang, 1931), but if the audience knows the words of the sextet – and in 1932 many of them would have done – the tune gains in significance: 'Who restrains me at a moment like this? Who diverts my fury?' The words might be thought to apply to Tony and his sister Cesca, with whom he has an unnaturally close relationship. They go on to predict her death in the final reel, which has Tony wailing with fear – mostly fear of loneliness – if not with remorse. The Donizetti sextet concludes: 'I am defeated … I am shocked! … I love you, ungrateful one, I love you still!' But back to Hitchcock.

In *Shadow of a Doubt*, the music – Lehár's waltz – is not, in the end, of any significance to the plot. It is simply present so that the audience will recognise it. Then, when we and young Charlie are finally shown the newspaper headline, 'Where Is the Merry Widow Murderer?', we say, 'Aha! So that's why she hasn't been able to get the tune out of her head.' But a question we are not expected to ask is how – and why – it got into her head in the first place. Back at the dinner table, young Charlie had wondered this herself, speculating that sometimes tunes can jump from one head to another. This is all Hitchcock is going to give us: Uncle Charlie is the Merry Widow Murderer – not that we know it yet – and therefore he has the tune going round in his own head. (Well he would, wouldn't he? It's his 'theme tune'.) Because he is close to his niece, who was named after him, there is some telepathic connection between them and now the tune is in her head too. It's nonsense, obviously, but we buy it. It is an aspect of what Hitchcock called a MacGuffin.

Before explaining that term, here's another example. At the

beginning of *The 39 Steps* (1935), Richard Hannay (Robert Donat) buys a ticket to the musical hall where he is just in time to catch the start of an act by Mr Memory (Wylie Watson), who daily 'commits to memory fifty new facts and remembers every one of them'. Mr Memory answers questions about football and racing and he answers Hannay's own question about how far it is from Winnipeg to Montreal. Each time he gives an answer, he demands to know 'Am I right, Sir?'

Hannay doesn't see the end of the act – no one does – because a riot breaks out in the theatre, shots are fired and Hannay goes home with the woman who fired them (Lucie Mannheim). She tells him her name is Annabella Smith. She also tells him that spies are trying to get important information out of the country. By the morning she has been murdered in his flat and Hannay is on the run, taking the 'Flying Scotsman' to Edinburgh. In the ensuing hue and cry across the Scottish moors, Hannay is handcuffed much of the time to Pamela (Madeleine Carroll), who believes him to be guilty of the murder and is magnificently unhelpful.

'There are 20 million women in this island and I get to be chained to you,' Hannay complains. Meanwhile, he finds himself continually whistling a jaunty little tune ('Oh do stop that whistling!' Pamela snipes at him).

The provenance of the tune is a mystery to Hannay, but Hitchcock certainly seems to have hoped his audience would recognise it as Mr Memory's signature tune. Back in the music hall the band had played it at the start of his act and then once more in an attempt to quell the riot. It had also featured, somewhat less jauntily, in the film's opening credits and yet again in the chase music on the moors. Still Hannay is puzzled.

'I wish I could get that damned tune out of my head,' he says. 'I wonder where I heard it.'

After Pamela overhears a phone conversation that exonerates Hannay and learns that the spies are headed to the London Palladium, she and Hannay make their way there, still unsure what they are looking for. The band strikes up Mr Memory's tune and suddenly Hannay understands: 'All the information's inside Memory's head!' He shouts out the question, 'What are the 39 Steps?' and professional pride forces Mr Memory to answer: 'The 39 Steps is an organisation of spies collecting information on behalf of the foreign office of ...' And with that he is shot.

So a tune has helped to stop a group of spies getting information out of the country. Except that it hasn't. It has been nothing but a diversion. Hannay goes to the London Palladium because of Pamela's tip-off. He doesn't know that Mr Memory will be performing there. It's only when the band plays the signature tune that Hannay exclaims 'Of course!' But 'of course' what? Yes, that's the tune he's been whistling, but this tune has changed nothing. If Mr Memory had had no signature tune for his act it would be all the same. The tune has been nothing but a delicious red herring, one that Hitchcock asks us to believe is significant right to the end of the film.

A MacGuffin is a plot point that is there to give the characters their motivation, the details of which need not trouble the audience. In *The 39 Steps* all we are told is that foreign spies are trying to steal air ministry secrets, and that is all we need to know. Mr Memory's tune has no relevance at all, save to stop us thinking too much about the MacGuffin. In *Shadow of a Doubt*, the waltz from *The Merry Widow* plays exactly the same role. In his famous and illuminating interview with François Truffaut, Hitchcock explained the origin of the term in a joke about two men on a train – a very Hitchcockian setting. One man asks the other what is the object on the luggage rack. The second man says it's a MacGuffin. The first man asks what that is precisely, and is told that it's 'an apparatus for trapping lions in the Scottish Highlands'. But there aren't any lions in Scotland, says the first man, to which the second replies that in that case it can't be a MacGuffin.

'So you see,' Hitchcock tells Truffaut, 'a MacGuffin is actually nothing at all.' And he remained of that opinion his whole career, never wanting to weigh down his viewers with unnecessary information and always happy to cut, often literally, to the chase. Sometimes, if the MacGuffin seemed likely to come to the fore, the director would even employ music or noise to cover up information. Perhaps he was concerned that close examination of his plot would reveal the holes, which are certainly plentiful, but he also wanted to maintain suspense, and he reasoned that plot details are dull. When Michael (Paul Newman) finally comes clean to Sarah (Julie Andrews) in *Torn Curtain* (1966), he is only telling her what we already know. Hitchcock didn't want to trouble us with the information a second time, so Michael leads Sarah away from the camera and tells her in the distance while we are treated to one of John Addison's musical cues and watch Julie Andrews throw her arms around dramatically. In *North by Northwest* (1959), the professor (Leo G. Carroll) needs to put Roger Thornhill (Cary Grant) in the picture. But the audience is already in the picture, so the briefing of our hero occurs as the two men walk across the tarmac at an airport and the propellers of an aeroplane start up, thus relieving us of the need to hear the details once more. And in the second version of *The Man Who Knew Too Much* when Ben and Jo McKenna (James Stewart and Doris Day) meet frantically at London's Royal Albert Hall, Jo tells her husband the little she knows, as we (who know far more than either of them) listen with growing alarm to Arthur Benjamin's cantata, *Storm Clouds*, and wonder how many more bars' rest the cymbal player has.

The Man Who Knew Too Much is the only film Hitchcock made twice. The first version was in 1934, a black and white film from Hitchcock's British period, while the second Technicolor version was made in Hollywood in 1956. Though the settings of the early parts of the films are different, in each case the Albert Hall and the *Storm Clouds* cantata provide the climax. In the first version of the film Bob and Jill Lawrence (Leslie Banks and Edna Best) are prevented from revealing secret information when their daughter (Nova Pilbeam) is kidnapped. In the later version, it is the McKennas' son Hank (Christopher Olsen) who is taken. Arthur Benjamin had composed the score for the first film, which included writing *Storm Clouds* for the climactic scene at the concert. Hitchcock had wanted a big piece – female soloist, large chorus and orchestra – more, one suspects, for the look of it than the sound. In the remake, Bernard Herrmann composed the film's score, but proposed retaining Benjamin's cantata for the concert scene. Herrmann was present, nevertheless, up on the podium conducting the London Symphony Orchestra, and we sight the composer Benjamin in the audience. There's a nice close-up of him wearing a silver tie and an ill-fitting grey jacket, with a handkerchief and pen in his breast pocket. (Incidentally, the piece itself is referred to as 'Storm Cloud Cantata' in the opening credits, but 'Cantata, Storm Clouds' on the poster outside the Albert Hall where Doris Day's taxi pulls up. Benjamin's publisher prefers the plural version, and so does this book.)

A foreign prime minister is attending the concert and revolutionaries from his country (together with 'English intellectuals') are going to have him murdered. In both films, the would-be assassin has been given instructions regarding the exact moment in the music at which he must fire. The same script is used in both versions of the scene. The gunshot should coincide with a cymbal crash to cover the sound and allow the hit-man to escape. In the 1934 film, Abbott (Peter Lorre) plays this moment to the marksman, Ramon (Frank Vosper), from a gramophone record. From just these few seconds of music, the man is supposed to know precisely when to fire, and we, the audience, are meant to recognise it too. It's a lot to ask, as Hitchcock himself must have come to realise, because in the remake he gives us far more to go on. In the 1956 film, Drayton (Bernard Miles) plays the same moment twice to Rien (Reggie Nalder) – and a third time, for the audience's benefit, after the gunman has left –

and he sends Rien off to the concert with a young female companion armed with a score of the piece. Once in the hall, Rien can hardly fail to spot his intended victim. The flag beneath the box in which the statesman is sitting consists of a diagonal white cross on a multi-coloured background. X marks the spot.

Everything to do with the music is spelt out more in the remake. The opening credits have Bernard Herrmann's music played by the London Symphony Orchestra, and the camera, never moving, shows us the percussion section of the orchestra in the Albert Hall. Being a Herrmann score, the percussionists are kept rather busy, but still there are moments when they are doing nothing at all and we are left watching the credits roll against an image of waiting musicians. This, of course, turns out to be significant. The main title music concludes with a mighty cymbal crash, the player holding out his cymbals, as percussionists will, to extract every bit of resonance from them. Against this image the following legend fills the screen: 'A single crash of Cymbals and how it rocked the lives of an American family.' So from the outset, we know what we're listening for.

In the 1956 version of the film, the Albert Hall scene is much longer than in the original. Hitchcock knew that suspense can be made greater by drawing it out and having the audience wait. Benjamin's cantata, four minutes long in 1934, was expanded by the composer to last nearly nine minutes in the remake. The later version has a great many more camera angles, especially for the choir and orchestra, and the performers are the focus of our attention. As the director realised, shots of an orchestra at work can hold an audience's attention, but if we know that the music they are playing will lead to murder, we don't want to take our eyes off them. For these nine minutes, we hear nothing but Benjamin's music. Once the performance begins, Hitchcock shows us around the audience and provides close-up shots of Jo and Rien and the prime minister's party, as well as the choir and orchestra. The film is in no hurry. Eventually, we settle on an elderly man at the back of the orchestra, sitting with his hands in his lap. The camera pans slightly to the man's left and we see two chairs beside him, each containing a large cymbal. In the 1934 version, the signal to fire had come from a rather smaller pair of cymbals, a gong and a bass drum, but twenty-two years later Hitchcock knew that simpler was better: just the cymbals, and make them big and shiny.

Soon we get more musical clues. As the choir sings, we see the gunman and his companion sitting in their box. She has the score open on her lap and we are shown a close-up of the page. She is following the choral part with her finger. Then we return to the cymbal player and Hitchcock gives us a look at his part: two pages containing nothing but rests, and finally at the end of the second page a single note, marked *fortissimo*.

Midway through the performance there is a loud timpani roll and the music picks up tempo. In the 1934 film, the concert is being broadcast on the radio and listened to by the other members of the gang. We cut to them at this timpani roll and hear one of the stooges ask, 'Was that it?' Peter Lorre, who is eating his dinner, waves away the question with a pained expression. In the 1956 film, this same musical moment is the occasion for James Stewart to arrive at the Albert Hall and have that animated exchange with Doris Day, and for a general ratcheting up of suspense. This involves Stewart's character running around the concert hall's circular corridors trying the doors of the boxes, but more importantly there is now a greater focus on the orchestra. The cymbal player has picked up his cymbals. There's a shot of the conductor's score, closer, then closer still, the camera travelling along a line of music. There's the conductor's view of the cymbal player, through his out-held cymbals. Then the reverse: the cymbal player's view of the conductor, of Bernard Herrmann, the man who will shortly point at the cymbal player and bring about the assassination. In the nick of time Doris Day's Jo works it out and, in the split second of silence immediately before the cymbal crash/gunshot, she screams – the first non-musical sound for nine minutes – ensuring the prime minister receives just a flesh wound. Hitchcock adds his own climax to the music (another joke that could not be passed up) with the marksman Rien falling from his box onto the audience below and, on cue, all the sopranos in the choir screaming in unison.

To call the musical performance in *The Man Who Knew Too Much* a clue is not strictly accurate. Neither Edna Best nor Doris Day knows what is happening when they go to the Albert Hall. They piece the information together as the performance gathers pace, and even then are not aware of the looming cymbal crash. But the simple plot – the MacGuffin that is the assassination attempt – is given vivid immediacy by Benjamin's score and, especially in the Hollywood version, by the way in which the music is shown to the audience. It is the music and the look of the music that provides the suspense.

Hitchcock told Truffaut that the MacGuffin in *North by Northwest* was his best, by which he meant the most meaningless. And it is perfectly true that even this film's title is meaningless. The pretext for the action involves secrets being smuggled out of the country. We never find out what the secrets are, where they might be headed or why, and of course, as the director wisely understood, we really don't care. But surely Hitchcock's best MacGuffin was itself musical.

'It's a tune,' explains Miss Froy in *The Lady Vanishes*. 'It contains – in code, of course – the vital clause of a secret pact between two European countries.'

In one of the best films of the director's British period, sound plays a vital role. The bulk of the film takes place on a train and the train's whistle not only alerts us to crucial events, but even causes a couple of them to happen. When Iris (Margaret Lockwood) is having tea with Miss Froy in the dining car, her companion says, 'I'm a governess, you know. My name's …' and the train whistle obscures her voice, forcing her to write 'FROY' on the window.

Later, the train whistle awakens Iris to the discovery that the old lady who was sitting opposite her has, indeed, vanished. And later still, back in the dining car, this time with Gilbert (Michael Redgrave), the whistle blows as the train enters a tunnel and the letters 'FROY' miraculously reappear on the window.

As for the tune, Miss Froy first hears it from a singer standing beneath her window in whatever Balkan country the early part of the film is set. Folk music features heavily in the film's first reels. Gilbert is studying the song and dance of this region and, much to Iris's annoyance, notating a clog dance in the hotel room above hers. The tune Miss Froy listens to isn't especially catchy and the singer's performance is laboured. Eventually Hitchcock has a pair of hands come out of the darkness and strangle him mid-phrase (one wonders if the makers of *The Body Snatcher* remembered this when they had Boris Karloff kill the blind ballad singer). At this point in the film, we do not connect the tune with espionage, so the killing seems merely like an extreme act of musical criticism. The punchline of the joke is the smiling Miss Froy, oblivious to the strangling, tossing a coin out of the window. We hear it clatter to the ground.

At the film's climax, when, during the shootout, Miss Froy – no longer vanished – is about to make a run for it, she begins singing this tune, over and over, to Gilbert. ('Hello, the old girl's gone off her rocker,' say Naunton Wayne tartly.)

'You're sure you will remember it?' asks Miss Froy.

'Oh, don't worry,' replies Gilbert. 'I won't stop whistling it.' And he's as good as his promise. So much so that Iris (echoing Pamela in *The 39 Steps*) is finally forced to complain: 'Can't you stop humming that awful tune? You must know it backwards by now.'

The final joke is that, back in London as they wait to meet the Foreign Office official and hand over the tune, Gilbert has forgotten it and can only seem to hum the Wedding March (by this time, things have taken a decidedly romantic turn). Fortunately, when the door opens and they walk into the room, there is Miss Froy seated at a piano, playing the tune. So 'the vital clause of a secret pact between two European countries' is now safe and, presumably, decoded.

*

Hitchcock's influence on other directors was immense, from his use of the camera to shock, to his juxtaposition of humour and suspense, to his thorough exploration of wrongful accusation – still a potent and recurrent element in the storylines of films. High on the list of Hitchcock's legacies to other filmmakers, though, is the use of sound and music, and the MacGuffin. Sometimes these were combined, as in *The Lady Vanishes*. The biggest musical MacGuffin of them all, though, is not in a film directed by Hitchcock at all. It's the one around which Steven Spielberg constructed *Close Encounters of the Third Kind*.

Aliens have chosen to make contact with Earth by means of a five-note musical motif, and suddenly all sorts of people have the fragment of melody stuck in their heads, from hundreds of chanting Indians in Dharamsala to a small boy with a toy glockenspiel in Indiana. A French expert, Lacombe (François Truffaut), attempts to teach the tune to a select group of important-seeming people – something like the United Nations – using the hand-signal method developed by the Hungarian composer and educator Zoltán Kodály: E rising to F sharp then falling to D, followed by the D an octave lower rising to A. Then he plays them the tape recording of the chanting Indians, who are singing in a different key. (This seems to be a continuity glitch rather than a subtle plot point.)

'We think it means something,' says Lacombe, not for the last time.

In the climactic scene, when the enormous alien mother ship comes in to land in Wyoming, one of the scientists plays the tune in yet another key (if these aliens can find their way to Earth, they can undoubtedly manage transposition). The mother ship responds in the voice of a tuba, and then proceeds to give an elaborate recital, the keyboard-playing scientist joining it in an inter-galactic jam session.

'What are we saying to each other?' one of the scientists asks.

'We have a translation interlock on their audio,' another answers reassuringly.

The point is that they are not saying anything to each other, at least not anything the audience need concern itself with. As we watch *Close Encounters of the Third Kind*, all we need to understand is that the aliens have come in peace and that, in contrast to what happened in *The Day the Earth Stood Still* (Robert Wise, 1951), this time we're not shooting at them. On the contrary, we are getting along so well with the aliens that we're all improvising music together. The by-now familiar five-note motif and its elaborations stand for communication where words would have been cumbersome. Even Kodály's hand signals are part of Spielberg's MacGuffin. They never had a serious function in the film, they just looked impressive. Kodály devised his brand of semaphore to teach music to the deaf. If you're wanting to teach a simple tune to people who can hear, these gestures will only be a distraction. Yet, as the motif is played over and over to the alien ship, Lacombe stands there clenching his fist and opening his palm, a look of spiritual ecstasy on his face. And it still looks impressive.

All of this serves to tell a simple story simply. Potentially tedious explanations have been averted by a very short tune and some hand signals. But John Williams's score for *Close Encounters* is also working at a deeper level, providing clues to the filmgoer that register in the unconscious. In contrast to the five-note motif, which is a plot point and given upfront, there are two elements in the musical score that recur. The first is a misty tone cluster that we first hear at the start of the film, coming from nothing, growing louder, then abruptly exploding in a startling *sforzando*. The second is the sonority of the tuba. Nearly all the film's music cues feature the tuba as a prominent component of the orchestration. We hear it particularly in the quieter moments, gently rumbling away in the lowest part of its register. It is a timbral presence colouring the whole sonority of the film.

When Roy (Richard Dreyfuss) and Gillian (Melinda Dillon) reach Devil's Tower, they recognise the national monument as the sawn-off rock they have been obsessively drawing and modelling. When that tuba solo blasts from the mother ship, we recognise it as the sound that has been insinuating itself in our memories for the last two hours. And when the ship opens to disgorge its cargo of blinking abductees, we recognise the glowing cluster of sound that was the very first thing we heard in the film. Spielberg and his composer do not require us to notice and register these musical elements, but they do want us to feel them. Sown as musical seeds at the start of the film they flower at the climax, bringing with them a sense of familiarity and inevitability that mirrors the feelings of homecoming Roy and Gillian have experienced.

In learning musical lessons from Hitchcock, Spielberg is in good and extensive company. As Hitchcock demonstrated, music is the most flexible of commodities in a film. Like film itself, it exists in time – it comes and goes – but it sticks in the memory. It is at once exact and yet it can be utterly imprecise: a good director doesn't reach for a musical cliché to bolster an emotion on the screen but uses sound and music to bring new layers of information to the film. Because it is non-verbal and invisible, music can co-exist with words as well as images: and it can enhance them or contradict them. Hitchcock used music in all these ways, playing with his audience's aural recollections, springing musical surprises, offering clues and red herrings and, time and again, allowing music to beguile and distract us so that we forget the mechanics of plot and experience the pure thrill of suspense.

The Sound of Voices

Herman Melville's novella *Billy Budd* is set on board a British man o' war during the Napoleonic wars. Billy, a popular, too-handsome boy, pressed into service from a passing merchant ship, is victimised by Claggart, the sadistic master-at-arms, and finally provoked into striking him. As a result of the blow, Claggart dies. Billy is found guilty of murder by a drumhead court, then hanged in front of the entire ship's company. The moment before his hanging, Billy asks God to bless the ship's captain. This is how Melville describes what happens next:

> The silence at the moment of execution and for a moment or two continuing thereafter, a silence but emphasized by the regular wash of the sea against the hull or the flutter of a sail caused by the helmsman's eyes being tempted astray, this emphasized silence was gradually disturbed by a sound not easily to be verbally rendered. Whoever has heard the freshet-wave of a torrent suddenly swelled by pouring showers in tropical mountains, showers not shared by the plain; whoever has heard the first muffled murmur of its sloping advance through precipitous woods, may form some conception of the sound now heard. The seeming remoteness of its source was because of its murmurous indistinctness since it came from close-by, even from the men massed on the ship's open deck. Being inarticulate, it was dubious in significance further than it seemed to indicate some capricious revulsion of thought or feeling such as mobs ashore are liable to, in the present instance possibly implying a sullen

revocation on the men's part of their involuntary echoing of Billy's benediction.

You would think this moment made for film, but in *Billy Budd* (1962), the director, Peter Ustinov, lets it go. In place of Melville's description of the inarticulate mass of protest, he has music. There's nothing wrong with the rather dissonant, angular melodic line by the composer Antony Hopkins. It's effective enough. But the book sounds better.

Whether consciously or not, Anthony Mann brings Melville's sound to life in *The Fall of the Roman Empire* (1964). At the death of Marcus Aurelius (Alec Guinness), the immediate sonic response comes courtesy of Dimitri Tiomkin's very strange score (complete with a prominent harpsichord). But in the following scene, the conversation between Lucilla (Sophia Loren), Livius (Stephen Boyd) and Timonides (James Mason) is underpinned by a relentless wind moaning outside, as though the elements were in mourning. This is more like it, and the sound returns at the end of the ensuing funeral procession, when we see the Roman legions standing in the drifting snow. But now it is not the wind we hear, it is men's voices. With their mouths hidden behind their shields, the soldiers stand motionless performing a horrifying ritual vocalisation, a wordless choral lament.

Human voices, massed or singly, have provided some of the most memorable sounds in more than eighty years of film history, but it is seldom remarked. In Fritz Lang's *M*, as early as 1931, voices are seemingly orchestrated, particularly in the crowd scenes. But the effect need not be so apparent or dramatic. Bertrand Tavernier often made use of a babble of voices to emphasise the solitariness of his central characters. *The Watchmaker of St Paul* (1974) begins and ends with scenes of a lot of people talking all at once. At the start we are in a café, at the end in gaol, the din of visiting time gradually clearing so that we can hear the conversation between Philippe

The Sound of Voices

Noiret and his son. In *Ça commence aujourd'hui*, it is the shrill racket of a primary-school classroom that gives way to something like an anechoic chamber in which we hear the private thoughts of a schoolteacher (Philippe Torreton). *Y tu mamá también* (Alfonso Cuarón, 2001) also places its voice-overs in a silent space. This is in contrast to the more or less constant chatter of the car trip through Mexico, where the three voices inside the car continually overlap with still more chat and music from the radio, even as the camera looks idly out of the window at the passing scenery.

In these scenes it is the sound of the voices that matters more than what is being said. Half the time, it is impossible to catch even the gist of the words. The voices provide a sonic continuum where, in other films, a musical score might be.

In *Magnolia*, soundscapes made up of various musical strands regularly provide this sort of effect, but there is also one memorable vocal continuum in which just a single voice – Earl Partridge (Jason Robards) on his deathbed – rambles on. It is part dying confession, part rationalisation, part regretful rant, and it runs on and on under several short scenes. Naturally, some of these scenes are distracting. We hear everything Earl is saying, but we only listen sporadically. We watch, for instance, as William H. Macy breaks into a house, and it is hard to pay full attention to Robards's speech, even though it is his voice we're hearing and not the sound of the breaking glass we are being shown.

The dull edge to Robards's delivery is part of the picture, and vocal monotony can be a useful device. In *Fahrenheit 451* (François Truffaut, 1966), Ray Bradbury's vision of a future in which the printed word is banned, books are burned and society, with no access to literature, is sensually deprived and culturally dead, finds its sonic counterpart not only in Bernard Herrmann's deliberately banal score, but in the way people speak. Their vocabulary is limited, as it would be, but more than that they speak in dull voices. As the fireman Montag, Oskar Werner's poor, heavily accented English (and maybe Truffaut's, too) helped him achieve this, but it's the two characters played by Julie Christie that are especially interesting in this regard. Linda, Montag's wife, speaks like an automaton, while Clarisse, the girl from down the road, is lively and engaged. Of course it turns out she's been reading books. It is the same in *The Stepford Wives* (Bryan Forbes, 1975). One knows a wife has been reprogrammed by the Stepford men from the change in her tone of voice. Suddenly we hear her speaking in a dull, soothing manner, occasionally exuding a sort of synthetic enthusiasm for all that is suburban: 'I'll just die if I don't get this recipe.'

Alice Harford (Nicole Kidman) in *Eyes Wide Shut* is also dull. She speaks very slowly and deliberately, because she is mostly either drunk or stoned or has just woken up from a nightmare. There are long pauses between words, and a slurred quality to her voice. Her husband Bill (Tom Cruise) speaks more clearly, but has an irritating tendency to repeat the things that are said to him. By the end of the film, in the scene in a toy shop, Alice is finally *compos mentis*, but by now she is repeating all the questions Bill asks her: 'What do I think we should do?' 'Am I sure?' It is hard not to wonder how much time might have been saved had she spoken a little faster and they'd both said everything only once.

In *The Sound Barrier* (David Lean, 1952), Ann Todd is Susan, the daughter of the aviator and inventor John Ridgefield (Ralph Richardson) and the wife the pilot Tony Garthwaite (Nigel Patrick). As its title hints, this film is, at least partly, about sound. It certainly makes us listen. When Tony first hears the roar of a jet engine from the test beds at Ridgeway's aircraft factory, he doesn't know what it is, but responds to the noise as though entranced.

'I think it's the most exciting sound I've ever heard,' he tells his future father-in-law, who soon signs Tony up to be one of his test pilots.

The emotional climax of the film, however, is not about the sound of jets, but about the sound of a voice. After Tony's fatal crash,

Susan, dazed, goes to the factory and walks in on her father sitting in his office listening to a tape of the dead pilot's final moments. As she runs away, horrified, Tony's voice follows her across the factory floor, growing louder, more reverberant (in the larger acoustic) and ever more anguished: 'Twenty-five thousand … Air brakes open … The controls don't respond. I can't hold her …'

*

When people talk about sound in relation to film, they seldom discuss tone of voice, and yet it is perhaps the most common sonic device of all. Speech is full of musical sounds: the way our voices rise and fall (pitch), how loudly we speak (dynamic), how quickly (tempo) and the syllables we choose to emphasise (articulation). In everyday life it is these musical aspects of speech, rather than the actual words spoken, that tell us if the person addressing us is happy, frightened, bored or confused, angry with us, in love with us or trying to deceive us. It is the same in films.

By way of an example, there's Julie Christie's voice-over narration in *Darling*. The voice-over is a common cinematic device and usually provides the viewer with a slightly different point of view from that of the characters on the screen, perhaps more detached. *To Kill a Mockingbird* is narrated by the grown-up Scout (Kim Stanley, unseen and uncredited), telling us what happened to herself as a young girl. In *Days of Heaven*, Linda (Linda Manz), like many a kid sister, is an acute observer. We see her on screen, sometimes behaving like a petulant child, but in the voice-over we hear her still childish voice speaking gravely and wisely.

For *films noirs*, the voice-over was a staple, and it was often a tired, cynical, male voice-over. One thinks of Fred MacMurray in *Double Indemnity* or William Holden in *Sunset Blvd*. MacMurray's narration is in the form of the insurance salesman Walter Neff confessing to his boss. We discover at the end of the film that it's his dying confession. William Holden's Joe Gillis famously turns out to have been dead from the start, narrating the film while floating face-down in a swimming pool.

The revelation at the end of *Darling* is subtler (and considerably more honest). From the start we have noticed a marked difference between the tone employed by Diana Scott (Christie) in her voice-over interview and the Diana Scott we see and hear on the screen. Although we are never privy to the questions she is answering, Diana's interview is clearly her life story, and she speaks in a considered and restrained manner. We notice that her voice is posher than the Diana we are watching, and we quickly work out that the interpretation she places on events is somewhat revisionist, peppered with justifications and very much to her own advantage. What the voice-over is telling us, though we don't know it until the end, is that having behaved like a princess most of the film, she finally is one. She's gone and married the Italian prince after all, and is giving her rather formal interview as his consort. There's more than a hint of Monaco about the whole story and a little of Grace Kelly about the tone of the voice-over.

Accents, posh or otherwise, are another aspect to the sound of voices. In British films, they can hint at class difference in a manner so subtle that you would need to be not just an English-speaker but actually British to infer anything from the sound. Subtitles certainly wouldn't convey the full effect, and it's doubtful whether Americans or Australians would always pick up on the differences in accent. At a less subtle level, of course, Hollywood has long used English accents to denote 'otherness', especially dominant otherness. So in *Spartacus*, the slaves are Americans and the Romans are Brits (and posh Brits at that).

In English-language films, non-English speakers tend to address each other in English, but with foreign accents. The two most common categories in which this convention has applied are native Americans in Westerns and Germans in Second World War films (we might also add aliens to the list). In making his revenge fantasy

Inglourious Basterds, Quentin Tarantino explained that he considered it unacceptably inauthentic for Nazi soldiers to speak English with a German accent, and so had put all their dialogue into German. The French characters, likewise, speak French and the Italians Italian. Linguistically, then, the film is relatively naturalistic, though it is hard to say why the director should consider this important in a film that misspells both words in its title and rewrites history to have Hitler killed by a Jewish bomb.

Timbre – colour – is a further element in the sound of voices. There are famous examples of actors altering their vocal timbre for roles. In order to play Othello, both Orson Welles (Welles, 1952) and Laurence Olivier (Stuart Burge, 1965) felt it necessary not only to black up, but to make their voices lower and richer. Woody Allen's whole vocal personality is so strong (timbre, accent and jumpy delivery) that actors who work with him – especially when playing the male lead Allen himself might once have played – regularly lapse into impersonation. Kenneth Brannagh did a spectacular job of this in one of Allen's most underrated films, *Celebrity* (1998). In *3:10 to Yuma*, Glenn Ford's villain speaks gently and seductively throughout, quite at odds with the character he is playing (although it sets up the last-minute change of heart). Anthony Hopkins played Hannibal Lecter in a similar manner, the softness of his voice somehow adding to his menace. John Malkovich is a master of this. Marlon Brando's gruff, wheezy Don Corleone in *The Godfather* is a timbral tour de force, as is Andy Serkis's hissing Gollum in *The Lord of the Rings*. Billy Bob Thornton's Karl Childers in *Sling Blade* (Billy Bob Thornton, 1996) is another brilliantly sustained piece of characterisation in which vocal timbre is one of the most important factors. Sometimes the sound of a voice can startle us. The only time we hear the 'wild boy' Victor speak in *L'enfant sauvage* he utters a single word, '*Lait*' (milk), in a high-pitched squeak. It comes as a complete surprise and the effect is comic.

In *Advise & Consent* (Otto Preminger, 1962), Henry Fonda

plays Robert A. Leffingwell, the nominee for secretary of state of a United States president. The action of the film centres on the Senate's confirmation hearing, in which a committee vets the nomination before consenting to it or rejecting it. Henry Fonda always plays good guys – everyone knows that – and so the Senate hearing, we feel, is bound to be a formality. But it's not. It is suggested that Leffingwell, in his youth, had communist leanings, and a man is mentioned, Herbert Gelman, of whom Fonda denies all knowledge. Then suddenly Gelman (Burgess Meredith) turns up to the Senate to answer questions. He speaks in such a fierce whisper that we instinctively disbelieve him, but in fact he is telling the truth. Leffingwell really is concealing his former communist sympathies. Vocal timbre can be misleading.

In *The Night of the Hunter* (Charles Laughton, 1955), Robert Mitchum gives a dazzling vocal display as the evil preacher, Harry Power. By turns wheedling and hectoring, pious and lascivious, he announces himself in the shadows with his creepy call sign of a hymn: 'Leaning, leaning, leaning on the everlasting arm'. Laughton drew a memorably cartoonish performance from Mitchum, though this does nothing to lessen his threatening nature. On the contrary, it makes him all the more threatening, because you feel there is really little about him that is rational. Finally – vocally – he turns into an animal. When Rachel Cooper (Lillian Gish) takes a pot shot at him as he comes into her house he scuttles away, yelping like a wounded dog. Listen to this sound, if you can, without shuddering.

Some of film's most memorable moments are when rational speech, or even irrational speech, gives way to sounds such as these, when words slip away and the voice is purely vocal. In the 1949 Ealing comedy *Whisky Galore!* (Alexander Mackendrick), the menfolk of the Scottish isle of Todday in the Outer Hebrides have been more dour than usual since their whisky ran out. The normal musical lilt of their speech is reduced to dark monosyllables. But then a ship is wrecked, the cargo of which consists of 50,000 cases of whisky. Once the Sabbath is over, the men row out to salvage the cargo. In the following scenes we don't see the whisky being poured or drunk: we hear the effects of the drinking in the men's voices, and it is not the expected sound of slurred speech, but of song.

The *puirt a beul* – traditional Hebridean mouth-music, wordless singing – starts off screen. Then we see an elderly man in bed. In an earlier scene he had been close to death, but now he is sitting up, much recovered and happily singing a little duet with his doctor. Other voices join in and now we see these men singing too. Eventually, it seems nearly all the men on the island are sitting or standing round the same table, clutching whisky glasses and singing together with broad smiles on their faces.

*

Finally, a few examples of the sudden transformation of voices into non-vocal sounds. In *The 39 Steps,* Robert Donat's maid enters his London apartment, sees Lucie Mannheim's body and lets out a scream. This is what we see: a close-up of the maid's mouth, wide and screaming. What we hear is the whistle of the Flying Scotsman as the film cuts to the train hurtling out of a tunnel bearing our hero to Glasgow. It's as though the train is coming out of the maid's mouth.

A similar moment occurs in *Don't Look Now*. John Baxter (Donald Sutherland) has found his daughter drowned in the pond in the big backyard of the family home. Stumbling and sobbing, he carries her up the garden towards the house. His wife, Laura (Julie Christie again), appears at the back door, unaware there is anything wrong. Then she looks up, sees her husband coming towards her with their dead daughter in his arms, and she screams. This time we do hear the start of the scream, but it is cross-cut with the sound of a masonry drill of similar pitch. Laura's scream gives us a jolt, and the screaming drill reinforces it. Since this drill is boring into one of the stones of Venice, it is also a marvellously effective way of changing location and jumping forward into the main part of the film. (There was a comic version of this same trick in the Marx Brothers' *At the Circus* [Edward Buzzell, 1939], when Margaret Dumont's Mrs Dukesbury opens her mouth to make a speech and an elephant trumpets on cue.)

In Satyajit Ray's first feature film, *Pather Panchali*, music often mirrors voices. Right at the beginning, Ravi Shankar's sitar playfully imitates the tripping speech patterns of Karuna Banerjee, who plays Sarbojaya, the mother of the Bengali family in the story. But the most powerful moment, which also involves Sarbojaya, comes near the film's end. Her husband, Harihar (Kanu Banerjee), has gone away in search of work, promising to return with money that will alleviate the family's poverty. While he is gone, his daughter Durga (Uma Das Gupta) becomes ill, develops a fever and dies. Harihar returns with gifts for all: a pastry board and a rolling pin, a picture of the goddess Lakshmi, a new sari for Durga … Sarbojaya cannot bring herself to tell her husband what has happened, but when she reaches for the sari her mouth opens and music comes out. It is the wiry sound of an esraj, a small stringed instrument fitted with a resonator (tar shehnai), and it is playing a great lament based on the evening raga *Patdeep*. We hear nothing of Sarbojaya's distraught tears, although we can certainly see them, and nothing of her husband's questioning. Soon, however, Harihar's repeated howling of his daughter's name overpowers the music and finally silences it.

Perhaps Ingmar Bergman remembered this scene (it is hard to forget it) when he was making *Cries and Whispers* in 1972. The film concerns Agnes (Harriet Andersson), who is dying painfully of cancer, and her sisters Maria (Liv Ullmann) and Karin (Ingrid Thulin), who visit her. It is not unusual for the characters in a Bergman film to say a good deal less than is on their minds, and this family has many secrets. Neither Maria nor Karin can bear to see Agnes in her final stages, and her death sends them further into their own worlds – especially Karin, who seems incapable of genuine communication with the others, speaking only of trivialities and household bureaucracy. She refuses even to be touched by Maria and, when her sister pushes the point, scorns her attempts at affection. Once outside the room, all Karin can do is scream. It proves cathartic. Maria comes to her once more, reaching out, and suddenly there is rapport. It is precisely at this moment, as Karin opens her mouth to speak tenderly to her sister for the first time, that the music starts: the *Sarabande* from Bach's C-minor suite for solo cello. Although the device is much the same as in *Pather Panchali*, the effect is almost the opposite; instead of grief, which, to this point, has permeated *Cries and Whispers*, we are witnessing affection, possibly even joy. Maria and Karin are smiling, touching one another's faces and speaking simultaneously, but it is only the cello we hear, the sound of voices replaced by something Bergman considered far more eloquent: a Bach *sarabande*.

The Sounds of Silence
(and Bumps in the Night)

Bernard Herrmann, that nonpareil among movie composers, died on Christmas Eve 1975, a few hours after putting the finishing touches to his music for Martin Scorsese's *Taxi Driver*. His career had begun auspiciously in 1941 with *Citizen Kane* and included such films as *The Ghost and Mrs Muir* (Joseph L. Mankiewicz, 1947), *The Day the Earth Stood Still*, *Cape Fear* (J. Lee Thompson, 1962) and *Fahrenheit 451*, as well as eight of Alfred Hitchcock's most celebrated pictures. Herrmann once insisted that music in a film was 'as important as photography'.

'Movies need the cement of music,' he said. 'I've never seen a movie better without it.'

Of course his own experience should have told him he was wrong about this. One of the films for which Hitchcock hired the composer contained none of his music, the soundtrack of *The Birds* calling only for a lot of electronic squawking, which Herrmann was paid to supervise. The film certainly doesn't suffer from a want of 'cement'. Quite the opposite: you only really notice the absence of music during the closing credits, and the effect of this, as Hitchcock doubtless intended, is sudden and chilling. Even in those films for which Herrmann or someone else had composed music, Hitchcock generally knew when a scene was more powerful without it. Herrmann eventually managed to persuade the director that there should be music in the shower scene of *Psycho*, and it would be difficult, now, to imagine it any other way. But the famous crop-duster scene in *North by Northwest* has no music, while in *Torn Curtain*, the film from which Herrmann was eventually sacked, the killing of the Stasi agent Gromek is all the more drawn out and gruesome for the absence of the composer's elaborate musical cue.

It is worth looking at this scene in some detail. Michael Armstrong (Paul Newman) is a rocket scientist who has apparently defected to communist East Germany. In truth, he is an American spy, intent on using his scientific training and knowledge to learn secrets. Gromek (Wolfgang Kieling) has been assigned to keep an eye on him, but Michael gives Gromek the slip and takes a taxi to a farm in order to meet another American agent. The farmer's wife who opens the door does not speak English and Michael speaks no German, so he draws the Greek letter π in the dirt with his shoe. It is the codename for the group of spies. The farmer is on his tractor and Michael climbs aboard for a brief MacGuffin of a conversation. On returning to the farmhouse, Michael discovers that Gromek has tracked him down and is chatting to the still-waiting taxi driver. Michael rushes into the house asking if there is a back door, and Gromek follows. The Stasi agent sees the π sign and works out that Michael is not what he seems.

So now three people face each other in the farmhouse kitchen. Gromek is at the telephone and already dialing Stasi HQ, while Michael and the farmer's wife exchange anxious glances: they know Gromek must be stopped, but they must stop him quietly or they will arouse the suspicion of the taxi driver outside. So sound is a crucial element in this scene, half the tension coming from trying to avoid making a noise (and remember, Michael and the woman can't speak the same language anyway). You can see why Hitchcock didn't want music.

Gromek turns out to be a hard man to kill. He has the constitution of Rasputin, surviving a glancing blow to the head from a pot of soup hurled at him by the farmer's wife, followed by a knife stuck in his chest. Michael has Gromek in a stranglehold so he can't shout, only mutter, but he breaks free and makes for the window.

Together, Michael and the woman manage to stop him opening it. Throughout the scene it is the muffled sounds of human struggle we hear: punching, kicking, grunting and heavy breathing.

Gromek now has his hands at Michael's throat, but with the woman's help Michael drags the Stasi agent across the kitchen floor to the oven. She turns on the gas taps and they edge Gromek's head inside. The camera looks down on this scene from immediately above the oven door. Gromek's head is no longer visible, just his hands, still round Michael's neck. Michael, red in the face, and the woman have all their weight against Gromek's body so that he cannot move. Gradually, as the gas takes effect, Gromek's hands loosen their grip on Michael; they twitch a bit, then one hand slips from view and we hear it gently thudding to the floor. Gromek is dead, and the gas taps can be turned off. Michael and the woman, who have only just met and never spoken to each other, have just completed a difficult and arduous murder.

Torn Curtain is a pretty disappointing film, but the killing of Gromek is one of Hitchcock's most memorable scenes. The absence of music is vital to its success, and especially to our appreciation of the sheer effort involved in the killing. Music would have made it seem too easy. But what we also learn from this scene is how the temporary absence of music can make us listen harder.

*

William Wyler's Cold War parable *The Big Country* is famous for its score by Jerome Moross. It contains some of the biggest and best cowboy themes ever composed and there's a relentless use of *leitmotifs*. Yet its most famous scene is almost devoid of music. The dawn fight between Jim McKay (Gregory Peck) and Steve Leech (Charlton Heston) is shot mostly from a great distance, looking down on the action. We hear nothing. We're not close enough. This is intercut with medium-distance shots in which the odd punch and groan can be discerned. As the two men become exhausted, slowly losing interest in fighting each other but continuing to trade half-hearted blows, music begins – a syncopated *ostinato* figure plays rather quietly as though mocking the contestants. It's the same when Henry Terrill (Charles Bickford) and Rufus Hannassy (Burl Ives) confront each other in Blanco Canyon: again no music, again distant aerial shots, again, after a while, the mocking music, this time disrupted by gunfire. Wyler's use of actual silence and just a few sound effects is an alienating device. As the camera stands back from the action, so do we. By refusing to involve us with music or sound effects, Wyler enables us to see that these people are behaving ridiculously.

But precisely the same technique can also increase an audience's involvement. This is certainly how the aerial shots, silence and sound effects work in *North by Northwest*. Roger Thornhill (Cary Grant) has arrived by bus in the middle of nowhere to meet a man named Kaplan, whom the audience already knows does not exist. He waits there at the bus stop, a mere dot on this wide expanse of landscape somewhere in the American Midwest. Occasionally a car passes, and in the distance there's a small biplane spraying crops, but otherwise we hear only the scuffing of Thornhill's shoes in the dirt and his hands plunging disappointedly into his trouser pockets as another car goes past and doesn't stop. At length, a car drops off a man at the bus stop on the opposite side of the road. The men stare at each other a while, then Thornhill goes over. But it's not Kaplan, and when his bus comes along, the other man climbs aboard, leaving Thornhill alone again.

A lot of directors would have started up the music at this point, because, in one of the most famous sequences in the history of film, the biplane is about to start its dive-bombing and machine-gunning. But no, Hitchcock has his star run into a cornfield and, besides the plane and its gun, offers us only the sound of fluttering corn each time the plane passes close overhead. The absence of music leaves Thornhill alone and very vulnerable.

Now he spots a truck coming in the distance and runs on to the highway, arms stretched out in front of him in an attempt to stop it. The truck screeches to a halt, Thornhill disappearing under the front fender, and the biplane, out of control, crashes into it, immediately bursting into flames. And finally Herrmann's music starts up again. For nearly nine minutes there's been no score and scarcely any dialogue, ratcheting up the tension even before the crop-duster began its attack. Now at the climax of the scene a flamboyant fandango – the recurring rhythm in this Herrmann score – bursts into life, along with the flames, and, rather than adding to the tension, it dissipates it. We can all breathe again.

Exactly the opposite effect is produced by the arrival of music in Michael Crichton's *Coma* (1978). The film concerns Dr Susan Wheeler (Genevieve Bujold), who finds herself increasingly worried about the number of people falling into comas during routine operations at her hospital. She begins to suspect some sort of malpractice and a possible cover-up. For the first fifty minutes of the film, there is no score, just Beethoven on the radio, aerobics music in an aerobics class, and Vivaldi in an operating theatre. With her suspicions growing, she decides, one evening, to speak to her boss, Dr Harris (Richard Widmark). He seems reassuring, in a patronising sort of way, but we can tell she does not feel reassured. Next we see her sitting in her car in the hospital car park. The car won't start. She gets out and in her frustration gives it a good kicking. Suddenly she realises she is being watched. At the same moment, Jerry Goldsmith's score creeps in (and 'creeps' is the word). We instantly know that the man watching her is not merely a passer-by beguiled by the sight of a woman kicking her car, he is something far more sinister. The watcher – like the music – is a new presence in the film.

So where, in *North by Northwest*, Hitchcock had brought Herrmann's fast, rhythmic music crashing in and so dispelled the tension that had been building, in *Coma*, Crichton lets the music slither in quietly and immediately increases the tension. This contrast is the

The Sounds of Silence (and Bumps in the Night)

perfect rejoinder to anyone who believes that music in cinema always behaves in certain ways. The effect of music, as these examples demonstrate, is dependent upon its interaction with all the other elements in a film.

In Joel and Ethan Coen's *No Country for Old Men* (2007), there is no score in the conventional sense, only the barely audible tones of Tibetan singing bowls. The sounds one remembers from the film are the desert winds and the sickening metallic chink of the bolt gun that Anton Chigurh (Javier Bardem) uses to kill his victims. But there is one very striking use of on-screen music, too. Llewelyn Moss (Josh Brolin), wounded, weak from the loss of blood and sleep, and trying to evade Chigurh, gets himself from West Texas down to Mexico, walking the last part of the journey. He finally falls asleep by a fountain, only to be awakened the following morning by a mariachi band, its members standing all around him. It's as much of a shock for us as for him, but like the music that accompanies the crashing crop-duster, it is a shock that allows us relief from the extreme tension the Coens have successfully created to that point. In fact, we laugh at the intensity of the performance, the smiles on the faces of the musicians freezing as Moss offers them a bloody $100 bill.

Few things grab our ears like the sound of music where there had been none before, unless it's a sudden and unexpected noise. There's a good example of this in the Coen brothers' first feature, *Blood Simple* (1984), when out of the blue a rolled-up newspaper slams into a screen door. At the last moment, we see it coming, cartwheeling through the air, but it doesn't alleviate the shock of the noise, which is followed immediately by the din of a jackhammer.

In *The Public Enemy* (William A. Wellman, 1931), the famous coal-truck scene makes use of one sudden sound effect to mask another. Tom Powers (James Cagney) and Matt Doyle (Edward Woods) are young gangsters who duck for cover in the street when they hear what appears to be machinegun fire. Of course it's the coal truck that Tom had seen earlier, unloading coal into a nearby cellar. Laughing at their foolishness, they get up and go on their way, but real machineguns are trained on them from a window across the street, and seconds later they open fire on the pair, killing Matt.

In *Some Like It Hot*, Billy Wilder paid this scene a small act of comic homage. The two musicians, Jerry (Jack Lemon) and Joe (Tony Curtis), have gone to a Chicago garage to pick up a car for an out-of-town gig. While they are having it filled with petrol, they witness the execution of several gang members by another gang in a version of the St Valentine's Day massacre.

'I think I'm going to be sick,' Jerry hisses urgently to Joe and turns his head away. We hear a splattering sound, then the camera pans across to show us petrol spilling onto the concrete garage floor.

Sound effects, misleading or mysterious, can quickly develop a storyline. The title, of course, is a clue, but even so, as we watch the opening seconds of *Witchfinder General* (Michael Reeves, 1968), with its bucolic greenery and fields of safely grazing sheep, the distant knocking in the background doesn't suggest anything in particular. It might be someone chopping wood. In fact, as we soon see, it is someone putting the finishing touches to a gallows, and in the very next shot a woman, screaming and struggling, is being led to it as a priest reads from the Bible. This all takes thirty seconds and jolts us right into the action.

Pickup on South Street (Samuel Fuller, 1953) has a slightly slower start, but no less powerful or pertinent to the plot and nature of the film. Following the credits, and a breezy, syncopated theme from Leigh Harline (the composer of 'When You Wish Upon a Star'), the first few minutes of the film play without dialogue. We are on a crowded subway train, coming into stations, disgorging and admitting passengers, and leaving again. Our focus is directed at the face of a young woman (Jean Peters) and the two men staring at her with what seems like more than casual interest. They are all standing in

The Sounds of Silence (and Bumps in the Night)

the crowded carriage, but she is oblivious of the men's attention. Although no one speaks, there is plenty to listen to. We hear all the sounds of the subway, the clattering over points, the squealing of breaks, the change in tone as the train moves in and out of stations, the opening and closing of doors.

We don't see Skip McCoy (Richard Widmark) board the train, but we notice him making his way towards us, up the carriage, finally stopping in front of the woman and unfolding his newspaper. Next we watch as his fingers move under the newspaper to open the clasp on the woman's handbag and, very delicately, begin to search inside for a wallet. (The sequence must have been an inspiration to Robert Bresson when he made *Pickpocket* some six years later.) Once Skip has the purse, the train lurches to a halt and he snaps the bag shut, exiting the carriage. The watching men quickly converge on the doors, which shut in their faces.

'What happened?' asks the younger man.

'I'm not sure yet,' the other replies. They both look back at the woman, who flutters her eyelashes, still unaware that she is being watched, let alone that she has been robbed.

We're not sure what happened yet either, but we're certainly interested. Samuel Fuller was good at getting his films off to a cracking start, and an arresting use of sound was part of his technique. We think of the way the first frames of *The Naked Kiss* crash in, mid-fight, mid-jazz solo. The actual music is immaterial: any loud, fast jazz would have done. Disorientation through sound – and jerky cameras – is the point.

Of course, as Ingmar Bergman knew, quiet sounds can be just as effective for this. Because his films generally used so little music, they offered a kind of blank sonic space in which something as simple as a ticking clock – a sound he returned to again and again – could play a vital role in establishing mood and focusing our attention. Bergman discovered that tiny sounds, heightened, created intense concentration.

The Finnish director Aki Kaurismäki's films are known for their dearth of dialogue and complete absence of music scores. In *The Match Factory Girl* (1990), there is remarkably little speech. Iiris (Kati Outinen) is the eponymous girl, and the first moments of the film take us to the factory in which she works. Before we are shown anything else, we see the complete process of manufacture from log to match to the labelling of the packages, and we hear the machinery. Then we see Iiris clock off, visit a shop, go home to the small apartment she shares with her parents and prepare them soup for dinner. She goes out dancing, but no one asks her to dance. In fact no one says anything to anyone in the first fifteen minutes of this film, and when Iiris herself finally speaks it is only to order a beer. When she buys a colourful new dress and shows it to her parents, her father slaps her face and calls her a 'whore'. It's the only word he speaks in the whole film. Her mother doesn't say much more.

What we do hear are tangos and 1950s-style surf guitar tunes (Kaurismäki selects and displays his musical choices as prominently as Wes Anderson and Quentin Tarantino). In fact it is not the 1950s – the TV news images of the massacre in Tiananmen Square tell us that much – and so the music choices seem more like a commentary on Iiris and her life. Equally disorientating is the radio in her parents' apartment. When we first meet her parents, the radio is playing a rugby league commentary from Sydney; later we notice news broadcasts in Russian and French. All this is barely audible and no one on screen seems to be listening. Anyway, there's no evidence that anyone in this Helsinki apartment speaks English, Russian or French. (On Iiris's birthday, she receives a book from her mother which we see, as she puts it in the bookshelf, is in Swedish.) But because there's really nothing else for the audience to listen to, we pay attention to these seemingly random sounds, and as the film goes on they build up a stifling atmosphere from which it seems Iiris might never break free, at least not without the help of rat poison.

One of the most celebrated quiet sequences in the whole of

cinema is the half hour without dialogue or music that Jules Dassin put at the heart of his heist movie *Rififi* (1955). The jewel robbery is planned in great detail and then the plan put into action. The four men – a couple of them experts in their field – have no need to speak. Each knows what he must do next, and so we observe them at work, admiring their skill and professionalism in much the same way that Bresson invites us to admire his pickpockets. These people are good at their jobs, careful and thorough. Not that we notice the absence of music, but it is impossible to imagine the scene with it. We are all of us – audience and thieves – concentrating intently. Music would be an intolerable distraction.

In contrast to the Gromek sequence in *Torn Curtain*, then, this scene isn't really about listening at all. It is simply about being quiet, about not making a noise. But there are entire films that deal with the business of listening. *The Conversation* (Francis Ford Coppola, 1974) is a classic, with a carefully modulated sound design by Walter Murch. Gene Hackman plays Harry Caul, a surveillance expert, and much of the film's plot hinges on his (and our) listening skills. In *The Lives of Others* (Florian Henckel von Donnersmarck, 2006), set in East Germany in 1984, the listener is the suddenly conscience-stricken Stasi captain, Gerd Wiesler (Ulrich Muehe). The plot of the Dogme-influenced *Red Road* (Andrea Arnold, 2006) is more concerned with watching than listening. The central character, Jackie (Kate Dickie), is a CCTV operator in Glasgow. But the sound design on the film is extraordinarily subtle and powerful and while Jackie watches in silence, the audience ends up listening.

Part of the power of *Red Road* comes from is its lack of a score. As with Kaurismäki's films, we find ourselves attending to barely audible sounds: sustained tones, electronic hums and blips, distant, indistinct voices. Against this background, when Jackie, for example, rubs her hands together, the sound is strikingly present. Ambient tones occur throughout the picture and so does the drone of traffic. Often the two blur, indistinguishably. Other high-pitched tones drift into earshot, as if extensions of the white noise from radio receivers.

Jackie recognises Clyde (Tony Curran), a figure from her past, on the CCTV and sets about gaining revenge. This involves seducing him. The film's climactic scene in her bedroom begins with Clyde referring to the distant howling of foxes on the housing estate. It concludes with his own ejaculatory howl morphing into another, rather louder, fox cry.

Red Road is a painfully sad film, but then so are *The Conversation* and *The Lives of Others*, spying being an essentially desperate act. Unlike *Red Road*, the other films both have scores, but they are used sparingly, making way for long scenes of eavesdropping. In *The Conversation*, which has a piano score by David Shire, the dominant music is snippets of the song 'When the Red, Red Robin Comes Bob, Bob, Bobbin' Along', played in the film's opening scene and heard again and again as Harry plays back his surveillance tapes. And then there's Harry's own solitary saxophone playing.

Nothing is as it seems in Coppola's film. Even the opening sequence, in which a young couple's conversation is recorded by highly directional microphones in San Francisco's Union Square, only slowly becomes clear. To begin with, the long-range microphones seem to be high-velocity rifles, complete with cross-hairs, and for a moment we think we may be about to witness an assassination.

Once Harry's recordings are made, we watch as he listens in his warehouse studio, mixing the three tracks in an attempt to keep the conversation clear and audible at all times. And we listen, too, as he goes over and over certain fragments of the conversation. The film's crucial plot twist is a sonic cheat, as others have observed, involving a change of stress in a sentence that can only be achieved by the substitution of a different recording: 'He'd kill us if he got the chance' suddenly becomes 'He'd kill *us* if he got the chance'. Does it matter? It probably depends on what you expect from a movie.

But throughout *The Conversation*, perhaps the most interesting aspect of the film – at least in terms of filmmaking – is that so much of the time we have the microphone's point of view. In the opening scene, we pass from microphone to microphone as the couple walk around in the crowd, but even later, when Harry is editing, piecing the information together, it is still the microphones that give us the angle, and we experience the story through them.

At the end of *The Blair Witch Project* (Daniel Myrick & Eduardo Sánchez, 1999), it is much the same. The three characters lost in a Maryland forest are filmmakers and they carry two cameras – one video, one film. What we see on the screen, then, is always shot by one or other of these cameras, so we have the point of view of whichever character is holding it. At the end of the film, Josh (Joshua Leonard) enters a derelict house at night. His fellow filmmakers Mike (Michael Williams) and Heather (Heather Donahue) follow him with the cameras. They go upstairs together, but then they hear that Josh is down in the basement. Mike runs downstairs with the video camera, and we have his camera's point of view as he reaches the basement and the camera suddenly falls to the ground (we infer that he has been hit on the head). Now we switch to the vision from Heather's film camera, but we retain the sound from Mike's. The effect is hugely disorientating: visually, we are Heather running downstairs, but our ears remain in the basement listening to her approaching screams.

Low-budget horror films such as *The Blair Witch Project* and *Paranormal Activity* (Oren Peli, 2007) can do a lot with suggestive sound. It's a tradition that goes back at least to Val Lewton. The films he produced for RKO in the 1940s were successful at the time and have attained cult status since, but they were intended as 'B pictures' and so made on the cheap. From film to film, the same directors, writers, actors and occasionally characters reappear. Even the scenery was recycled. So low were the films' budgets that hand-me-down sets were sometimes used, including the grand staircase from *The Magnificent Ambersons* (Orson Welles, 1942), which appeared in both *Cat People* and *The Seventh Victim*. Lewton's theory of filmmaking was simple. Things – supernatural things, zombies, big cats, murderers – were generally scarier if you feared they might be out there in the dark somewhere, but couldn't actually see them. It was a philosophy in keeping with his meagre budget.

The need to find non-visual methods of terrifying the paying public was behind the employment of many a sound effect. *Cat People*, directed by Jacques Tourneur, was the first of Lewton's pictures and remains the best known. We remember the air brakes on the Central Park bus, not to mention the deep growling amid the flickering shadows of the swimming pool. But Mark Robson in *The Seventh Victim*, his first movie for Lewton (or anyone else), offers a masterclass in how to scare people on the cheap, and it's nearly all a matter of sound.

Mary Gibson (Kim Hunter) has come to New York City to look for her sister Jacqueline (Jean Brooks), who has disappeared. She stumbles on a bunch of devil worshippers – forerunners of Mia Farrow's neighbours in *Rosemary's Baby* (Roman Polanski, 1968) – who have her sister in their thrall. The last ten minutes of the film begin – at night, of course – with all the satanists gathered together in a room. Jacqueline is with them and they are trying to convince her to drink poison. Roy Webb's typically resourceful score is supplying some subtle tension, but not all his music is on the soundtrack. Seated at a piano, one of the assembled guests, a one-armed woman, is thoughtfully adding a few chords to the mix. At the climax of the scene, the poisoned glass is knocked over and Jacqueline leaves the house.

As she walks away from the front door, street lamps cast alarming shadows around her. Almost immediately we are jolted by an off-screen crash, shown to be the lid of a garbage bin dislodged by a dog. A man emerges from the shadows to follow Jacqueline, and we hear the play of their footsteps, her high heels clacking, his feet barely audible. She goes to step off the curb and a car's brakes screech (we don't need to see the vehicle). She pauses outside the stage door of a theatre, chirpy music and audience laughter coming from within. We hear the creaking of someone's shoes close by. As Jacqueline reaches out in the dark, she finds the hand of a man. We see and hear his switchblade open but a sudden off-screen peal of female laughter signals the actors emerging from the theatre, still wearing their costumes (doubtless from another RKO production). Jacqueline goes with them to a bar, but doesn't follow them in. The strains of stride piano are heard.

Finally returning home, she meets a distracted-looking woman on the landing outside her room. It is Elizabeth Russell, a Lewton regular.

'I'm Mimi. I'm dying,' she tells Jacqueline.

'I've alway wanted to die,' Jacqueline admits, and when she opens the door to her room, we see a noose hanging from the ceiling.

Meanwhile, a psychiatrist and a poet are quoting phrases from the Lord's Prayer to the satanists (to the accompaniment of Roy Webb's strings quoting the 'Dresden Amen'), and Mary and Jacqueline's husband are confessing their love for each other. The final shot is of Mimi, all dressed up, going out for her last night on the town. As she passes the door of Jacqueline's room, we hear one final off-screen sound: a chair being kicked over. Mimi pauses briefly, then continues down the stairs.

The sound effects in *The Seventh Victim* and other films from the Lewton stable are generally heightened, exaggerated, amplified. They are made to stand out. A stage beyond that is the elimination of other noises so that a particular sound dominates a scene. One rather beautiful example of the technique is the scene in *Trilogy: the Weeping Meadow* (Theodoros Angelopoulos, 2004) in which the violinist Nikos (Giorgos Armenis) dies amid the gentle flutter of a hundred bed sheets hanging out to dry. Certainly the smudges of blood he leaves on a few of the white sheets are eloquent in their own way, but the sound of all that flapping is poetic – both a benediction and a sign that life and laundry go on.

This technique is bolstered when a kind of artificial muting is applied to all but one sound in a *visually* noisy environment. The fight sequences in *Raging Bull* (Martin Scorsese, 1980) make good use of this technique, the crowd noise receding, sometimes disappearing altogether, returning as a great roar, and then an individual punch given sickening prominence.

In *The Road to Perdition* (Sam Mendes, 2002), John Rooney (Paul Newman) leaves O'Neil's bar with his entourage of six bodyguards carrying umbrellas. It is nighttime and raining steadily. The rain, indeed, is all we hear. But now comes a slow cross-fade as Thomas Newman's score replaces the rain. By the time the party reaches Rooney's car and discovers that his driver has been shot dead, the rain is still coming down, but we are hearing only music. Now we watch as Rooney's henchmen are gunned down by an unseen and unheard machine gun, collapsing, one by one, on the wet street. At last, Michael Sullivan (Tom Hanks) appears. He walks towards Rooney and as he does so, Newman's music slowly fades away, and the sound of the rain returns.

The slow-motion prom scene in *Carrie* (Brian de Palma, 1976) is another example of this technique, but involving the disappearance of the music as well as most of the sound effects. When their names are read out, Carrie White (Sissy Spacek) and her date, Tommy (William Katt), walk up to the stage, smiling beatifically, accompanied by Pino Donaggio's cloying music. It is surely meant to be too sweet. We know there's a bucket of pig's blood waiting for them, but we don't know when it's coming. De Palma delays the moment as long as he reasonably can, but once Carrie has been crowned prom queen the bucket must drop (still in slow motion). Donaggio's string orchestra falls quickly away in a downward glissando as we hear gasps from the crowd and the blood splashing onto the stage. And then, far more arrestingly, the creaking of the empty metal bucket swinging on a rope – like a body on the gallows – and banging against something solid. The other sounds have drained right away.

The creaking and the banging are all we hear. Then the bucket falls, hitting Tommy on the head and knocking him to the ground. Now there is total silence. We see Chris (Nancy Allen) laughing hysterically, but we don't hear her. Bit by bit, an elaborate collage of sound comes forward, made up of voices from earlier in the film (including Carrie's mother's warning, 'They're all going to laugh at you') and the crowd's raucous laughter. From here on, as Carrie takes her indiscriminate telekinetic revenge on her teachers and schoolmates, the sound effects, though still exaggerated, more closely relate to the images on the screen, underpinned by the return of Donaggio's score, now all long, low single notes on cellos and double basses.

In *Samson and Delilah* (Warwick Thornton, 2009), this same technique is used to take us inside the head of one of the main characters. Samson (Rowan McNamara) is lying on his mat, and we are hearing the simultaneous sound of a reggae beat and country music. The reggae is coming from outside on the veranda, as it does almost continuously during the first part of this film; the country music is on the radio just beside Samson. Samson covers his ears and immediately we share his experience, the music remaining as a distant blur. When he uncovers his right ear, he and we hear the reggae, when he uncovers his left, we hear the country music, and we hear each in extreme stereo from either side of the screen. We are now in his head, listening through his ears. Talk about point of view!

*

Among the roles played by sound effects in films are the development of character and the facilitating of plot. Both these are achieved with a train whistle in *Call Northside 777* (Henry Hathaway, 1948). To be honest, it is a poorly written, lumpily directed, sanctimonious drag of a film about a '*Chicago Times*' reporter, Jim McNeal (James Stewart) trying to uncover evidence that will gain a pardon for a man wrongly convicted of shooting a cop, but the train whistle is worth hearing. Searching for the perjurer, Wanda Skutnik (Betty

Garde), McNeal finally traces her to an apartment on the wrong side of the tracks. Specifically these are Chicago's L-tracks – the city's elevated railway – and as McNeal enters the apartment, the noise from the trains is given increasing prominence. It provides more than local colour. Skutnik screams at McNeal and, as the two argue, the climax of their fight coincides with a train's piercing whistle, all but drowning their voices and completely obscuring the entry of a man in the doorway with his gun pulled on the reporter.

It's hard not to believe that Reginald Rose, who wrote first the teleplay (in 1954) and then the screenplay of *12 Angry Men* (Sidney Lumet, 1957), did not have this scene in mind (or at least at the back of it) when he invented one of the major plot points in another drama about mistaken identity. This was the fact that the noise from a passing L-train must have obscured the shouting that a witness claimed to have heard. (Incidentally, two of the jury members in *12 Angry Men* – Lee J. Cobb and E.G. Marshall – had also been in *Call Northside 777*.)

There's another memorable L-train in *The Godfather* when Michael (Al Pacino) shoots McCluskey (Sterling Hayden) and Sollozzo (Al Lettieri) in an Italian restaurant. There are no trains at all in the scene until just before the climax; in contrast to the scene-setting whistles in *Call Northside 777*, this time the trains serve no purpose but to heighten the drama. After Michael has located the gun behind the toilet cistern, he prepares to leave the bathroom and return to the dining area of the restaurant. The first train passes at this point, the sound growing quite loud but then retreating into complete silence. Back at the table, while Michael summons the courage to shoot, another train approaches, its breaks screaming as Michael pulls out his gun and begins to fire. If anything, the noise from these trains performs the role of a score in the scene, Coppola holding off the actual music until Michael throws the gun down when he leaves the restaurant.

In *Outrage* (Ida Lupino, 1950), Ann Walton (Mala Powers) jams a truck horn to attract attention when she feels threatened, but the sound of the horn continues into the score, forming a kind of pedal point. It is an example of a sound effect blending with and becoming part of the music, here with disastrous results. The score absorbs and neutralises the truck horn, and by the time a man finally takes notice and looks out of his window Ann, off screen, is being raped.

Akira Kurosawa liked the sound of rain almost as much as Bergman liked clocks. The beginning of *Rashomon* (1950) features a torrential downpour and so does the end of *Seven Samurai* (1954). Before we arrive there, however, the rain is foreshadowed in the score. The film starts with taiko drums, ominously quiet, playing throughout the opening credits. They might almost be a musical representation of rain. In the last part of the film, the drumming has been transformed into the hooves of galloping horses, the sound finally climaxing in that pounding rain. In *Black Narcissus* and *The Sound Barrier*, it is wind and jet engines that inspire the score. Malcolm Arnold's music for the latter has made a feature of its orchestral piccolos even before we are properly exposed to the jet whistle itself. In *The Red House* (Delmer Daves, 1947), Pete Morgan (Edward G. Robinson) tries to stop young Nath Storm (Lon McCallister) from taking a shortcut home at night.

'You can never run away from the scream,' he warns him. 'It will follow you through the woods. It will follow you all your life …' He might have added, 'It will follow you in the score.'

A more thoroughgoing and recent instance of sound effects entering and even becoming the score is in Dario Marianelli's music for *Atonement* (Joe Wright, 2007). The film is about writing – more and more so, as it turns out – and it begins with the sound of a typewriter carriage being whacked into position, followed by typing. The typewriter in the film is an instrument of creativity, destruction and ultimately a form of atonement, but it is also a percussion instrument, continually finding its way into the music. After Briony (Saoirse Ronan) falsely denounces Robbie (James McAvoy) for having raped Lola (Juno Temple), the typewriter's rhythmic motif joins with piano and strings. The music settles onto a single repeated piano note (which we briefly see Briony playing, as though she might be tapping away still at her typewriter). When Robbie is driven away by the police, his mother (Brenda Blethyn) beats repeatedly on the bonnet of the car with her umbrella, adding a new percussive strand that is also taken up in the score. Later in the film, at the wedding of Lola to the real rapist, Paul Marshall (Benedict Cumberbatch), the typewriter suddenly erupts again into a fierce tattoo of condemnation.

If sound effects can become music, the opposite is also true. One might argue that much of the time in blockbuster action films, the continuous stream of music ceases to function musically and, instead, provides a continuum of sound that somehow supports the action (and possibly papers over the cracks in the script). But in Michael Mann's *Collateral* (2004), this is done quite consciously as a dramatic device.

As the hit-man Vincent (Tom Cruise) and his unwilling companion, taxi driver Max (Jamie Foxx) enter the Fever Club looking for Vincent's next victim, loud, pounding techno music is playing. It is Oakenfold's 'Ready Steady Go'. The club is packed with cops and FBI agents as well as hundreds of dancers, and the chances of Vincent finding the man he is looking for – or of the cops finding Max, who they think is Vincent – seem small (shades of the Grand Hotel tea dance in *Young and Innocent*). Vincent, Max and the cops all move through the surging crowd, trying to see above hundreds of bobbing heads, the rhythmic music loud and relentless. The sequence resembles nothing so much as the final street carnival in *Les enfants du paradis* (Marcel Carné, 1945), with Baptiste (Jean-Louis Barrault) watching Garance (Arletty) disappearing in the distance as the whirling dancers seem to carry him backwards and away from her. The lively, joyful tarantella is at ironic odds with the desperation on Baptiste's face. He is surrounded by the joy of the revellers, but for him the music is a terrible noise bringing the destruction of all his hopes.

The dance music in *Collateral* is equally at odds with the shooting that now breaks out in the Fever Club. At first, the music serves to disguise the gunshots and the dancing is undisturbed, but as the violence increases, a full-scale panic breaks out on the dance floor. And of course the music continues its relentless techno beat amid the shooting and the screaming. It is at this point the music ceases to function as music at all, its very incongruity turning it into nothing but inappropriate noise, the meaningless soundscape against which the killing continues on screen.

FIVE DIRECTORS

Bruce Beresford

One of a handful of film directors also to have staged opera, Bruce Beresford has a strong musical sensibility. Indeed his respect for music is such that he uses it sparingly in his films and never in an obvious way. But his films are full of evocative sounds, from the wind on the veldt in Breaker Morant *(1980) to the sub-Arctic winds of* Black Robe *(1991). We recorded this conversation at his home in Sydney in 2007.*

ANDREW FORD: Maybe we should start with a general question about the role of music in films. Do you have any theories about this? Do you have fixed ideas about how music works in films?

BRUCE BERESFORD: My feeling about music in films is somewhat ambivalent. When I did a lot of the early Australian films, I didn't really use scores at all. There's no score in *Breaker Morant* – it's only got a brass band. In things like *The Getting of Wisdom* [1978], all I used was some of the music the girls were playing, because I felt music was terribly *over*-used in films. I used to get very irritated by these scores that drowned out all natural sound, and I started off by wanting to make my films using just the sounds of life around the characters. Even *Don's Party* [1976], all I used – ever – in the music, apart from a piece of Janáček on the end, was the discs that they were playing. And then you can hear other things; you can hear the wind in the trees, you can hear dogs barking. If you do put scores in, they tend to drown out everything else. The other day I went and saw *The Bourne Ultimatum* [Paul Greengrass, 2007], which has got non-stop music – it just goes from beginning to end, and it just becomes like wallpaper – you stop hearing it after a while, and you start to wish: 'Can't I hear anything else except those throbbing drums?' So I used music very sparingly, because I was trying to use other effects. But then when I started doing Hollywood movies, of course they get very anxious if you haven't got scores; they put heavy pressure on you to use scores, and they think there's something really wrong with a film if it's not drowned in music, with the music spelling out every emotion in the film, or perhaps even providing the emotion which isn't there, and providing the thrills which aren't there. So I had to start using scores, and then I sort of hunted around for composers whose music I liked in films. And Georges Delerue, at that point, moved to Los Angeles, and I used him I think for six films. Since he died I've been scrabbling around a bit trying to find other people.

AF: Maybe we should deal with these things one at a time. Let's go back to the earlier films, the ones where, as you say, there's practically no music, or to put it another way, the music that you use in the films is real music …

BB: Source music, yeah.

AF: *Breaker Morant* is a good example. The brass band. One of the things I like about *Breaker Morant* is at the end where the prisoners are being taken off to be executed and you see an empty bandstand. It's as if you're telling us there'll be no more music now.

BB: I only ever wanted the brass band. And I didn't get really much objection from the Film Commission, except once or twice. I'd have the band playing and then the music would go over another scene, and someone said to me, 'Won't everyone think that the brass band is playing out in the countryside?' I said, 'I don't really think so. I think it's a film convention that you can still hear the music.' But you see it was effective, because the brass band was really used as a symbol of the authority of the British. And I thought, if I try and put a score on it as well, it's going to turn out to be a smorgasbord. It'll be a mess. And it was great to have the sound of hoof-beats and footsteps and the wind across the veldt and all that – all of which would've been greatly minimised if I'd put a score in the film.

AF: And it's the same deal in *Tender Mercies* [1983], isn't it? The songs are sung by Robert Duvall, and in a couple of cases actually composed by Robert Duvall. But there was a score written for that film – I'm sure I've seen a version of that film that actually has a card in the opening titles reading 'Music by George Dreyfus'. But there isn't any of his music.

BB: You're right. There was a score written by George Dreyfus and when I put it against the images, I thought somehow it demeaned the film. Not that the score wasn't well done – it was well written – but I thought the film was so simple, about characters who were … I was going to say uncomplicated, but they weren't uncomplicated. It told the stories of their lives in such a straightforward kind of way, and with such insight that I thought, 'I don't want any adornment on this, I don't want to do anything that adds anything to the emotion other than what the characters are saying to one another.' I felt that the music added a kind of Hollywood falsity to it, so I took the score away, and decided, before we mixed the film, that I'd only use the guitar music and songs that the central character was playing.

AF: Well, that's one of the things that the film is about, so why would you put other music in there muddying the waters?

BB: Yeah, well ultimately I didn't. See, I was under some pressure to put a score on it, and so we did actually record George's score. It's even available on a disc. You can buy the soundtrack music from *Tender Mercies*, and there is no such score on the movie.

AF: I noticed his name had been removed from the DVD I watched recently.

BB: Well I saw a DVD recently and it's very strange, because at the very end of the film there was a country and western song, but on the new DVD that country and western song is not there. And there's a very strange bit of music – which is not by George Dreyfus. I don't know what it is, or where it came from, or who put it there, but it wasn't me!

AF: Hollywood likes a lot of music, as you say, and they like it to fulfil certain functions. Perhaps we could talk more generally about some of these? I suppose the most obvious is that it's there to reinforce what's happening on the screen. Can you think of some effective example of this in movies, where the scene would've been weaker if you'd taken away the music?

BB: I think music's done a lot for some films. I remember in England some years ago, seeing a screening of *Chariots of Fire* [Hugh Hudson, 1981] before the score was put on. I thought that the film was sort of okay, but it somehow didn't hang together, and the story seemed fairly slight. Then when later I saw it with the score by Vangelis, he had managed to tie all the elements of the film together. Somehow the film was more gripping with that music. I think there must be other examples like that. The Morricone scores on those Spaghetti Westerns are extremely well done. He added almost an epic quality to what were quite simple, low-budget films. They were well directed, but I think if they hadn't had those amazing scores by Morricone, they'd never have achieved the notoriety that they did. The scoring was so unusual and the orchestration was so clever and so odd for the time. I think it's been copied a lot since, but they made a tremendous impact. And then you've got a lot of those scores by people like Hans Zimmer, who came in with these electronic scores and did films like *Gladiator* [Ridley Scott, 2000], where the rhythmic, pounding quality of the score seemed to shore up a film, which was certainly brilliantly directed, but had a rather silly plot. Somehow those scores help carry you through a lot of stuff. And then, of course, they become clichés. There's lots of composers now who write sort of faux-Hans Zimmer scores.

AF: Let's stick with Hans Zimmer because he did the music for *Driving Miss Daisy* [1989]. One of the things I notice, Bruce, when you *are* using scores, is that you dole out the music in quite a stingy way. And very often it comes in late in the film. You've been watching a film for a quarter of an hour before you hear any music, and hardly ever do you put music under the credits, as though it would be a cliché to do so. So in *Driving Miss Daisy* by the time the credits come the music's actually stopped.

BB: Maybe that's not conscious if I've done that. I know I'm always very conscious of the fact that if you have the music there, pounding away all of the time, the audience stops noticing it, because it really does just become wallpaper and you stop hearing it – you hear the dialogue and things, but you don't really hear the music. So I think what I consciously do is try and use the music sparingly, so when it is used it makes an impact; the music's actually doing something, because it comes in in certain scenes, or it underlines certain points. If it's there all the time, it becomes harder and harder as the film progresses to use the music effectively, because it's just washing over everybody. If it's there all the time, you can't say to yourself, 'Well I'll use a piece of music here to make a certain point', because it's there constantly anyway, so it's not doing anything.

AF: Did you give Hans Zimmer some kind of brief for *Driving Miss Daisy*?

BB: Yes. I think that was his first film in America. I wanted Georges Delerue to do the score, but the producer's wife had dug up Hans. She said, 'There's this wonderful German composer here and we want him to do it.' I thought that Hans's computer scores were not really suitable, so I had to work with Hans a lot going through it all. Yes, I was quite specific about what I wanted it to be like, although I tried not to overdo it. He ultimately didn't do a bad job, but I hated the sound of it being synthesised. I said to Warner Bros – in fact Hans did too – 'Let's record this with an orchestra.' And they refused. It was only a low-budget film, they weren't that interested in it. And I said, 'Look, you've *got* to do it with an orchestra,' and Hans backed me on this. They said, 'What's wrong with it?' I said, 'It sounds mechanical. It needs to have real people playing; it's going to be much better for this film, which is such a touching film about these people – that kind of sound is wrong.' Anyway, it was impossible trying to convince the studio heads of this; we never did succeed. But when we were doing the score, Hans sort of did it scene by scene, and I'd go through and listen to it. And he was quite clever, because I'd say, you know, 'I don't think that this bit is vivid enough, or it should be more "Southern" …' I remember one bit: I said, 'There's something wrong with the travelling theme, it's just a bit mundane.' And he went back through it and added a banjo, just plucking out a tune here and there. He was very clever; it worked very well. *Now* if you try to get Hans, there's a kind of Hans Zimmer factory. You'll be very lucky to get Hans himself – it's usually someone else. But he worked pretty hard on *Driving Miss Daisy*. I don't think he's done any other scores like that. All the others have been big blockbuster scores. This one was much simpler.

AF: What about the business of 'spotting', of deciding where the music goes – I mean *exactly* where the music goes. Do you have strong feelings about this?

BB: Yes – the spotting I usually do. What I'll do is go through the film on a television at home, and I'll mark up exactly where I want the music to be, and what I want it to do; and then I'll go through it with the composer. Now, in that process you usually change bits. Sometimes they'll say, 'Could it begin a little earlier and go a little longer?' or 'Could it do this instead of that?' or 'Could I bring back this theme or that theme?' But I do spot it very specifically. And about 90 per cent of the time, that's the way it stays. Occasionally when I've got the music in I've shifted it around; I've used bits in different scenes, or I've cut bits up. Sometimes, when I've looked at the whole film back in the studio, I've said to the mixer, 'I really don't think that bit of music works in that scene.' Because when you see it all the way through, instead of in fragments, you get a different sense of it. So then I've said, 'Let's go back and drop that bit, and drop that bit, and let's add a bit to such-and-such a scene.' That happens. I think in *The Contract* [2006] I did that quite a bit – we added bits and pieces all over the place. But it was more of a genre film, you know. As you get to more personal films, it tends not to happen so much.

AF: There's a lovely bit in *Driving Miss Daisy*, about midway through. It's a crucial scene where Miss Daisy [Jessica Tandy] thinks that Hoke [Morgan Freeman] has stolen the can of salmon, and then he turns up with it. At the end of the scene, the Dan Aykroyd character is left standing in the kitchen holding this can of salmon, feeling foolish, and at that point you start up the introduction to 'Song to the Moon' from Dvořák's *Rusalka*. It's wonderfully effective, and it goes through the following scenes. But maybe you could talk about why *Rusalka* in the first place, and also about the fact that it starts when it does.

BB: Well, I can tell you why it starts when it does. It's because I didn't want to start it just on the shot of the radio, because I wouldn't have enough time in the film to get enough of the aria across for the thing to work. If you pick it up when she's listening to the radio, and then you cut to the next scene, which I think is in the cemetery, you'd only have a fragment of the music. So I thought, 'It's going to be more interesting to begin the aria earlier, and have people think, "What the hell is this?"' So you've got a certain tantalising quality to it, and then you realise she's listening to it on the radio. As for the aria itself, it's fairly simple. See, Alfred Uhry, the writer, wrote it about his grandmother and her chauffeur, and he said, 'She *always* listened to the Metropolitan Opera broadcast on a Saturday afternoon.' In fact, Warner Bros wanted me to change it to a country and western song, and I said, 'But look, she's a cultured old Jewish lady who was a school teacher. I haven't put the aria in because I like opera,' (because that's what they'd accused me of). 'It's in the original script from Alfred.' They hated that aria, you see. I wanted to get an aria that was attractive but not that well known. Now *Rusalka*, at that time, had not been performed very much, and I thought, well, the 'Song to the Moon' is a fabulous aria; it's very melodic. Although, when the people at Warner's saw the film, they said to me, 'You've got to take off that *atonal* music!' [Laughs]. I said, 'What atonal music?' I really didn't know what they were talking about. And they said, 'Oh, that thing she's listening to on the radio, what is *that*!?' And I said, 'Oh God, that's not atonal, it's a *gorgeous* thing.' Luckily, Dick Zanuck backed me up and we never did take it off. But I just wanted to pick an aria that was not that well known but that was beautiful. I nearly picked one from [Mozart's] *Zaide*, but I thought that might be a harder sell with Warner's. But then of course, *Rusalka* became so popular that people actually started reviving the opera. It's been performed quite a lot now.

AF: And it works beautifully under the changing seasons, the passing of time …

BB: Yes, it works beautifully. That was a Czech recording we got of that; I think we got it for next to nothing. There was a lot going on in Prague at the time; we had terrible trouble getting the copyright. We were ringing Prague when there were tanks in the streets, but we got through to someone, and got it cleared in the midst of gunfire in the background.

AF: There's another use of music that is the opposite of reinforcement, where the music undermines what's on the screen. It's an operatic device in a way, you know, where the words are telling you one thing, but the music is telling you something else. Is it something you've done?

BB: Perhaps at the opening of *Double Jeopardy* [1999]. We've got all these idyllic scenes of beaches and sand dunes and sunrises, and it's all beautiful – filmed in the islands in Vancouver. But I said to the composer, Normand Corbeil, 'The music shouldn't be just beautiful.' I said, 'You can do an attractive melody, and make it sort of idyllic, but at the same time, it should have a sinister quality.' He did it very well, actually. Because the music was, on the one hand, attractive and pretty, but there was something about it that was rather creepy, so we set up a good mood for the film. I've done that kind of thing.

AF: Sometimes the music can do the work for you, can't it? You can actually have the music push the film along.

BB: Oh yes! In fact, they're huge on that in Hollywood. I mean, they believe – and I don't *think* it's really true – but they believe that if a film is a bit slow or repetitive, you can put on a score that drives it along because there are these thumping 'boom-boo-ba-doom', especially the electronic scores. I'm rather dubious about this. I know an editor said to me once, 'If the scene is slow when you look at it on the editing machine, printing it in colour properly and looking at it on a big screen with a pounding score will not make it any faster.' And I've always thought he was right. And I've been very careful to make sure that the pacing is correct even before the music's put on. In *The Bourne Ultimatum*, I'm sure they believed that the relentless score was giving the film pace. But I still found it very boring, because it was just one fight after another; it had no script development and I don't think the music did anything to drive it along at all.

AF: When do you start thinking about music in the filmmaking process?

BB: Sometimes even when I'm shooting the film, but mostly when I'm editing. Because what you have to do now for the studios in particular is put on temp scores. These can be really a two-edged sword, because they tend to temp the films with music that's from other films. The favourite temp score for just about every film is the Morricone score from *The Mission*. They put *The Mission* on just about everything. And then when you put your own score on, they say, 'Oh, can't you get the composer to copy the score from *The Mission*?' Temp scores can be very, very misleading and a lot of composers hate them. They say, 'Don't let me see the film with the temp score on it because it inhibits me. I really want to think of my own score.' And I think they're right, but of course you have to put the temp scores on for the studios.

AF: Have you ever been in the position where you've been unable to get rid of the temp?

BB: Only in the sense that they wanted it copied. I've had scores dropped too. That's a problem. That happened to me on the film *And Starring Pancho Villa As Himself* [2003]. Studios can't really interfere with you directing the film, because they really don't know how, they haven't got the knowledge. But when the film's finished they all think they know about music, so they come in and change it. When I did the Pancho Villa film, the HBO head guy said to me, 'What do you think of the composer Joe Vitarelli?' And he played me this music by Joe Vitarelli, and I thought it was fairly bland TV music, you see. And I said, 'Look, it doesn't really mean much to me. It's competent enough, but it's sort of fairly uninteresting, TV, chewing-gum-for-the-ears type of music.' It didn't really do much. I said that I wanted to use a composer called Stephen Endelman. Well, someone rang me one day and said, 'Bruce, I just want to give you a bit of advice.' I said, 'Who is this?' And he said, 'Oh, it's just someone else in the studio, you don't need to know who it is. I just want to tell you something.' So I said, 'Well, what?' He said, 'No matter who you use to score the film, Joe Vitarelli's music will be on it finally.' And I said, 'But they've agreed to using Stephen Endelman, and we're going to Prague to record the score.' He said, 'It doesn't matter what you do, you won't end up with Endelman's music.' So we recorded Endelman's score and put it on the film. Then I left LA. And they went in and they took it off and put on the score by Joe Vitarelli [laughs]. Which was, I thought, awfully bland. But that was evidently what they wanted. It happens on a lot of films.

I had a composer friend whose job was – he worked for Harvey Weinstein – to re-score movies that Harvey had bought. So Harvey'd get some film and he'd bring in this guy, and he'd say, 'Do a new score.' And the guy said to me that the problem was the scores were fine. He said there was really no reason to do a new score; nine times out of ten he thought the scores were really good. I mean, he re-scored that Australian film *The Castle* [Rob Sitch, 1997]. And I said, 'What was the [original] score like?' And he said, 'I thought it was excellent.' And I said, 'So why did Harvey want to change it?' And he said, 'I don't know!' He said, 'So all I did was, I copied it' – it cost like seventy or eighty thousand dollars – 'I sort of copied the score and we recorded it again and put it on!' He said it was like a non-job [laughs]. It was pointless! And he said, 'I was doing that for film after film', just changing scores for no apparent reason. A very strange thing to do. Of course, there's been some famous examples, like the score for *2001* that was dropped, which was by Alex North.

AF: Maybe we could talk about Georges Delerue, because here is a composer you've worked with half-a-dozen times. He came to you with an enormously impressive CV of work, including some of Truffaut's greatest films. How did you hook up with him?

BB: I'd always loved his scores. He always wrote music that was very suitable for the movies. I mean the Truffaut scores were often very light and melodic, but then he wrote amazing scores for things like *The Conformist* [Bernardo Bertolucci, 1970], which had a sort of pastiche of 1930s music and was very well done. He was one of the few Hollywood composers who did all his own orchestration – most of them didn't – and I heard that he was moving to LA, so I got in touch. He didn't speak English at that time, and in fact he never learnt it very well, but he did learn it. When I think of all my efforts to speak French ... But he had a great understanding of films. You could show him scenes and discuss them, and he'd say, 'What about this?' And he'd play little things on the piano. He was very quick. And with Delerue it always seemed to work. He always had attractive tunes that weren't trite. Looking back over the years I realise he certainly borrowed from other composers. But maybe they all do that ...

AF: Let's talk about some of the work he did for you.

BB: It started off he did a very light and attractive score for *Crimes of the Heart* [1986]. It was very melodic. It had a sort of Southern feel to it, without being pastiche, and it had a light touch, which is what the film had. Then when I did *Black Robe*, and I wanted a score that was much more serious. The film was set in North America in 1629, and so I played him bits of French music from the early seventeenth century – a lot of choral stuff – and he was very quick to get on board with that. A lot of historical films look correct but the attitudes are the attitudes of today, so I wanted everyone to have the attitudes of the period and the beliefs of that period. I mean the Jesuits genuinely believed they'd save these Indians and they'd all go to heaven and all that kind of nonsense, and the Indians had a different sense of belief. So I told Georges that it's not just about religion and faith, on either side, it's also about courage and adventure. I wanted the music not to be too sombre, but to have a thrilling feeling. These Jesuits, they came from France. They were in this wilderness with these guys who must have been unbelievably tough and ruthless, and they set out in these little canoes and paddled up the river. I mean the courage that that took! In that climate! I wanted the music to reflect that courage, and Georges wrote this wonderful theme as they're setting out, which really captured the spirit of those people. He came up with it straightaway. He said, 'I see what you mean, what about this?' And he played me this music. And I said, 'You've got it exactly.'

AF: *Paradise Road* [1997], based on a true story, is a bit like *Tender Mercies* or, indeed, *Breaker Morant*, in that it comes with its own music.

BB: Yes. *Paradise Road* was about a women's choir in a Japanese prison camp [during the Second World War]. One of the women in the camp had been a professional musician before the war, and she had a phenomenal memory and was able to write out a whole lot of well-known pieces of music – things like Ravel's *Boléro*. Then she worked them out so they could be sung by voices with no accompaniment whatever, because they never had any musical instruments. So the voices were the instruments. She wrote out dozens and dozens of bits of music, and it all still exists. The choir had the effect of building morale in the camp, because the women were from all over the place. A lot of them were Dutch and English. There was a lot of tension and they were all starving, and the choir gave them something to do and focus on, and in a way brought them all together. And even the Japanese guards used to come and listen to it and loved it. We've got a sequence in the film where one of the guards tries to persuade them to sing some Japanese songs, which they refuse to do. After the war, a women's singing group was formed in Holland which continued to perform the music from camp, and we got hold of them and they recorded the music for the film. But I felt that the film needed a score as well. Then I heard on the radio the first symphony of Ross Edwards, and it made such an impression on me – it was so powerful and so melodic and had such intensity – that I thought he sounded like a very interesting composer. I tracked him down and asked if he'd like to do the score for the movie. He hadn't done film scores before – I think he might have done a documentary or something – but he said he was interested. So I said to Ross, 'I think we should put on music that sounds very English' – because the majority of the women in the camp were English – 'and it will contrast with the Japanese and the tropical setting.' And so he wrote quasi-Elgarian pieces. But they had his great gift for melody and they were beautifully orchestrated. I thought the string pieces were very effective.

AF: So it was a similar approach to the one you took with *Mister Johnson* [1990], using English music in Africa.

BB: I knew you were going to say that. Yes, it is a very similar approach and for much the same reason. *Mister Johnson*, which is set in West Africa, is about an African who wanted to be an Englishman, and so I used it there for ironic effect.

AF: We should talk about *Double Jeopardy* and *The Contract*, which have the same composer. They're quite conventional thrillers, but the music is not necessarily what you expect.

BB: Yeah, Normand Corbeil is Canadian, lives in Quebec. He's the first one I've found really since Delerue died that I thought was a fairly original film composer. I heard his music on a film called *Screamers* [1995], a Canadian science-fiction film which I think is extremely good – it's got a very tense story and is extremely well directed by another Canadian called Christian Duguay. So I just called Corbeil. I said, 'I suppose you get a lot of people calling you up who've heard your music in films.' And he said, 'You're the first one who's ever called me.' So I got him to do *Double Jeopardy* for me. I knew I'd have trouble with a big studio because he was unknown, so I did a very clever thing. I got Normand to send me music he'd written for other films and some stuff he'd done for me, and I temped *Double Jeopardy* with Normand's music. I didn't tell the studio people what I'd done, but they all liked it. And then I said, 'Well now we've got to get a composer.' And they said, 'Well we want the score to sound like what you've temped it with.' So I said, 'It's interesting you should say that, because that's Normand Corbeil who I want to compose it.' So they had to agree. And Normand's very good. He works on a synthesiser, but he's a proper trained composer and he orchestrates it himself: He's not one of these people who hits a few notes on a piano and then turns it over to an orchestrator. He can write attractive love themes – gentle stuff – and then very dramatic stuff that doesn't sound melodramatic or corny.

AF: There's a particularly effective scene near the end of *Double Jeopardy*. Tommy Lee Jones is chasing Ashley Judd down Bourbon

Street, or somewhere in the French Quarter of New Orleans, and you hear the music blasting out of various bars and they go by.

BB: When I was in New Orleans on a location survey, I was walking down Bourbon Street. And it's quite a funny experience, because as you walk along you hear a bit of music from here and a bit of music from there. There's someone playing jazz …

AF: Someone playing Cajun …

BB: Yes, really a tremendous sort of cacophony. So I thought, what I'll do is recreate this feeling in the film. It's almost like a piece by Charles Ives: you're just getting bits and pieces all intermingling and overlaying one another. So all of that track was just put in later. We got all these tracks and mixed them together with a lot of noise and created, I think, a very effective atmosphere. We actually filmed the sequence in Vancouver, not in New Orleans. We got some alleyways and dressed them up.

AF: Are there moments in films – either yours or other people's – where you feel that the absence of music has been particularly effective?

BB: Yes, there's a Korean film that I wrote about recently called *Musa: The Warrior* [Kim Sung-Su, 2001], which does in fact have a wonderful score, but it's used quite sparingly. There are long action sequences in it where you're just hearing the whiz of arrows and footsteps and people running through the forest and brushing against trees. Somehow that made it more tense. The music's not drowning out the natural effects. And then when they do use music, you really notice it.

AF: There's a fair bit of that in *Black Robe*, too.

BB: Yes, I had long sequences in *Black Robe* without music. You know it was great to be able to use the sounds and the loneliness of the wilderness, because when you put music on it's not lonely any more. So at the end, when the priest is reaching the Huron village, all you hear is the wind whistling. There's no music. It's just this sound of ice crunching as he walks in the wind. If you put music on it you'd lose all that.

Sally Potter

First coming to public notice with her film Orlando *in 1992, the British director Sally Potter immediately established herself as an original voice in cinema. Based on Virginia Woolf's novel, the film itself was original enough, with a century-hopping central character played by Tilda Swinton, but for anyone who looked closely at the credits, there was something almost equally striking. The director was partly responsible for composing the music. I met Sally Potter in her office in the East End of London in December 2006.*

Andrew Ford: You don't just write and direct films; in some cases you compose the music. Where did this start for you?

Sally Potter: I think music's always been somewhere at the centre of my life. My parents both loved music. My father used to conduct to records, and it was his great grief that he couldn't play an instrument – but he was a brilliant conductor of records! My mother's great dream was to be an opera singer and she did train as a singer late in life, and certainly performed on the amateur stage, and briefly professionally even. I learnt the violin from the age of seven, the piano from the age of fourteen, but in a way those facts are less important, perhaps, than my own relationship with music. So, whoever it was who said that all the arts aspire to the condition of music, I agree, in the sense that you can't pin music down to a story, a representation of something else – it's not 'a thing', it's an experience through time that is itself. That therefore opens up an enormous metaphysical, emotional, mental space in which it's possible somehow to contemplate the condition of being. Maybe that's a rather pompous way of expressing it, but the feeling, in fact, with music is completely direct. You respond to it with your whole body, and with your guts, and with the rhythm in your feet.

AF: And film and music of course both exist in time, don't they, unlike pretty much any of the other arts. You can read a play, you can read a script and make some sense of it, but with music or film you have to wait for the composer or the filmmaker to give you the next bit.

SP: Yes, it's equally ephemeral in that sense. Music exists on the page as notation or as an object, a CD or something, and film exists as a DVD, but you can't touch it or taste it, it only exists as it unfolds in front of you in real time as music does. That's why I think they are ideal travelling companions – even and including a film that uses no music on the soundtrack; you're still making music decisions all the time, because you're dealing with phrasing, with timing, with the equivalent of a melodic line, whether that's through the human voice, or through the kind of narrative thread that takes you through time – so to speak the top line. But you're always dealing with harmony, with layers: layers of image, framing, character, plot, costume, sound effect … this enormous score of lines that go around the line that takes you through time. So there are incredible parallels, actually, with music.

AF: I read that you wrote *The Man Who Cried* [2000] as you were listening to and discovering and absorbing yourself in various sorts of music, and that this contributed to the script. You made certain script decisions based on the opera, or Gypsy band that you were listening to at the time. Can you talk a bit about that?

SP: It was, in particular, Gypsy music, which I was discovering bit by bit and becoming completely entranced and inspired by. And, in parallel, some Yiddish music, klezmer music. And hearing some of the links between the two, and knowing the narrative of the story, which was the links between the Jewish experience and the Gypsy experience in the Second World War in Europe. They seemed to make a lot of sense, intuitively – to find the roots of that commonality in their music. The opera was a slightly different case, because they were decisions that were made much later in the evolution of the script – about which operas [to use]. Initially, in my early drafts, it was all Wagner, actually, because it was going to be the real opposite of … not the opposite, but the kind of polarity with the other music, and of course all that Wagner signifies. Sometimes when I look back, I think I should've gone with my first thought, but to listen to it, it's heavier and denser and you can't quote from Wagner in the way that you can from Puccini and the others. But yes, the starting point was music. In the instance of *The Man Who Cried,* I then worked with Osvaldo Golijov, the composer whose work I'd first heard as an arranger in fact, when he was arranging things for the Kronos Quartet, and the Kronos Quartet did a concert with the Taraf de Haïdouks who were by then my favourite Gypsy music, so I thought 'Aha!' and it went from there.

AF: And 'Gloomy Sunday' is the other important musical link in that chain, isn't it?

SP: It was an extraordinary link, because I had a particular Gypsy recording – not the Taraf obviously, but another Gypsy recording – of 'Gloomy Sunday'. And Osvaldo Golijov had done an arrangement of 'Gloomy Sunday' for the Kronos Quartet, based on that same recording, which is a quite obscure and rare recording. That was one of the tunes I'd been listening to again and again while I was writing, so then I thought, 'Well, everything's come together in a most extraordinary way.' That sequence of coincidences all pointed in the same direction.

AF: And with the opera ... I can see that *Il trovatore* was an obvious choice because it's got gypsies in it, but why did you end up with the bits from *Tosca* and *The Pearlfishers* in particular?

SP: *The Pearlfishers* ... there's a quality in the particular piece that's quoted from so often, of melancholy and of longing that seemed right for those reasons above all. I'm trying to remember if there were any particular thematic reasons in addition, but I think they were in a way pure music choices there. Then I started to do research into the great Yiddish cantors, and some of their early recitals, and I discovered that these cantors weren't just singing prayers, they weren't just singing for the congregation, they were also singing arias from operas. And so this incredible crossover between the cantorial, the spiritual voice, the religious voice, or song as a form of prayer, a form of calling out to your God, whoever you think your God to be ...

AF: And of crying, indeed ...

SP: Of crying ... So that kind of crossover between opera, and particularly the male voice actually, and prayer. So then we did a Yiddish version of *The Pearlfishers* – I think it was the first time that *The Pearlfishers* has ever been sung in Yiddish. As for *Tosca*, well there are themes in *Tosca* that seemed very appropriate: themes about betrayal, and ideals and principles, and imprisonment and death and the schism between your political principles and your love, your romantic love and all that. But I was also looking for the classic tenor moment.

AF: And the aria 'E lucevan le stelle' is a kind of prayer anyway, isn't it?

SP: It is. It's got that same quality of yearning. In the storyline, the tenor is a bit of a brute, but when he sings, he's an angel – that those two facets can co-exist in one person relates for me in a very hidden way. I remember reading George Steiner writing about the Nazis in the camps, who could do unthinkable and unimaginable deeds in the daytime in the camp, and go home at night and listen to Beethoven, knowledgeably, and maybe even play in quartets and so on. And so Steiner's meditation was, how can these two sensibilities co-exist in one human – and let's give up all romantic notions that the arts can somehow humanise. That isn't what the arts are there for.

AF: Your films seem to me to be about, if not clashes of culture, at least meetings of cultures – eras, in the case of *Orlando*. Do you think you use music partly to spell those meetings out, as it were, to demarcate the different cultures in the films?

SP: I think that music can be both a demarcation and a bridge, because essentially it's a language that goes beyond languages. It is the international, universal form of speech. So I can listen to a qawwali from Bollywood, from India, or I can listen to the Taraf or one of the other Romanian groups singing in Romany, or indeed an Italian aria, or a Sardinian folk song, or whatever, and I can relate, as an individual. I can understand and feel and empathise with the experience, whether I can understand a single word of the language being sung or not. So there's that bridging sense that then makes a nonsense of the phoney barriers of nationalism, terror of differences, demonising of other cultures or other beings as somehow incomprehensible, or inscrutable, or generally weird, or even evil. That gets cut through at a stroke once you hear the human pulse of music. But there are of course other borders which are important and useful borders: the *necessity* to know your own difference and your own roots and celebrate that, so that everything doesn't become one great big, globalised, homogenised mass, where everybody's singing the same tunes, drinking the same wine, and eating the same food out of the same packaging. So the border as a form of protection of the beauty of multifariousness is a good border. And the border that's saying, 'We're the best, and we need to eliminate you because you're weird and different' can be transcended by music.

AF: On a fairly basic level, you use music sometimes to establish mood. I'm thinking of, for example, the beginning of *Yes* [2004] – there's B.B. King and there's a Chopin waltz, and they obviously do different things.

SP: Well, there are many ways that you can use music. The B.B. King is very specifically a character reference, because the character, played so beautifully and subtly by Sam Neill, is a man who had his moment in the late '60s, early '70s perhaps. He was an idealist, he was a young man. Let's imagine he was at university, and thought if he went into politics he could change the world and do good. And in his spare time he was in a rock band, and if he'd been any better at the guitar would probably have preferred to be a rock star to a politician. So [he was] somebody that we can recognise, but also somebody that we can empathise with. He wakes up thirty years later and finds he has become the enemy, at least in his own home, and is the one doing all the things that he was sure he would never do and could change. But the part of him that has remained somewhere in his core is the rock guitar, the blues, but all he is left with is playing air guitar in his suit, alone in his sitting room. That's dropping a clue to us, the audience, at the beginning, that this is some of who this character really is, despite what he appears to be. It also sets a mood of course, of the blues, but more importantly it's unconsciously giving us a clue about the identity of this man. The Chopin waltz is about the ambience of that situation, which is classic architecture, big gathering, cocktails, champagne, the clinking of glasses, long table, formality, a kind of looking back to another epoch. Not that Chopin was doing that, but that's how that particular kind of group of people – politicians and their spouses – would like to identify with [this music], and think that Chopin belonged to them.

AF: Part of the sound of *Yes* is the language itself. More than virtually any other film script I can think of, there is a musicality to the way it's written. You must have answered this question a million times, but why did you decide to versify the script?

SP: In a funny way I didn't decide – it was the way that it needed to be written, for these characters to be able to say what they needed to say out loud. A lot of what they say is what would normally, in a so-called naturalistic script, be buried, as a kind of subtext or something we'd glean maybe from body language. Or it's things that are impossible to talk about but which are the deeper themes of the film as a whole or something. There's something about the form of verse that allows you both to go big and small. From one line to the next you can deal with an incredible scale of things, from God to dust, you know, and with a fluidity that, it seems to me, is perhaps closer to the structure of unconscious thought, where we meander and flow seamlessly from one level of thought or feeling to another.

The structure of verse is somehow close to the way that we really think and feel, if we could put a microphone inside our brains and listen to the thoughts, the rapidity with which they move, and the grace with which they move, compared to which most of us are stumblingly inarticulate when we try and get those thoughts out into speech. We're groping really, because it's so much slower than the speed of thought. So verse, somehow, allows you to write in a way that carries that flow, and with a tone and a rhythm that tells us something about the inner rhythm and phrasing of the person, of the character. It was a very joyful way to write, but of course a complete taboo from the point of view of film financing, and some critics also took against it. But for others I think it is what has drawn them most into what the film's really trying to do, and has made it a much more profoundly emotional experience for some. It's been an interesting reaction. But from the point of view of the impulse to write, it wasn't like, 'Oh, I think I'll write a film in verse', it was more a feeling of poetic necessity. But also, this is the only way I can write for these characters about this particular strange bundle of subjects that's been kicked into being by the events of September 11th 2001.

AF: The maid's wonderful asides to the camera, did they come out of the verse? It's such an Elizabethan, Jacobean conceit.

SP: The film started with the scene which became, in the end, the classic climactic moment, in structural terms, of the film as a whole, which is a long argument between the two central characters in a car park about what's really going on for them, what they really believe, and what's led to them finally coming into a state of deep conflict. That was the starting point for the whole film, and I started with it as a short, as a kind of pilot for the longer idea. And then I started developing the lives of these two characters that I had found, if you like, at this moment already well into their relationship. So I asked myself: are they married, are they single, what kind of houses do they live in, what are their jobs? And so on. And I found, if you like, the people who were in their lives. And one of the people in the life of the female character was this cleaner. So I wrote a lot of their monologues, soliloquies, really in parallel, without the idea of a narrative yet. So I had piles on the table – on this very table – of the cleaner, the husband, the niece, the goddaughter, the friend, the guys at work and so on, and found each of their voices, and then wove those together into a story. It worked that way around.

AF: You wrote some of the music in *Yes*, and the same is true of

Orlando. This is unusual. There's only been a handful of directors who composed their own music: Clint Eastwood, John Carpenter, Charlie Chaplin …

SP: Mike Figgis …

AF: Mike Figgis, of course. But it's very unusual. Maybe you could talk not so much about how, as why?

SP: In the case of *Orlando*, it was because we'd run out of money in post-production, and we couldn't pay for the existing music by the end. For the kind of production values on the screen, it was an incredibly, insanely low budget, and of course money runs out when you're at the very last stages. And I was saying to the producer, Christopher Sheppard, one day, 'What are we going to do?' And I said to him, 'I can *hear* it in my head, I can hear what the score should sound like, I don't know who we can get to do it and who would work for no money.' And he said, 'Wait a minute, you can hear it in your head? Okay, well go into the studio and do it.' So … I did [laughs]. I can read music, though I'd never written in the sense of writing notes in a score, but for many years I was an improvising singer in groups where my job was to improvise the top line and the lyrics (which is another reason why *Yes* ended up being written in verse, of course), so I went and sang on multi-tracks the different parts that I could hear in my head for some of the scenes. I worked with David Motion, who is an arranger and who had a little studio, and we worked in his downtime. We worked through the nights doing this, and then he took some of those lines that I had sung, and rearranged them for instruments, and then I directed or edited things that he suggested, and we ended up with a lot of material. I got Fred Frith in to improvise lines, but according to specific directions and within a harmonic chain of key changes that I had scored already. And then the final stage, if you like, of this way of composing, if you can call it that, was that all the material was there, and I moved it around, took a line from here, a note from there, pushed this to there, that little guitar note on that movement of the eye, and this there, so it was like working with music as material, or building blocks. Really, it's kind of composing by editing, I don't know how else to describe it. And that became the basis of a method for all future films. I would score it in terms of the key changes, then I would work with improvising musicians that I know well and direct them just as I would direct an actor. Different lines, so I would have multiple choices, and then use that as substance for the final score.

AF: So you have their parts on different tracks as well, so you can move anything anywhere.

SP: Yeah, I separate everything out onto tracks and then sometimes create whole new cues out of elements from other tracks. In the case of *Orlando*, my own voice ended up as a sometimes barely audible kind of wall of sound, as a texture. Because I was also looking for a texture, having tried already tons and tons of different kinds of music, orchestral, piano, guitar, flute, voices, rhythmic, non-rhythmic, ambient, floating, pulsating, whatever, in order to find what is needed, what becomes obtrusive; trying always to avoid the kind of wallpapery music, you know, that's just plastered all over something because it's too empty; trying to avoid anything that says, 'Aha! This is how you should be feeling in *this* scene, dear audience'; trying instead to work in counterpoint with the image, or in a musical dialogue with the image. In the end what I discovered with *Orlando* was that we needed a unifying sound that was going to take us through 400 years, so you never wanted to be too located in any one period. We could *refer* to the period, just as we were referring with the costumes and other things to each period, but you couldn't be jumping from one musical era to another. The unifying thing was this texture of a seamless and floating wall of sound that didn't have specific barline moments.

AF: You've raised so many possibilities for using music that maybe we should look at one or two of them, and perhaps cast the net wider to include other people's films as well, and the way in which music can be used. Do you have some favourite moments in films, your own or other people's, where music plays an absolutely key role, where it changes something in the film, changes the course of the film in a sense?

SP: The most obvious is musicals, where music is at the very centre of the story and is carrying us energetically through. Let's take a film that everybody knows, like *Singin' in the Rain*, with numbers that have become iconic. When you look closely at the form of that particular musical, it's both an incredibly intelligent commentary and deconstruction on the history of cinema itself – silent film to sound, you know, there's all these wonderful jokes on sound, in synch, and out of synch, which, looked at in a certain way, were very avant-garde, very strange. And then the numbers themselves are full of enormous joy. That's kind of conscious, in-your-face use of music, as an inherent part of the form that you're watching and, in many ways, is some of the best use of music in film, and you go back to those and of course to Bollywood. If I think of some of the early Bollywood films, the early black and white films and the use of music – I'm thinking of one called *Paper Flowers* [Guru Dutt, 1959] – I remember the opening sequence of that, which set a tone of such utter languid beauty that you were propelled into this journey for the rest of the film by the atmosphere of how the music was set up at the very beginning. So that would be one kind of example, then another would be Emir Kusturica in *Time of the Gypsies* [1988]. The use of the music there that breaks your heart, the particular sound he was using of one young woman singer … I'm trying to remember the tone … it's like a kind of boy soprano sound, the purity of the voice and absolute unsentimentality, heartbreaking unsentimentality, and there the music carries you a lot. Woody Allen often uses the same period of music but uses it very well, often uses it contrapuntally, so you've got very up-tempo something happening at a very difficult existential moment for the character, or something like that. So it's a very intelligent use of existing pieces, well-known pieces, jazz in particular – which of course relates to what he does himself, playing the clarinet. It's music he knows, music he loves, music he's got in his ear.

I also very much like the Dogme films that don't use any music. I find them intensely musical experiences through their refusal to do the easy thing. The refusal of sentimentality, the refusal of the idea that music in a film is there to be *not* listened to, which is what I also hate. I detest music in restaurants, for example, I detest music in supermarkets, I detest music when I go into an elevator. If music is there, I want to listen to it. I don't want to train my ear to not listen, which is what bad film music does. Dogme films, which only use music if the source is there – if you see somebody playing – when the music does come into the film, makes it kind of astonishing. The silences, where you would expect music, open your ear in a way to the music of human speech, or to the sounds that you're hearing. Which brings us to another subject, and I know I'm taking a little walk with this subject away from your question, but in my view you can't actually separate music from sound effects when you're working on a film, and you have to *score* the effects and the voice with the same mentality as the music, which may be why I'm so directly involved in the music myself, either putting it together, or choosing the music and scoring it, or working with a composer. I don't want to take credit for the work that they do, nor over-inflate what I do, that's why I tried to describe carefully how I do it, but nevertheless I'm very involved in it. In the same way, I sit with the sound editor and we work on the sound effects, we tune the effects. So if there's a car horn – *'daa daa'* – okay, should it be *'daa'* or *'daa'* or *'daa-daa'* [imitates car horns in different pitches]? We tune it, we see where it should be, what's happening before, what's happening after, what was the last note you heard, the last car horn, or the last piece of music, or the next and so on, so that you end up with a kind of integrated sound world, in which the sound of children playing – as we have outside here now – or the creak of my chair, they're all a kind of music.

AF: Yes, that's a very John Cage attitude, isn't it, it's an inclusive attitude. The opposite of what you're describing is the classic action-movie use of music where you have often quite an elaborate, sometimes even orchestral score being absolutely smothered in sound effects, which have no relation to the score at all. I'm thinking of the boat sinking in *Titanic*, where somewhere in the background is a James Horner score, but with all sorts of explosions and whatnot happening on top of it. How much more striking it would've been anyway to have that boat go down with no music.

SP: Well, *Titanic* is a particular case because it's all about more, bigger, bigger is better, and then a bit more would be better still, so let's add a bit more. It's about massiveness, isn't it, and that is consistent with the theme and the name, *Titanic*.

But a root of classical film music for which I have enormous respect would be, for example, Morricone. What can be more memorable and more cinematic than [whistles the opening of the theme from *The Good, the Bad and the Ugly*]? I mean it's genius, it's absolute genius, and correct for what we're seeing. It gives you this feeling of the huge, huge spaces that the film is occupying, the geology of the land somehow even, the man in the landscape. He's a genius. And the score of *The Third Man* which again takes a simple idea [sings the theme], a simple melody but also a single instrument and then takes that idea and develops it and its many variations and so on. But the identity of it is so strong, it's not pretending it's not there; you hear it, you're meant to hear it, you want to hear it, you're dying for it to come back again, and it doesn't take you away from what you're watching, nor does it just underline it, although it does somehow give you this anxious nostalgia at the same time for the era. It's just brilliantly written and brilliantly conceived, both of those examples.

AF: And there it's actually the quality of the sound as much as anything, it's the quality of the sound of that zither. Before you actually string the notes together and you hear the melody, the sound itself does it, doesn't it?

SP: Well, I now realise in the examples I've picked out they are about the choice of instrument, and a lot of 'classic' film scoring – classical in the sense of not classical at all but boring film scoring – is just the full orchestra. The full orchestral sound is not, in my view, the most interesting sound for film. Whereas when you *cast* your musical instrument in the way that you cast your actors, there's an identity, and an incredible identity. Morricone always does that, he uses a full orchestra, but he'll always find a sound as well that's the right sound, that will unlock the key. Those three examples that I've mentioned – the Kusturica, the sound of that girl's voice, *The Third Man*, the sound of the zither and the whistling in the Morricone – I think that makes a huge, *huuuuuge* impact, because each instrument brings with it a world, a sound world, and a historical root and a cultural root. So, in *Yes,* for example, one of the men is in Beirut at an Armenian christening, and she is in Cuba going out to a dance hall – we used a Cuban song, a *son*, but we brought into it the Armenian duduk. It must be the first time that there's ever been a duduk in a salsa, but I think when you hear that you can feel where the characters are, you feel both this split and this musical marriage of two cultures. I find that very exciting, choosing the instruments.

AF: And it's another example of you bringing different styles together. I'm thinking, in *The Man Who Cried*, of the Yiddification of *The Pearlfishers* and also the Gypsy instruments joining in with 'Dido's Lament'; it's bringing these cultures together in another way.

SP: Quite consciously in that one, probably more subtly in *Yes*. I think the whole area of fusion music is a dangerous one, I have to say, despite the fact that I've done it myself in the ways that you've described, but I find very much of what's called fusion music to be just a horrible mishmashy compromise of everything, and you lose what's beautiful about both. I think when it's done well, though, when it's done with enormous respect and care for whatever the elements are that are coming together, it has a much greater chance of working well. Ry Cooder did that very well with *Buena Vista* and with others, but sometimes people call something fusion – let's say tango stuff, I happen to know a lot about tango, so when I hear a so-called tango fusion, I usually groan. Nevertheless, in the context of a film, you're doing something different, people are speaking to each other, and in the case of these examples that you're picking out, it is people particularly from different cultures who're finding a way both of speaking to each other and listening to each other, even more importantly.

AF: You've mentioned the Dogme films of course, but are there any other favourite moments in films where music is eschewed and the effect heightened because it's not there?

SP: [long pause] This silence is me thinking … I'm thinking of a rather odd example, actually: some of Eisenstein's films which in fact did have scores but which I first experienced as silent films and then later on heard with scores and was very disappointed and felt that they were films that worked better silently, and the scores made them far too descriptive and less interesting. I think that it may've been by watching a lot of early silent cinema that made me think a lot about what sound do we need. Do you need somebody sitting at a piano, if the action's fast, going, 'da-ra, da-ra, da-ra, da-ra, da-ra' [sings] if it's a horse? Or is it more interesting to have your inner ear *hear* the silent hoofs and feel the rhythm through how the film's been edited or how the action's been put together? Or maybe it's more interesting, if you're seeing a horse go *'da-ra, da-ra, da-ra, da-ra'*, to hear *'aaaaaaaaaaaaaaaaah'* [sings an unchanging, continuous sound] across it, and then you feel some kind of underlying, other rhythm of continuity. I think silent film has a lot to teach us about what we don't need. I seem to be talking about silence a lot for somebody who really loves music, and loves working with music in film, but I think, unless you respect the silence, you don't know what you need with the music. Also what you do find, when you're in the cutting room, is that the temptation is to use music to fudge things that don't quite work, to make a transition that isn't really there, and so I'm very strict about forcing myself and the editor to look at things under the worst conditions without any props of sound effects or music to make it all work. So that then when the music does come in, it has a value, but you're not leaning on it as a crutch.

AF: What about naturalism? The Dogme films aim to be as naturalistic as possible with all of that natural light, and the only music comes through radios and whatnot. Watching your films, watching *The Man Who Cried,* for example, it seemed to me that the whole film in a way is operatic, not just the bits where you're actually watching opera, but there's something stylised about the entire film, and I think probably your work in general. I wonder whether that in a sense relates to your use of music almost being the opposite of Lars von Trier or whoever.

SP: Well, the Dogme idea that the films are naturalistic is absolute bollocks. No film is naturalistic, not even a documentary is naturalistic; as soon as you've got a camera in the room you're looking at one thing and not another thing, you're not in real life, you're in the real life of a film. But what the Dogme proposition or manifesto gives you is it helps you to become conscious of the language you're using, the means you're using, and is a kind of choice of limitation, because with all films you're dealing with the limits of time, space, your ability, the actors' availability, the money you don't have, the light that's falling, and so on and so forth, and so, in reality, in a shoot you're in a desperate struggle all the time against obstacle and lack, out of which you then have to make something that's very convincing. What the Dogme principle allows you to do is to say, 'I choose this limit, I choose this constraint, I choose this lack, what can I do with it?' So there's a kind of vitality in the choices and in the decision making of the filmmakers that comes out of that feeling of power, really. But it's nothing to do with naturalism. It's just somebody who, instead of using a tripod, is moving the camera around, instead of moving a light towards the actor, you move the actor towards the light, you know, or whatever it may be. But I still find it very interesting indeed.

AF: What about the other part of the question about your use of music. Lars von Trier is aiming for something naturalistic – I absolutely agree with what you say – but are you aiming for something which is not naturalistic?

SP: I don't think Lars von Trier is aiming for something naturalistic. He may say he is, but even that's a kind of manifesto. What he's aiming to go away from is sentimentality and a kind of falseness. And I'm not aiming for something unreal, I'm aiming for the real for which there is no voice; the inexpressible, giving it a form of some kind, that chaotic inner, heightened drama in which we each live and nobody else seems to notice. The definitions of what's real and what's not real, of naturalism and non-naturalism, for me they're aesthetic devices to frame a way of telling a story, or a way of describing an experience ... that's why music is so useful. Nobody says 'That's natural' or 'That's not natural', it's just one piece of music or another kind of piece of music, which has a history and a formal structure. Real? Not real? A piece of music's a piece of music. Of course it's real. I think also one moves then into a kind of political dimension of what's real and what's not real, because, for most of the world's population, the reality of their experience is neither expressed, nor listened to, nor even considered real – it's invisible; most people lead invisible lives. Once you start listening to those invisible lives, they are incredible dramas with incredible narratives, with incredible musicality in them, with unbelievable leaps through time and space and emotion and fantasy and what one might even call madness. Most definitions of reality are simply a norm, a standard written by the educated voices of the dominant culture, one way or another. So bollocks to reality! Heightened reality, or even magical realism – the Latin American writers: that tradition is probably closer to many people's real experience of their sense of self, their sense of themselves as the player in their story, in their life, and the sense of the emotional canvas, let's say, within which they live, and the metaphysical and spiritual canvas within which they live. The direct experience that I've had, that I'm kind of on the right track with some of that, is through the feedback that I've got from *Yes*. We have a website and people write in to the website, and so many times, after screenings and on the web, people say, 'This is my experience, this is me' or 'This is the first time I've seen this aspect of my life on the screen.' Now this is a film written in verse that's considered completely artificial, with these various other criteria for non-realism but in which people are finding themselves.

AF: Is there anything that we ought to talk about that we haven't talked about?

SP: I always feel that I want to give more credit to the musicians that I work with, and the composers and the arrangers of the pieces that I use. I think that the musicians and the contribution that the individual musicians make to a score, to a recording or to a piece, is very under-credited. Of course you've got pop stars who are idolised, or big composers' names, but the unsung skills of the singing voices of the musicians, and the intelligence that they bring to the process, is extraordinary, and, for me, one of my favourite parts of filmmaking. When I go into a recording studio with some musicians whose work I love, I'm in a kind of rapturous condition. I just adore it and have incredible respect for what they do. Some of my particular collaborators, such as Fred Frith, the guitarist, Thomas Bloch who I've worked with several times now, Osvaldo Golijov, obviously, from *The Man Who Cried*. And, in the case of *The Tango Lesson* [1997], which we haven't talked about, the innumerable, hundreds upon hundreds of recordings that I listened to, of the orchestras of the 1940s, '50s, '60s and '70s, Pugliese in particular, Troilo, D'Arienzo, all these extraordinary musicians whose work hadn't travelled much out of Argentina then, and it has now. There is a sort of glorious wealth in their recordings, and I was very happy to be able to have some of their music in my film.

Wim Wenders

*The name of the German filmmaker Wim Wenders is strongly associated with music. Not only has he made films about music (*Buena Vista Social Club *in 1999 and* The Soul of a Man *in 2003) but the film that brought him worldwide fame has an instantly memorable soundtrack. Ry Cooder's slide guitar is probably the first thing people think of when they recall* Paris, Texas *(1984). Wenders was in Sydney in 2003 and I interviewed him for* The Music Show *(ABC Radio National) at the Museum of Contemporary Art.*

ANDREW FORD: You've said that you *listen* to films more and more, as well as watching them, even more perhaps than watching them. Could you explain what you mean by this?

WIM WENDERS: A whole deal of work goes into the sound today, much more than ever before. When I started to edit films, you'd spend like eight, ten, twelve weeks on editing your picture, and then two or three days on the few tapes that you needed in order to mix the film, three or four tracks plus a music track. Everything was mono, and the mixing would take a day or two. And to prepare the mix you can just do it in a day or two. And today it's the other way round. You edit the film and, well, maybe [it takes] the same time, but you spend three times as long to work on your soundtrack and to work on the mix, and you have up to 100 or 200 tracks, and you pre-mix your effects and you pre-mix your dialogue and you pre-mix the music, and actually you spend so much more overall on the sound than on the image that it's sort of just the other way round than twenty, thirty years ago. So sound has undergone incredible changes. The picture [editing] is only now starting to be as [flexible], you start to be able to manipulate it as much as the sound. And most theatres have invested incredibly over the last ten, fifteen years in the sound system, and the projectors are still the same old projectors.

AF: Has this change in the structure, the multi-layered nature of sound, has this affected the way that you shoot the visuals?

WW: Not really, I think. But it affects a lot the way you see them in the theatre, and sound is sometimes the bigger adventure and the bigger experience in contemporary films, and you're mostly overwhelmed by the sound. It's like a wall of sound, and some people sometimes can't take it, because it's just too much. Music plays a more important part than ever, and most movies are marketed with their soundtracks and sometimes soundtracks are more successful than the films themselves. You can even finance the film partly with your soundtrack.

AF: What do you use music for? Because you use a lot of music. I'm thinking not at the moment of the films that are obviously *about* music, but where you use music; what's the role that it plays in the film?

WW: Difficult to give a generalised answer, because music in almost every film has a slightly different function. Overall I think I use music differently than it's used conventionally in film, and mostly it's there in general in films, it's there to reinforce the dramaturgy of the film and to reinforce tension or whatever the film is about. And in a way in my films music is more part of the subject of the film, and I use quite a lot of instrumental music of course. I think of Ry Cooder's work for *Paris, Texas* or *The End of Violence* [1997] but I also have started to use more and more songs made for the film by all sorts of artists, in order to help tell the story. I think music and rock-and-roll are so much the art of our contemporary lives that it's almost unthinkable for me to not have music become part of what the film is about, and part of the contemporary landscape, so to speak. And it's also, for me, the most fun part of the entire process of making a movie and the most privileged part. I know that other directors don't deal with it, or don't want to deal with it, or cannot deal with it, and there's people [who] only – I mean, [whose] whole business it is to select music for movies and market movies and music together, and that's the last thing I would let anybody do for me, because that's the most fun [part]: to choose and to talk to musicians and find with whom you want to work on a particular [film], or on a particular scene. And mostly I use musics that don't exist yet [...] I listen to music all the time [...] when I'm shooting and when I go home and when I drive my car back from the set, and when I sit at home and work ... I listen a lot to music, and mostly the music I'm listening to while I make the film then becomes the core choice for the musicians I approach.

And then of course you have to turn them on and make them understand the climate of the film and what you really expect. On the other hand, you don't really want to be too specific because there's nothing worse than music that's too much on the nose, especially if the lyrics start echoing what the scene is about – then you're lost, because then all of a sudden it shoots backwards.

AF: I assume that you don't have an enormous sympathy for the filmmakers of Dogme 95, who eschew the use of music. But presumably you would go along with them to the extent that it is possible to use music in a film badly or manipulatively; it seems to be what you're saying in fact about not having the music mirror the action.

WW: I had long discussions with Lars about this part of the Dogme rules, and I said I could easily do a Dogme film, but I would have trouble with that one rule that you cannot add music afterwards. So the music would have to be playing in the scene and then of course it's very tough continuity-wise, and I explained to Lars, and Lars laughed and said, All these rules are only there to be broken. I mean there is music in Dogme films, but it's got to be played inside the film, or it's got to be recorded as you go, if you go with the rules, but then again Lars broke a lot of his own rules, all the time.

AF: What's the difference between working with songwriters like Peter Gabriel or Nick Cave on *Until the End of the World* [1991] and *Faraway, So Close!* [1993], and working with a composer such as Jurgen Knieper, who's been behind the music on a number of your films, going right back to *The Goalkeeper's Fear of the Penalty* [1972]?

WW: Well, even *The Goalkeeper's Fear of the Penalty* … actually it's haunting me now because I can't show [that] film any more. We used a lot of existing music such as Roy Orbison and Van Morrison […] stuff that I could never pay for, because at the time I wasn't so much aware that you had to buy the rights to all this stuff. I mean it's very different work[ing] with [a] composer because that is sort of a unifying element for a film if you find a theme or two and even if you go as far as with *Paris, Texas*, where there was only one music, there was not a single additional song. It was just with Ry Cooder – there was not a single note from anybody else in the film – and that of course then gives the film a very special flavour. Sometimes I feel it's just as important as your director of photography and his camera work. When Ry Cooder was recording the score for *Paris, Texas*, he did [it] in front of the screen like those musicians in the silent-movie times who were recording to the picture, or improvising to the picture; Ry proceeded the same way. I had the strangest impression that he was sort of re-shooting the film with his guitar and it was really very much linked to the camera work, in that the guitar and the camera had a sort of very magical link to each other. It is the most important ingredient to the film once you've started to assemble your story and you have a first cut. [The music] then adds so much and changes the tone so much, you've got to be very careful because it can quickly be too much, and before you know it, it's just a sauce over everything. I know many great movies that had too much music, and we're suffering from it, and it's unfortunately a very contemporary abuse of too much of the good thing.

AF: In *Paris, Texas*, it seems to me not that there was too much music, but that in a sense the film ended up being as much about the sound of that guitar. That slide guitar became a kind of *leitmotif* in the film, and it also became a part of the landscape. And speaking of landscape, here I am with my elbow on a book of photographs you've taken which are mostly landscapes of a sort. Do you think of music and landscape as being rather similar?

WW: I think of music [as] having a strong sense of place, and I like music that really comes from a very specific area and that could only come from that town or from that country, like in *Lisbon Story* [1994] for instance, we used the music of fado and that is their town and there is no other place in the world where they would play that sort of sad, almost blues-like music that is the father of the Portuguese fado. And of course *Buena Vista Social Club:* this music could never exist outside of Havana. And Ry Cooder's slide guitar is so much the landscape of the American West. This bottleneck guitar I should rather say. So I think music can be rooted in a particular place, and I think it's very important, and I like music that I know has a history and has a strong connection to a certain place and is very specific. I don't like music that is sort of generalised and could come from anywhere. A lot of contemporary American films actually avoid any specific places because they want to appeal to the lowest common denominator all over the globe, and so they don't want you to actually know where it takes place – it's nowhere, and the music also comes from nowhere.

AF: I suppose *Buena Vista Social Club* is as much a film about Havana as it is about the music; what about the new film, *The Soul of a Man*? Is there a sense of place here?

WW: A very strong sense of place. It's shot in Mississippi, most of it, a bit of it also in Chicago. And it's about three musicians who lived and recorded in the '20s, '30s and '60s. It's about Blind Willie Johnson, whose song 'Dark Was the Night' was actually the inspiration for Ry Cooder's soundtrack of *Paris, Texas*. It is about Skip James, who recorded in the '30s, was then completely forgotten – nobody even knew that he was still around – and was rediscovered in the mid-'60s. And another totally forgotten musician, J.B. Lenoir, who was an important influence on many people, for instance Jimi Hendrix, and way ahead of his time. He sang about the war in Korea and Vietnam, he sang about the black liberation movement, he sang about social issues before any white singer ever brought that up. But he died completely unrecognised, poor and miserably. So I made this film about my three blues heroes because I felt they deserved better. And I had the help of lots of musicians who came in to record their songs. I had great people come in. Nick Cave did a beautiful J.B. song. Bonnie Raitt, Lou Reed, Lucinda Williams, Los Lobos – it's a great list, an impressive list of people. Cassandra Wilson did one of [their] songs to pay tribute to their inspiration.

AF: But you chose these three figures. I have to say I'm one of the people who doesn't know about J.B. Lenoir at all, but Blind Willie Johnson has, apart from his guitar playing, this amazing gravelly voice. And Skip James is surely one of the saddest, bluesiest blues musicians ever. There's this wonderful Skip James song, 'I'm So

Glad', which is if you listen to it the height of desperation. Were you attracted to these people because of their extremes?

WW: Yes and no. They first of all wrote fantastic songs, and I'm so glad Skip James lived to know that ['I'm So Glad'] was recorded by Cream. He didn't live long enough to really make use of the royalties, but it became a worldwide hit when Cream played it. He wrote a number of very, very sad songs; he had a pretty miserable life. J.B. Lenoir wrote a number of very funny and very lively songs. 'Mama Don't Talk to Your Daughter' is an outrageously funny song. And I hope that all three of them will get the recognition they deserve. The film is called *The Soul of a Man*, but it's not a film that stands on its own. It's the first in a series of seven films [called *The Blues*]. They are produced by Martin Scorsese and my company in Berlin. Clint Eastwood made one on the history of the piano in blues music. Scorsese himself did one about the African roots of the blues. There's also Mike Figgis. There were seven altogether, and everybody chose his own favourite subject in the history of the blues, and it just turned out that we didn't overlap at all.

Peter Greenaway

If Wim Wenders's international career began with Ry Cooder's guitar, Peter Greenaway's started with Michael Nyman's homage to Purcell in The Draughtsman's Contract *(1982) and his name remains closely linked to Nyman's, though it is twenty years since the two of them worked together. He visited Australia for the Melbourne Festival in 2009, where his installation* Leonardo's Last Supper – *an exploration, animation and celebration of Leonardo da Vinci's famous fresco – ran in North Melbourne Town Hall. I spoke to him there, just prior to the opening.*

ANDREW FORD: Let's begin with this project, *Leonardo's Last Supper*. Tell us if you would about its origins. How did it start?

PETER GREENAWAY: I'm trained as a painter, certainly painting for me is the prime visual means of communication … Whenever I'm given a commission or opportunity to put these two great loves together, one painting, the other cinema, I'm going to grasp it. I'm very concerned about our attitudes towards cinema, which I believe is a text-based medium, not an image-based medium. I think cinema knows this; this is why it's always going back to the bookshop for its subject matter. And so the whole process is really to conduct a dialogue between what painting does with imagery and what cinema does with imagery. And in practical terms, it is to create a dialogue directly between cinema language and paintings *per se*. So we project directly onto original paintings.

AF: You once said something like 'filmmaking is too important to be left to storytellers'. But you're a storyteller, aren't you?

PG: Yes, but also, if I could quote somebody else in return for your quotation of me, John Cage – who primarily is a composer, but more importantly for me a great guru and thinker – suggested that if you introduce more than 20 per cent of novelty into any art work, watch out, you're going to lose 80 per cent of your audience. So you're going to create consternation in your audience. I cannot, and never could, command a Spielberg audience, but it was never my intention to. I think, as a European filmmaker, we've done comparatively well. The last film that I really did with Michael Nyman would have been *The Cook, the Thief, His Wife & Her Lover* [1989] and that gathered together an audience of about 25 million people in the Western world. Not necessarily all at once, and not certainly in one massive weekend.

AF: But the music that you work with in your films, most famously that of Michael Nyman, but also Wim Mertens, for instance, in *The Belly of an Architect* [1987] …

PG: Yes, and John Cage himself, we worked together, and Philip Glass and Steve Reich and Louis Andriessen, and more recently Goran Bregovich, a lot of Balkan composers … so there's a whole series of music-makers. I have to be careful here a bit because I would much rather (and I hope this isn't cultural snobbism) work with composers than people who write music for the cinema. As I'm sure you know, music is often extremely badly used in the cinema, because it's very much the slave of everybody else: 'Give me twenty-five minutes of pathos'; 'Give me fifteen seconds of excitement'; and that most crazy paradox of all, 'Give me three seconds of silence'. That's not the way, I think, that music is best used. So I always try to establish a relationship with a composer that gives them the maximum amount of freedom to do what they do best.

AF: And why would a capital-C Composer be better at that than somebody who writes for film?

PG: Because he understands the disciplines more, his breadth of knowledge, his musicological associations are likely to be far more profound.

AF: I suppose the most obvious uses of music in film – you've just said it, really – is to reinforce an emotion that the filmmaker is trying to stir in the viewer. Have you ever done that?

PG: I don't think consciously, but there is inevitably that, I suppose, in some cases – I'm thinking now of the extraordinary music that Michael wrote for *The Cook, the Thief*, which had huge emotional import I think. But there was always a sense I suppose of the particular use of Michael's music. In a sense it was counterpointing what I wanted to do. Michael's music is very ironic. It's very difficult to put irony into music, but he is one of the successful composers who have done that. So often we would deliberately play opposites in order to express, I suppose, intellectual ideas about the usage of image and music. I've often tried to fight against that emotional manipulation in order to give far more credibility to [a] great range of music, not just simply as support for you taking out your Kleenex.

AF: Yes, but of course music is going to be emotionally stirring whether you want it to be or not.

PG: Yes, but the great thing about music – I mean, I've always wished to be a composer – it can be both. You [composers] have put yourselves into the extraordinarily greedy position of having the most abstract of structures and the most intellectual of propositions in association with the highest emotion.

AF: The way in which Michael Nyman is ironic, at least in the music that you used, is primarily by taking other composers' music, much older music, as a starting point. It makes it much easier to be ironic if you're dealing with Purcell or Mozart. And in a way, that's often been your approach as a filmmaker, hasn't it?

PG: Yes, but you must agree that the musical tradition is full of massive quotation, you're always massively quoting one another, it's a bit like painting. Painters are great quoters of one another's imagery. It's part of belonging to the club; we all want to belong to this club. Certainly if Mozart's a member I'd like to be a member of the same club, and you must feel like that. And if Rembrandt's a painter and I essay some opportunity to manipulate visual imagery, then I'm more than proud and excited as an act of humble homage to be associated, indeed, with that club.

I think [these are] the processes by which we build constantly, like a dwarf sitting on the shoulders of a giant, forever and forever and forever. And if you're talking about Purcell, I'm a great lover of English baroque music and certainly of Italian baroque music. We have just finished post-production of *Leonardo's Last Supper*, and we have essayed a dialogue between a famous painting by Veronese called *The Wedding at Cana* and the music of Gabrieli and Vivaldi, to great effect.

I've just received an Australian commission to make an opera, which I'm going to call *The Marriage of Christ*, which we're going to organise with the music of Gabrieli and also an Italian contemporary you might know, a man called Giovanni Sollima, a great cellist. The central figure of the Veronese painting is actually a self-portrait of Veronese playing a cello, so there are all sorts of looping references that we can make here, and I think that's also very, very important.

I think Veronese used the idea of music in that particular painting to indicate notions of concordance, of harmony, of people gathering together.

AF: One of the things that I think of as a correspondence between Nyman's music and your films in your collaborations is the fact that he constantly refers to seventeenth-century music, and you seem to be particularly drawn to seventeenth-century art. Do you know why that is? Why Vermeer, why Rembrandt …

PG: It's probably a mistake, maybe related to distribution patterns. We've made fifteen feature films now, and only four of them are historical movies. It just so happens I think that the historical movies have been the ones that have been best distributed. But having made that statement, I do think that the period – shall we say from 1600 to 1700 – was an incredibly fertile period, politically, socially, historically and culturally, in [the] English tradition. It's the beginnings of English supremacism, if you wish. Maybe that has all sorts of unfortunate connotations, especially if I speak here in Australia. But it is the time when first notions of atheism, first notions of capitalism, first notions of parliamentarianism are all establishing themselves, and culturally it's incredibly fertile as well. The beginning of the century would find Shakespeare still alive and then you would begin, at the end, Restoration drama, notions of all sorts of new thinking, the birth of the novel, et cetera, so culturally, politically and socially it's a very fascinating time. And, it could be said, the beginnings of modern notions of Englishness. So a fertile time which is incredibly useful to be mined and exploited and deconstructed.

AF: And in terms of the paintings, good for cinema. All of those shadows, all of that candlelight.

PG: Yes, well some people believe, don't they, that cinema began in 1895 with the Lumière brothers, but I think maybe we can posit it back contemporary with maybe Rembrandt, so we're talking 1630s – going back into my favourite century – when there were a whole series of European painters who were, for the first time, seriously painting artificial light. And what is cinema? No more than manipulation of artificial light, both at [the] source from the camera, and then when you project it. So we'd be talking, first of all, about Caravaggio in Italy, Velasquez in Spain, maybe Rubens in Flanders and certainly Rembrandt in Holland. It is relative to the development of all sorts of new technologies; I often associate the development of the mirror (this might surprise you) and the development of the candle. Of course there have been mirrors and candles way back to the Greeks but there were particular technologies at this particular time – mainly in Germany and not in Holland – which were developing artificial light. Candles were very, very expensive; consider how many bees are necessary to make a wax candle. The only people who could afford candles, essentially, were the church and the aristocracy. But suddenly they introduced animal fats and tallow into the manufacture of candles, and the bourgeoisie and in some cases the rich proletariat were able to afford to use candles in their domestic lives. And this period, from about 1590 probably to about 1650, saw an enormous burgeoning of the whole concept of artificial light, which really continues now, when we have twenty-four-hour lit cities. It's the beginning, literally, of being able to burn your candle at both ends, an incredible enfranchisement of our ability, in a sense, to appreciate our working life. We were not limited any more like the poor old farmer, who has to get up at dawn and go to bed at sunset. So our literary and cultural life extraordinarily benefited. And I mention the mirror, too, because it's the beginning of intense introspection, the first time we could really seriously look at ourselves. Rembrandt painted himself fifty-seven times, almost obsessively, as though he'd suddenly discovered his own persona because for the very first time he could see himself clearly.

AF: You've been talking, with regard to *Leonardo's Last Supper*, about taking a painting and moving it in time. I get the impression, watching your films, that you sometimes want to do the opposite with a film: that you want to make it more like a painting, that you superimpose, you write on your images. But of course it is a linear form – a film lasts ninety minutes or 112 minutes and it goes from beginning to end, and music is linear as well. But music has this wonderful ability to be abstract, almost by definition. Is that something that you aim for?

PG: I suppose, in the last ten years, my scripts have become far more like music scores, so they are deliberately organised with regard to abstract values so that there will be themes and ideas and variations, based upon a proposition. (I am obliged, although I feel very paradoxical, to write a script, because I cannot go to a studio with four paintings, three lithographs and a book of drawings and say, 'Give me the money' – they won't understand what I'm on about.) So I'm more than happy to play with notions of taking a theme, giving it to the violins then passing it on to the percussion, then making a solo voice and giving it to the choir – which means that often there will be a lot of real legitimate reasons for repetition, for continually arguing and pushing the same point of view from all sorts of different angles.

This, of course, is not exactly what most cinemagoers have been accustomed to expect. I think most people go to the cinema really to be given an illustrated nineteenth-century novel, and I say that, I suppose, with a bit of chagrin because we haven't even moved into the twentieth-century illustrated novel – the ability to translate Borges and Perec into cinema has not at all been successful – so most cinema is still illustrated Dickens and Zola and Tolstoy. That has got a lot to do, I think, with the timing of cinema as the manufacturing industry. It's always been relevant to me to think that Freud created his first paper on the hysteria of women six months before the Lumière brothers invented the notion of cinema. So somehow, psychoanalysis and our understanding of characterisation, good and bad and evil, and, you know, that Jesuit thing that all our relationships are related to the first three years of our life, has been part and parcel of the way we organise cinema. Which seems to me to be old-fashioned, unnecessarily recidivist and rather unfortunate, and we must do something serious about it.

But there again, you know, every medium has to be relative to all the technologies and the philosophies of the age in which it's invented. But we've had enough of it now, and I think we ought to change and I seriously believe that cinema is dead. I always give, rather facetiously, the date of the 31 September 1983 when the zapper, or the remote control, was introduced into the living rooms of the world, because immediately you do that you indicate choice, [and] the beginnings of interactivity – and cinema cannot be interactive, because it's supposed to be viewed by a crowd and in a sense democracy denies the ability to make it your product.

I live in Amsterdam, [where] they have the worst statistics of going to the cinema in the world, which I would cheer. The average Dutch citizen only goes to the cinema once every two years. That's not because they are not watching audiovisual excitements, but they're not watching them in those curious places called cinema. And I think the whole fragmentation of notions of attention span, the ways that we now receive our audiovisual material are entirely different, and if something is to succeed the 114 years of cinema as we've known it, it's got to take account of these things. Now I am constantly associated, I think, with a paradox, if you like: I think cinema's wasted on cinema. The tools are so much more sophisticated than the uses to which we put them, because basically our cinema now is bedtime stories for adults, and we've seen all the tropes and paradigms, we've used up all the potentiality; every time you see a film, within five minutes you know what's going to happen, you understand the genre it's connected with, you can probably anticipate the ending, and we really need to find new ways of manufacturing forms of cinema [and] audiovisual phenomena. The two great things of the twentieth century which should never be forgotten are that music has given up harmony, and painting has given up figuration. Now we need to show that cinema can give up narrative.

AF: Coming back to the idea of repetition in your work: the composers you work with are almost all composers who employ a lot of repetition in their music.

PG: I think they're all related to minimal music, not that any composer wants to be associated with minimalism anymore …

AF: No, although Nyman of course invented the term.

PG: Absolutely, yes, and there is a way that a lot of the composers I associate myself with are in some curious way related to that tradition – second-generation, third-generation, fourth-generation, even fifth-generation minimalists! There is a lot of music coming out of the Balkans now which is related to this association. We've just come out of making a huge project called *The Tulse Luper Suitcases*, where I work with a lot of Balkan composers who, rather latterly, have put – okay, let's be bland – a Gypsy association of bittersweet music together with minimalism, often to extremely good effect. I don't know whether you'd agree with me but the music of our formative educational years always stays with us. I am born in 1942, I come of age in '63, I'm twenty-one in '63, and this is the big time indeed of New York minimalist music, coming out of Cage, so my enthusiasms I suppose are from Cage, up to … I'm not so sure that I would particularly enjoy Philip Glass now, but certainly music of that particular period, and those associations and that ability to organise music in that way is still, indeed, very much with me. But you know, I've also been associated with Bono and U2 and Brian Eno, and the music, again, which was alive and well and kicking when certainly I was a young man of – what? – nineteen to twenty-seven.

AF: Most filmmakers lay music against their films, but I get the impression that in some cases you have laid your film against music, that you've choreographed scenes to music.

PG: Well, Michael and I – I always used to go back to that famous example (I'm not so sure it's true, and it might very well be apocryphal) of Prokofiev and Eisenstein working on *Alexander Nevsky*. The story goes that Eisenstein never turned a frame of imagery, and Prokofiev supposedly never wrote a note of music, until they'd established a good relationship about what they thought they were on about. It's rather interesting, isn't it, that Prokofiev's *Alexander Nevsky* score is played far more times than Eisenstein's film is ever seen in a cinema.

AF: Yes, that is interesting. But a lot of Michael Nyman's music existed in some form before you used it in your films.

PG: That sometimes is true, but the opposite is also true. I think Michael and I met outside the Royal College of Music one winter's afternoon almost by accident. We knew one person in common, I think, but he'd had no particular essays in cinema before, and my music enthusiasms at that time were probably more to do with Schoenberg and Berg. I was a great Berg and Webern fan. I suppose, [as] I had an association with a Dutch composer, Louis Andriessen, it was Berg and Webern that came to the fore more than the minimal music tradition. Curiously, Michael introduced me to Steve Reich and I introduced him to Stockhausen. It seems rather strange, retrospectively, but there was a great coming together of ways of organising and structuring. Michael in a curious way is like a music editor, and certainly my disciplines are coming out of the notion, I think, of the editor. But the editor-at-large, now, is a profound gatekeeper in the twenty-first century. We need editors in everything, there is so much information. The editor is somebody after all who creates structures and strategies to understand the information coming at us.

AF: Have you edited your films to music? Have you made a cut here because there is a strong beat here?

PG: That's often true but also the opposite is true. I'd go back to the composer and say, 'Look, I want to organise my structuring this way; can you fix your music to accommodate me?'

AF: One of the best uses of music I often think in film in general is when the music is doing something which is apparently unrelated to what's happening on the screen – it can give you different information.

PG: Well, that comes back to a sense of irony again – you know, terrifying things might be happening in my film but, to put it simplistically, most delightful things are happening on the music track.

AF: Are there examples from other filmmakers you can think of?

PG: [Jean-Luc] Godard, for example, in I suppose some of his earlier films. *Pierrot le fou* [1965] has a brilliant use of snippets and montaging of music. He had a great understanding of notions of quotation as well. [The] problem with quotation, of course, is that you need to know the source. It is no good being a blasphemer unless you are talking to an audience of believers.

AF: Let's talk a little about Louis Andriessen, because now we're suddenly moving into an area here, with *Rosa* and *Writing to Vermeer*, which is operatic, where the music is paramount. The most important part of the opera is the music. Does that leave you working differently?

PG: Yes, there's a problem here, isn't there? There's nothing to indicate with the word 'opera' about music at all. The word is Latin, Italian origin, which simply means 'work'. And should we in fact have an opera-devised work where indeed the composer is king? That's only something that people like you have taken over, and sometimes I think rather in a negative way. Are operas meant to be visual phenomena, or musical? Going back to what we just said about Prokofiev and Eisenstein, Prokofiev somehow lives more satisfactorily than Eisenstein does. Music is a very, very quick and immediate communicator, especially if you think about contemporary mechanical reproduction. Sting, on a Friday night, makes a track; on the Sunday morning it's in Beijing. That amazing ability, certainly in the twenty-first century, to make that move so quickly. You can't make painting move that quickly, and you certainly can't make literature move that quickly, because of all the barriers.

So, there is a way that that sort of immediacy could be put to good use, but I'm very much aware that cinema is a medium of the past tense: in a sense, you know, *Casablanca* to me is very boring, because it's always the same. And these notions of how we can manipulate time, which of course music's been able to do for years and years and years, is very important. I think probably, and I'm sure you'd agree, that basically the opera tradition died during World War I: it had a long, long, innings, 300 years or more, and I suppose, in some curious way, it's no accident that cinema took over the responsibilities of what opera did, the notion of the big audio-visual spectacle. I'm not interested in the Menotti opera, which has dialogue lines like 'Please pass me the salt, darling.' Opera for me has to be a grand event where excuses for melodrama can be accommodated like they could be accommodated in no other art form. And the two operas you mentioned, certainly *Rosa*, was an extravagance of an extraordinary grand opera tradition.

The guts and the relevance of operatic communication has now really basically disappeared from our lives. There are still people making operas, of course, and still embracing, indeed like we did, modern means of communication with projection, and all sorts of electrical apparatus. But I suppose it's also relevant to the manufacture of opera houses. There are opera houses, aren't there, all over the world in some belated excitement somehow. Even though opera was dead, essentially, people went on building opera houses, which is always a rather curious paradox. If you think about opera, for example, in Australia – what on earth are you worrying about with opera in Australia? You're a brand-new nation, let's forget these old fossilised activities, which basically only pander to a very elitist audiences with a lot of privatised knowledge.

AF: But you're talking about …

PG: Well, wait a minute – I'd been given the opportunity to play, if you like (you know, the English play very seriously), with the notions of what opera can mean, and, let me repeat, this notion of being able to encompass melodrama like no other art form possibly can. We spent a lot of time talking about Michael Nyman, but that's really where we basically parted company. In *The Cook, the Thief, His Wife & Her Lover*, the last reel, the last twenty minutes, is really totally operatic. Shallow stage, we even made references to everything being [the] 'plush red' you associate with opera houses. People move very, very choreographically, they don't exactly sing but their statements are deliberately artificial, and it posited very much in the tradition, I suppose, of … why is it – maybe on another occasion you can answer me these questions – why [is] most grand opera about the humiliation of the female, time after time after time after time? And *The Cook, the Thief* is about the humiliation of the female, so it makes all sorts of connections there.

But after that, for several years, I really gave up making cinema and, as you've indicated, moved directly over into opera houses. There was one film I made, I don't know whether you ever saw it, it created a lot of fuss, called *The Baby of Mâcon* [1993] – again nobody actually sang in an operatic way, but there was huge amounts of different kinds of music in it and it was organised very much on a sort of musical ritualistic basis. Its subject matter offended people enormously so I don't think that film had a particularly wide distribution. It's one of my favourite films. I was then taking up citizenship in Holland, where I am now, living in Amsterdam. There was an extraordinary entrepreneurial theatre man, a man called Pierre Audi, who used to run theatres in East London very successfully and then was appointed the head of the Netherlands Opera and has done extremely well, and it was through him I met Louis Andriessen, though we had made films before. There's a movie called *M is for Man, Music, Mozart* [1991] that was our first collaboration.

But then again, and here I'm being confessional, I always fall out in the end with composers. Regularly as clockwork. And you probably know, though Michael Nyman's very much part of our conversation, we had the most extraordinary and violent divorce because we both wanted different things out of the media we were associated with.

AF: It was *Prospero's Books* [1991], wasn't it?

PG: And in the end of course I absolutely had an enormous bust-up with Louis Andriessen, so again a violent disagreement. It seems to be that composers and filmmakers have enormous egos.

AF: One of the things that struck me though about seeing *Writing to Vermeer* was that there didn't seem to be an enormous difference between it as an opera and the films of yours which I had seen. It seemed a really quite seamless transition from the screen to the stage.

PG: Well, there was certainly a lot of screen organisation, indeed, and many, many projections. Though I'm a little surprised about your comment because that extraordinary *coup de théâtre* at the end, where the huge heavens open and enormous amounts of water go splashing down on the stage, was a very, very physical operation, which would never have been successful in the same way if we had made it a cinematic venture, because suddenly our huge cast of female performers got thoroughly, thoroughly drenched, and you felt for them in some curious way which made again an association with that extraordinary music by Louis very, very pertinent as a live event.

AF: Opera is a tradition, of course, and I think it's probably the tradition that you object to mostly, but you can have people singing and acting and moving around and shine lights on them, and so forth and …

PG: You're being very derogative.

AF: No, no, not at all.

PG: I can see that you have some problems. Again you're trying to assert the supremacy of the composer in the world of opera!

AF: [Laughs] Possibly, but I don't think so; I think what I'm saying is that surely it's what you make of it, that opera *per se* is neither good nor bad, it doesn't really exist …

PG: I think Messiaen said, out of all the thousands of operas, there are only five good operas ever. I think that even the most famous operas that we know, from *The Magic Flute* to *Rigoletto*, still don't fulfil the demands of this extraordinary medium, which is deeply, deeply artificial. And the notion of suspension of disbelief is very important in cinema, but good lord, it's even more important in that great tangle of artifice that's represented by opera.

AF: The fact that it, as you say, has become something which is associated with 'elites' (I hate that word), people with a lot of money who can afford the tickets, is actually not opera's fault …

PG: Well, I'm not sure about that. It's to do with the cult of the singer, isn't it, the notion of [the] diva came out of the opera house and that word's passed into common parlance, as something rather unfortunate. So maybe opera has encouraged its own demise as regard to those characteristics.

AF: But given that you don't much like opera and you think that cinema's dead …

PG: Well, I'm not very fond of cinema even when it was so-called alive.

AF: … it is more than a little paradoxical that you've spent your life working in these two media.

PG: Yes. I think I'm working in an antique art.

AF: But you'll keep doing it?

PG: Well, the language is so amazing, the way that we can manipulate not only imagery, but also sound now in the contemporary world is just amazing, you know. We can all – excuse the parallel –

become living Picassos, the ability to manipulate these vast vocabularies is deeply, deeply exciting. But let me repeat, you know, I do sincerely believe that cinema is wasted on cinema, and we must find better uses for the tools.

Peter Weir

Peter Weir's films make imaginative use of sound, from barely audible rumbling to the full-blown use of scores and often famous pieces of classical music. Some of the most memorable scenes in his films are those with music. The following interview took place at the director's home at Sydney's northern beaches in mid-2008.

ANDREW FORD: Most people, asked to nominate the sound of a Peter Weir film, probably go for panpipes. So maybe we should start with *Picnic at Hanging Rock*. Panpipes were an unusual choice, but they've stuck to that film like the zither sticks to *The Third Man*. How did you come up with the idea?

PETER WEIR: Bruce Smeaton had done the score, as he had on *The Cars That Ate Paris* [1974], my first film – this was my second film. We had had a very successful collaboration; I was very pleased with his work. But we were missing something, a kind of emblem, a theme. Bruce was reaching the end of his patience with it, and one of the producers said he'd heard this music the night before, on the ABC, on some terrible disaster in Africa, I think, a drought or something like that. We got hold of it, laid it in, and Bruce said, 'Well, I hate to say it, because I'd rather compose it, but it's a damn fine piece.' So we contacted the people in Paris – Gheorghe Zamfir on the panpipes and Marcel Cellier on the organ. Zamfir was very difficult. He said, 'That's my old music – you want my new band,' and so forth. After some negotiations we managed to get it. We just took a dub off a track from a fresh new

LP from Folkways or something, and there it remained in the film.

AF: And why was it right?

PW: It's really hard to put words to a thing like that. You might be tempted to say, with such an ancient instrument, that it was connecting to the side of the film that was really touching on the power of nature, on the great unknown of this country, at that particular time. Here was European culture in the outback, as it were; without playing the didgeridoo – which wouldn't have worked – it invoked, I think, a hidden world.

AF: You've had a few moments in films where the music has been quite a hit. Maurice Jarre's music for *The Year of Living Dangerously* [1982]: you'd hear it on the radio all the time. It must be one of the last film themes to have that kind of exposure. And the barn-raising scene in *Witness* [1985], likewise – the music was popular. Does that help a film?

PW: I don't think so. For the composer it may mean something. Let's take the barn-raising cue – that became part of, not just the album that was released (with the rights going significantly to Maurice, and rightly so), but he would also incorporate it into his live concerts. It would be not as well known as 'Lara's Theme' [from *Doctor Zhivago*], but it would certainly be recognisable.

AF: And there are other examples of you choosing bits of music that were already famous. I suppose Górecki's third symphony at the end of *Fearless* [1993] wasn't actually that famous when *Fearless* was made, but it certainly became ubiquitous ...

PW: No, it was – it was in America. My wife heard it in a store, in some interesting little boutique shop in San Francisco, and she got hold of it and said, 'It's so powerful.' I talked to the man in the shop and he said it'd become a hit of the FM classical world. He said he'd known people tell him that they'd pulled off to the side of the road when it played, simply because they just couldn't concentrate on their driving, they were so absorbed in its power. Interestingly, I finally met the composer on a trip I made to Israel. It was the evening of Holocaust Day, of all things. I was promoting *Fearless*, and somebody said, 'Górecki's here', and we went to a concert and met afterwards. We had to speak in sort of wobbly French, and he told me he was inspired by a visit to Auschwitz. He hadn't seen the film at that time. I did in fact see the piece against Holocaust footage later, and didn't think it worked, because it was too much, it was too powerful, it was like doubling. You could've put a fly buzzing on the soundtrack and it would perhaps have been more effective.

AF: That was that Tony Palmer film [*The Symphony of Sorrowful Songs*, 1993], where he took the entire symphony and put that footage against it. When you have a very famous piece of music in one of your films, there is the recognition factor, isn't there? That must be a bit of a problem for a filmmaker if people go, 'Oh! It's *that* music!'

PW: It's true. If the film is popular enough, or if it becomes a classic, then that piece – let's pick an obvious one, *Thus Spake Zarathustra* in *2001* – becomes really the property of that film. That would be the rare case. If the film sinks without a trace – and that is what most films do; they're meant like wine to be drunk in the year – then people don't even remember that it was used. But it's always a problem for a director with my particular taste. I would really like to be able to compose the music. For me, music is the fountainhead of all the arts. I've never known a good arts-worker, if I can put it that way, who didn't love music. I'm sure there's an exception, but it's something to do with its mathematics and its rhythm and its utter mystery. I want to say this quote, which became very important to me, from a Gwen Harwood poem – she's no longer alive but she was a Tasmanian poet:

> ...words can never
> contain, as music does, the unsayable
> grace that cannot be defined
> yet leaps like light from mind to mind.
> [from 'Four Impromptus']

That's why in one sense it's hard to talk about music, as we are today. I think you call it in; I use it when I can't say it in any other form, either visually or through the dialogue. I bring it in like the cavalry, and this creates some problems for the composer. There are directors, they may even be in the majority, who hire the composer, they get somebody respected, somebody who they admire or trust, who composes a score. They will go and listen to the recording, they are probably involved in earlier try-outs on the piano, which is usually the instrument of the composer, and they make their comments. But you're in a foreign world, it's like someone speaking a foreign language. You might say, 'Could it be a little slower?' or 'I like that one but not the other one.' And then you get the score. In my case, I will have laid up a temp track, which most directors do – you can't bear to have sections which are embarrassingly silent, they're meant to have music and you lay something in. So I become a sort of radical DJ in the cutting room – that is, I'll sometimes find scraps of music I've been playing on the set or whilst writing the screenplay. In fact, I play them at dailies and, in the end, my gift to the crew isn't a T-shirt but music from the set – I'll often play it on the set, and it will basically be a CD-load of esoteric and sometimes very well-known pieces. Some of those end up finally in the film – it's happened a number of times. [When we were filming] *The Year of Living Dangerously*, [I was playing] the Four Last Songs of Richard Strauss, and eventually Linda Hunt, who played the male character opposite Mel Gibson, said to me, 'What is that you're playing?' I said, 'I just find this piece somehow sums up a great deal to do with you, and particularly the scene we're doing tomorrow.' And she said, 'Well, can I have a listen?' And she loved it – I never pushed it on anyone else. She said she *really* loved it, she'd been playing it all night. I said, 'Well, maybe you should play it to Mel if that's something you love', and so it got into the film.

AF: Going back to that Gwen Harwood quote, about music being able to articulate the inarticulable, of course what you do, when you put it against your film, is you give it meaning that it doesn't have. Music doesn't have specific meanings: a Mozart sonata is a Mozart sonata – it isn't about anything except itself. But when you put the Albinoni *Adagio,* for example, against *Gallipoli* [1981], you're not only giving it this connection for the audience possibly for the rest of their lives (as happened with *Also sprach Zarathustra* in *2001*), but you also say, 'This is sad music', or whatever. Your pictures illustrate it.

PW: I think that's perfectly true, but it's also true that there are pieces of music that you've heard at specific times in your life – let's talk about classical music – that had some meaning for you that's really quite impenetrable. I first heard Beethoven's fifth piano concerto as a young man. My mother would bring home the odd classical record – really three or four pieces, because she felt we should have culture; it was kind of a sweet Australian thing to do in the 1950s, so we wouldn't be too Aussie or something – and I was really struck by this piece. Wilhelm Kempff was the pianist, and I can recall the album cover to this day. Many years later, in 1975, working on *Picnic at Hanging Rock,* we were missing a piece that somehow needed to sum up some sort of loss, without overdoing it, of the girls not having been found. I recalled the piece, asked for the Wilhelm Kempff, got it, played it in the cutting room. It worked immediately, the slow movement, and we bought it. And of course what happened is they said, 'Well there's a cheaper version, or we can get someone to record it.' I listened to a couple of other versions, but it had to be that version – something about his timing. The same happened with the Yo-Yo Ma cello piece that the doctor plays, or apparently plays, at one time in *Master and Commander* [2003]. Richard [Tognetti, the violinist] got someone to come in and play it, a wonderful cellist, but it was just something about that Yo-Yo Ma recording that meant very much to me. You can say it's a matter of taste, but I also used that Beethoven in *Dead Poets Society* [1989], and I could still sit with that music and still explore it like a series of interconnecting caves under the ground in which you only ever reach so far, and there's still more to explore in it. Yet it's such a simple piece – well, the whole piece is not simple, but that section is.

AF: It's in *Fearless* as well, isn't it?

PW: [Laughs] I'd forgotten about that. I think it might be, yeah. It's probably playing here in the house somewhere today.

AF: Let's talk about something which is about as close to music as a filmmaker gets, which is timing, and when you decide to use music. You mentioned *Master and Commander,* and there I think there's almost no music until the Fantasia on a Theme by Thomas Tallis [by Ralph Vaughan Williams] comes in, which is a very striking moment. In *The Year of Living Dangerously* we're actually in the second half of the film before you hear the famous theme – up until then we've heard bits of the Four Last Songs, and the colonel playing his bagpipes, but we haven't heard the tune, and suddenly it comes at a key moment. 'Spotting' is what it's called, isn't it?

How do you decide where to bring something in and how long to leave it out?

PW: That is the phrase – a horrible phrase. 'Let's spot the music' – it always feels too technical for me. But you do it with a composer: he has to know where you want it to come in and where you want it to go out, and usually it changes by the end of it. Maybe half of that spotting session is ever accurate. So I find that period uncomfortable … Where to put the music and so forth. Firstly, let me go back to what has always been an ambition of mine, which is really to make a film that didn't require music. It might have and probably would have source music in it – we call it 'source', which means somebody's either playing it on a radio, or literally someone in the street is playing with their hat on the ground for a few coins. But I would love the film not to need it, because I don't enjoy [music in film] for itself – I think it is part of the whole. In one way it shouldn't be noticed, and if it is, perhaps it should be featured, which I've done, and have loved when others have done. Of course, anyone would think of Ennio Morricone with his Westerns with Sergio Leone. I think the same about the James Bond theme – they touched something there. Those little signature things, the zither, as you've mentioned before, in *The Third Man*. But if you set out to do it, it never happens. If you set out and say, 'In this film I'm going to have a zither-type motif', the poor composer goes home and he thinks, 'Oh my God'. Those things just occur, you know, they're like a natural event. A tsunami of creativity. So mostly you don't have it. I'd love to do it without music, but in the end I'm so grateful to have pieces that I love to play, because they're just doing things the film is failing to … what is not being brought out by image or sound.

AF: The moment [in *The Year of Living Dangerously*] when Mel Gibson gets into the car, outside the embassy I think it is, and Sigourney Weaver sits in the passenger seat, and the music starts – it's like the beginning of another act in the film, suddenly they're going to be living *really* dangerously, not that the music tells you that at all, it's rather light, tuneful, unemotional music …

PW: Oh no, it's got a real pulse. It's actually a Vangelis piece and it was used in the trailer. I'd met Vangelis – he was then a very big name, *Chariots of Fire* being of course his famous piece – and I went to him because Maurice had tried to replace that piece of music that was in my temporary track; he couldn't do it, it just had a sort of throbbing power to it. So I spoke to Vangelis. Poor Maurice – he was very good about my doing things like this in amongst his score – he said to me, 'Peter, you know, someone the other day said to me how could I rip off Vangelis? I said it *is* Vangelis!'

AF: Well, I didn't realise that, *I* thought he'd ripped off Vangelis.

PW: Vangelis didn't want a credit. Interestingly.

AF: The use of music to reinforce emotion, to tell the audience what to think, of course, is the great trap of the filmmaker. It's something which you deal with in *The Truman Show* [1998], particularly at the moment where Truman meets his 'father', that reunion scene. You see Christof, the director of 'The Truman Show', almost literally manipulating the music, almost conducting the music, bringing it to a climax and timing that moment to perfection. And then, at the end of the film, you bring back that same music, and it works on us, the viewer! In other words, you do to us what Christof has done to his TV audience, which I think is a very nice conceit. But it's an issue, isn't it, this manipulation?

PW: Well, it certainly was in that film, and that piece was composed by Burkhard Dallwitz – he shared the credit with Philip Glass. We talked about it and agreed that he was to write it within the style of the show, but with great sincerity, because I would often talk to an actor or a crew member from the point of view of Christof the director, so I could assume what he wanted. I thought he was in a sense a director that I would respect [even] if I found his ethics revolting in that show, but he had ideas and taste and passion. As you note in the film, that moment when they meet, the father and son, Christof – Ed Harris – was in a sort of ecstasy of creativity and is conducting the piece. At one stage one of the crew there on camera says, 'Shall we zoom in now?' and Christof says, 'No, no! Hold it!' He just waits for that exact moment in the music: 'NOW zoom in close!' I loved doing that because it was a sort of delightful parody of what we all do.

AF: There's also a very, very brief shot of Philip Glass looking at the screen in another part of the film and playing the music live, as it were.

PW: Yeah, he loved doing that. I said I thought it was great fun – given that it was a 24-hours-a-day, seven-days-a-week show – that he would be one of the rostered musicians on the show.

AF: Let's talk about Maurice Jarre a little more. First of all you used his son's famous *Oxygène* for the running music in *Gallipoli*, then after that I think you did five films with Maurice Jarre, and this is, as you mentioned, the composer of *Lawrence of Arabia* and *Doctor Zhivago* and some terribly famous film tunes. How did you work with him? What did you tell him when you were working on a film?

PW: The reason I went to him was because of the range he had. If it had just been *Doctor Zhivago*, I would probably never have dared to approach him, but then I saw Maurice's credit in one of the films of the German filmmaker Volker Schlöndorff. I sort of enquired whether it was the same Maurice Jarre – I thought it was great music. It also had interesting use of ethnic instruments in it – there was really no one like him for grabbing something from the street, as it were. Here I was, doing a film that was going to have gamelan in it, and fortunately he was available. We really had a rapport from the beginning. He was very generous, and I say that because I am this infuriating director who does lay up a very good temporary track. I say to the composer, in Maurice's case that first time, 'Do you want to hear it without the temp track – will it affect you?' He said, 'No, I'd rather know what you're thinking, it'll be a shorthand.' And then he came out of that first screening and said, 'Gosh, you made the job hard, you've really chosen from world music', and I said, 'I don't want you to just repeat it or copy it – you may do something quite different, but you can see what I'm trying to do.' So he could accommodate that, and it didn't throw him, even down to that particular Vangelis piece. So, given the freedom he gave me, I tried to give as much to him. I think the next time we worked together was *Witness* and he was determined to do something to beat that temporary track, and did, in a way. His barn-raising was far better than whatever I had there, and he was so proud when he played it to me. At that stage he was immensely adaptable; he had moved from orchestration to use electronic instruments. Despite his classical training and maybe even some prejudice, he adapted to the new technology and inspired those players. And subsequently there were some very, very famous people who played on the track of *Witness*, four or five of them, and they could make any sound you wanted. It's an awful thing but it's true: they'd sample classical instruments, or folk instruments, and some poor Bulgarian man would come in and blow a few things through a comb or something and they'd say, 'Thank you very much', and they'd pay him and they could use that forever, that sound. Maurice worked with these five guys, and they got this very big sound, a very beautiful building sound that became the barn-raising theme. I couldn't thank him enough; he gave me more than

I expected. So we had a very good relationship, but I think I was pretty difficult as a director.

AF: What about those sections in films where you're not using music as such, or certainly not themes, but more soundscapes? *The Last Wave* [1977] is mostly soundscape; there is a composer on the film who I've never heard of ...

PW: His name was Groove Myer, he chose to go by the name Charles Wain on the credits. He was a very, very successful composer for commercials at the time, but I don't know that he did other films.

AF: But that film is all rain and thunder and hail and frogs ...

PW: I think that films have sounds that are fundamental to them. I'll give you an example: I was working on *The Thorn Birds*, I was going to direct it as a movie for Warner Bros, and I was in Los Angeles working on the screenplay, having a terrible time – I really should not have taken the job on. I think it was the only time I took something on because it was irresistibly exciting, it was the big thing at the time, the book a huge seller – but not right for me. I was waiting for the writer to come for a meeting at the Polo Lounge in Beverly Hills and I was getting close to pulling out of it. I knew it'd be embarrassing. I thought, 'What is it that's not in this thing?' Now it happened I'd ordered a cocktail, and I had a swizzle stick, the classic plastic long swizzle stick, and I was playing with it in my mouth, you know, like a cigarette holder. I happened to close my jaws on the swizzle stick and tapped the end of it. Well, of course, it vibrated inside my skull, a *brrrr* sound, you know, with echo. And I thought, 'My God! That sound isn't in this film! And I have to have that sound! I always have that sound!' It was repetitious, it was tense, it was bass, and the sound was perfectly musical, as the swizzle stick made it in my mouth, and I knew I would never make the movie –

which I didn't. And I saved the swizzle stick and stuck it in my diary. [Laughs]

AF: And now whenever you're about to start another project, you put the swizzle stick in your mouth? [Laughs]

PW: A kind of tuning fork, yes! But I do find, when I'm looking at a script, that there's a certain kind of music I always play. If it's vocal I like it in a foreign language that I can't understand, so I don't get distracted by the sentiments. But I play a lot of African music. I used to play folk music, but [now] I tend to play a lot of African pop music, and Arabic music, particularly that qawwali sort of music. Music with a passion in it, or feeling, but you don't know exactly what it is they're saying or what it means. I find that that music helps open the unconscious and the creative process. On a shoot I'll play my music that I've collected. Almost every evening with a glass of wine after rushes and dinner, I sit on my own to think about the next day's work, put the music on in headphones so that I don't have any other sound, hit certain tracks, seemingly at random. I think what it does is jam the radar. I think it stops you making sense and I think it allows the unconscious to open its doors, to daydream as it were, and I mean the word with a different kind of weight to it, to daydream. I get, I think, some of my best ideas through using music in that way.

AF: Is that why you play music on the set as well?

PW: I'll play it on the set to blast away the tendency to entropy that occurs. Two or three hundred people doing things around you ... the music silences them sometimes, for a start, particularly on the opening day or when we're very tired, and often they'll know the piece. Pink Floyd is wonderful for this kind of hosing down of the set [laughs] because they're pretty hard to resist, they're completely ageless, and some of it's so strange and powerful. So I'll play that and suddenly anything might happen on that day. We've got our script, we know what we're shooting, people are wardrobed and made-up, but that music introduces a kind of controlled chaos, a sort of anarchy. Quite often, if the actors are a bit stiff, I'll play the music through the take so they can hardly hear each other. Of course it ruins the sound take, but you can always dub it later, but generally it starts off with such a reckless feeling: we're part of a tradition of creativity stretching back through the ages and others have created things like this piece of music we're playing. And isn't that a great enterprise to be involved in, the enterprise that is the creative enterprise? And then I'll say, 'Let's switch the bloody thing off', and they'll act away. But it's sort of introduced this irreverence and this sort of sheer delight in making something.

AF: I think *Fearless* is a film which is interesting from a sound point of view. The opening scene is very impressive. That's I guess a combination of sound effects and music – is it Maurice Jarre's music? It sounds a bit like Penderecki.

PW: It is Penderecki. This was a Warner Bros picture and they had the rights to a piece of his music that Stanley Kubrick had used in … I think it was in *The Shining*. It is the most powerful and strange piece of music, it is like flies released from the depths of hell. I wanted something that let loose the dogs of war – all is chaos, there is no north or south in the opening of that film – and this music provided it. But there are sound effects woven in amongst it, as you say. I did my first film in '67, so it was really not long after sound, and you could meet people who'd worked in the silent industry, and they were still working – Hitchcock for example. You were born in an industrial age; the city is full of sounds which became a new kind of music. The rattle of the blade of an electric fan, the throb of a refrigerator; people have made experimental works out of this kind of sound, but this repetition that is there in a lot of mechanised sound I think peculiarly suited film – not all films, but some films. But when you take that repetition you create a tension. And film – part of its DNA is tension. Will they kiss? Will she turn around? Will he walk away? Will the bomb go off? There's a tension in it which you're always making play of, whether it's comedy or drama you're working with, and so sometimes that kind of *dom-dom-dom-dom-dom-dom* … my swizzle stick example is what you're dealing with. It can be badly used, I'm not saying it works automatically, but I think I've been drawn to that cyclical music. When it breaks out of its cycle, of course, it has great power. Just a change of a note or of a chord progression makes a difference.

AF: There's a moment in *Fearless*, I can't remember whether there's music or not – it's the bit where Max, the Jeff Bridges character, is walking across the ten-lane highway, and gets to the other side unscathed – you certainly hear a lot of traffic and a lot of honking horns, and then the sound drains away completely, and although he's still by the highway, it slowly goes to silence. That's a very striking moment, and there's a bit of ambient melody that comes in, and you hear him breathing closely miked, and the sequence finishes with a close-up of his ear. That moment of silence is very powerful, and other directors have done the same thing, have taken everything away for effect. What is the effect, do you think? What are you after there?

PW: Well, apart from trying to give an idea of the character's mental state, we all know that after loud explosion there's a silence; those who've been close to bomb blasts often say there was just a flash of white and then a sort of silence: 'I didn't hear the bang …' But to a degree I think you're playing with the audience in the theatre. I think that when it goes quiet in the theatre it creates another kind of tension – you can be just on the edge of [being] aware of other people in the theatre, and then the sound comes back and you're taken back into the story. It's perhaps heightening their senses: we listen in a different way when it's quiet, and when the sound comes back we hear it slightly differently. So it's probably altering, to some very minor degree, the way your senses are absorbing the picture. I've experimented with that because I love sound so much, and I'm interested in this area. For example, on *Picnic at Hanging Rock*, I knew I had a mystery which did not have a solution, and that intrigued me, but I couldn't assume it would intrigue those who'd been to mystery stories in which there was a solution – it might be irritating, which it was to some, I suppose. So I had to let them know, halfway through the picture at least, not to expect the conventional ending. There were ways I did that visually; less known are the ways I did it on the soundtrack. For example, we took an earthquake. I think there are certain sounds that we humans have filed away somewhere, that we know are extremely dangerous. One of them I think is an earthquake, the deep rumble of what will shortly be the earth moving. Most of us have not experienced that, but I think we carry the sound. Anyway, I laid this earthquake sound in on the optical track, just at the threshold of audibility. If I'd made it too loud it would've been noticeable and distracting, but only good sound systems could pick it up, so you only ever heard it in good theatres. But it was there. Somebody once said to me, maybe there was a subway under the theatre, and I said, 'No, that is my sound.' I just wanted people to experience it as a child experiences something, and therefore not expect Inspector Plod to turn up at the end and say, 'Those girls have been taken off in a spacecraft' or whatever. They've just disappeared.

AF: It's a not dissimilar device to the growling of the animals that are the cars in *The Cars That Ate Paris*, which is also at quite a low level, and you keep thinking, 'Those cars sound like beasts.'

PW: Yes, I've not kept a record of things that we've tried, and I've worked with some very good people – like Lee Smith, who then went on to cut many of my films, but he did a lot of my sound. Sometimes, despite all of the advances that we've made optically, now moving toward 3D and CGI, I think there's been less done with sound. David Lynch is the only person I know who's been particularly interested in it to a great degree. I mean, he has done fabulous things, and we shared the same sound designer on two films, Alan Splat, who unfortunately died – he was quite extraordinary in putting tracks together and making sounds, an extremely sensitive San Francisco gentleman who would play the cello to relax in the evening. He'd been at film school, I think, with David Lynch – they had done many things. So he was doing *Mosquito Coast* [1986], then he did *Dead Poets Society* for me. *Mosquito Coast* had more range for his talent, but he told me about David Lynch. He said he was working on *Blue Velvet* [1986], but he said, 'The sounds that I was creating were so awful, and so horrible, and David was loving it, that I became ill and I couldn't finish the film. They had to get someone else, the sound made me sick.'

AF: Who are the other filmmakers who've used sound well, or strikingly?

PW: I think a one-man film school is Alfred Hitchcock … there's hardly a filmmaker, I think, who hasn't looked at his key films. Then I would say Stanley Kubrick, who was really quite an inspiration for me. I was fortunate enough finally to meet him. We had exchanged odd letters – you know, he saw everything, and of all things, he'd seen my very first film, *The Cars That Ate Paris*. I loved the way he used sound. He had the same kind of difficulties with music that I faced. I think we were rather similar in that – as someone said, Stanley would have liked to make the coffee on set, 'cos he could make it really well [laughs]. He was like that, I think, just a perfectionist in the best sense. So music became a thing that he could hardly just assign to someone, and if you follow all the stories of his films, there are certain difficulties that he had with composers. He would junk whole scores and so on, and often he would end up with his temp tracks, or bits of them, and then re-record them in a different way, constantly experimenting, but his sound is also very very good.

AF: Did Kubrick like *The Cars That Ate Paris*?

PW: He said so. I saved the letter, of course. I was only just getting started – I just couldn't believe I'd gotten a letter from Stanley Kubrick. I'd written him one about his film *Barry Lyndon*, which I'd just been to see in Sydney: I described the projection and the sound. He was well known to be obsessive about how his films were projected, whether the prints were in good condition in far-flung regions. So I wrote and said, 'You'd be pleased to know I saw it in Sydney, and it was well-projected and they watched the focus, and thank you for your wonderful films, yours sincerely Peter Weir.' And that was it. But he was a man who had a kind of internet before the internet; he knew things, he had contacts. So he wrote back and said, 'I know who you are, I saw your film.' [Laughs] And then he saw *Picnic at Hanging Rock*. He was about to do a Stephen King – *The Shining* – but he'd also been looking at another Stephen King book called *Salem's Lot*, a vampire film. He passed on that one and said, 'No, I'm going to do *The Shining*, but you should offer that to Peter Weir', and they said, 'Who's that?' at Warner Bros. And he said, 'Go and look at his film *Picnic at Hanging Rock*.' So they called me up and said, 'Stanley's recommended you for this job.' [Laughs] So I went and saw them. I didn't end up doing it, I didn't like it, but I used to call him the un-met friend.

AF: I watched *The Cars That Ate Paris* a few days ago for the first time in a long time; I hadn't remembered how funny it was! I'd remembered how sinister it was, but I laughed and laughed, and a large part of that actually is the music, which is beautifully done.

PW: Oh, it's fabulous! That was a case where it was Bruce from end to end – he just took that and ran with it, Bruce Smeaton. As some French journalist labelled it – I think in a rather snobbish way, at the Cannes Film Festival – 'humour noir, des antipodes'. [Laughs] And I think that's how it was seen by the French.

AF: The idea that you can take 'Little Brown Jug' and turn it into the most sinister tune ever composed …

PW: Yeah, that was a wonderful cue. That was a lot of fun to do … What am I saying? 'A lot of fun to do'! I'm repeating some cliché. It was so terrifying and hard. I don't think there is a more difficult film than your first one. Four-week schedule, six days a week. You've done short films, but to go out with this first film shot in Panavision, wide-screen, anamorphic: it was overwhelming. And I thought, how do people make a life of this? How can they survive? (I was twenty-nine.) This could kill you!

Epilogue: The Shared Experience of Sound

Did we not live in an age of DVDs and downloads, this book wouldn't have been written. At least, not by me.

It isn't so long ago that old films were hard to see, apart from the obvious classics. A comparatively small range of work was available on video and you might occasionally stumble across a forgotten gem on late-night or day-time television, but to undertake anything resembling systematic research into films of the past – even the quite recent past – you would have needed access to a film archive.

This really only changed at the start of the twenty-first century. As people acquired wide-screen televisions, many also began to build their own DVD libraries. In response to this demand, thousands of previously unavailable films were commercially released on DVD, often quite cheaply. Suddenly, we were all film historians.

Although I watched the great majority of the films discussed in this book on DVD, I would like to end with a short paean to the movie theatre. Watching a film at home is like listening to the recording of a symphony. It's better than nothing. There are even advantages over hearing an orchestra play it live. For one thing, you will probably hear more detail on a CD, concert hall acoustics being notoriously variable. Certainly the ability to listen a second (or hundredth) time can't be lightly dismissed. But there is also something inescapably inauthentic about the experience. As much as anything, it is about the way we *feel* a symphony orchestra in concert, or a movie in the cinema.

The kind of concentration engendered by a large audience, fully focused on a film, is impossible to replicate in front of your television. What's more, one's fellow audience members can become part of the sonic experience of cinema. I'm thinking of a sharp intake of breath from a hundred or more people, or a shared guffaw of relief, even a sudden scream.

I remember seeing Peter Weir's *Fearless* in the cinema. In the sequence where Jeff Bridges steps out blindly into the midst of heavy traffic on a multi-lane highway and the film's sound is reduced to nothing at all, I could hear the breathing of the audience around me. It was noticeably shallow. After a few seconds, it seemed, we were all of us holding our breath as one.

Pretty much the opposite of this experience was watching the start of *A Knight's Tale*. When the groovy mediaeval crowd at the joust beat and clap their hands to Queen's 'We Will Rock You', the noise resounds through the whole cinema. There is an almost visceral quality to this moment in a cinema with good sound equipment, the thumping, clapping and singing of the on-screen crowd being felt by members of the off-screen audience, the physical sound going through one's whole body. But there's more to it, still, because the general urge to sing along, even if not acted upon, adds a further level of excitement. It would not be the same on telly.

This is not to say that cinemas will always give you the best experience. The first time I saw *Casino Royale* (2006) I was forced to imagine the brilliant ending. I'd gone with my father-in-law to his local cinema in Eastern Finland, where, it turned out, they have a tradition of shutting off the film and bringing down the curtain the very instant the credits start to roll. So the triumphant return of the James Bond theme went for nothing in that town. What *coup de théâtre*? And when one thinks of how many movies of the past twenty-five years have ended with a hit song that functions almost like a clincher to the action, one can only conclude that these cinema patrons are missing the point of quite a lot of recent films.

Epilogue: The Shared Experience of Sound

My favourite story of a trip to the cinema is second-hand. In 1966, my family was preparing to move from Liverpool to London, and my father was already working in the capital, coming home to us only at weekends. During the week, he amused himself by going to the pictures a lot. I was only nine, but already in love with the cinema, and I used to look forward to hearing reports of these films seen in the Big Smoke. I vividly recall one description. It was a film which, in the course of researching and writing this book, I realise must have been John Schlesinger's *Darling*. I'd never seen it before, but when the final scene came round, I recognised it from my dad's account, forty-four years ago. It is the scene I described at the end of Chapter 9, in which a beggar woman sings 'Santa Lucia' at Piccadilly Circus.

Now, with any picture set in a big city, there is something wonderful about going to see it in a cinema in the middle of that same big city. For example, I've always loved seeing Woody Allen films in New York. You leave the stylised depiction of Manhattan on the screen and within seconds you're outside in the genuine hustle of Bleeker Street or wherever the cinema is.

That autumn night in 1966, as my dad and his fellow patrons of the Odeon, Leicester Square, emerged from *Darling*, into the cool, acrid city air, they were at first bemused to hear 'Santa Lucia' being sung across the street. It wasn't just the song that was familiar; it was the voice too. There she was: the same beggar woman, now a movie star. She was wearing much the same clothes she'd worn on screen, and giving a live rendition of her immortal performance for the astonished filmgoers. I assume she was also doing good business.

You'll never have an experience like that if you watch all your movies at home.

Some Further Reading & Acknowledgments

As mentioned in the introduction, there is very little published writing about the uses of sound and music in film that isn't solidly academic, and much of that is solid only in the sense that it is impenetrable. Too much academic writing about film and music consists of lists and descriptions disguised by jargon, and I quickly decided that *The Sound of Pictures* should discuss actual films and not other people's theories about them.

But I would like to recommend a few volumes, and top of the list is the book-length Hitchcock/Truffaut conversation. Originally published as *Le cinéma selon Hitchcock* by François Truffaut (1966), it was translated into English two years later, called simply *Hitchcock*, and later revised. For my money, there is no better single volume about filmmaking. The book ought to be on the shelf of anyone interested in cinema, and although it is not specifically about the uses of sound or music, it has much to say on the topic.

Staying with Hitchcock, Jack Sullivan's *Hitchcock's Music* (2006) stole a little of my thunder in that he addressed point after point that I was intending to make about the director's films in the present volume. It wouldn't have been so bad had I disagreed with his conclusions, but I didn't. My resentment about this aside, I must say that Sullivan's is a brilliant book, intensely readable and refreshingly free from academic obfuscation. In the end it forced me to concentrate on the area of musical information in Hitchcock's films, and so probably did me a favour.

The other essential book, besides Truffaut's *Hitchcock*, is another series of conversations, this time squarely on the subject of sound in film, between the novelist and poet Michael Ondaatje and the editor Walter Murch. In *The Conversations* (2002), Ondaatje leads Murch on an informal but detailed discussion of his work. Of particular interest are his films with Francis Ford Coppola: *The Conversation*, *Apocalypse Now* and *The Godfather* (Parts I and II).

Other books I dipped into were Anahid Kassabian's *Hearing Film* (2001), Philip Brophy's *100 Modern Soundtracks* (2004) and K.J. Donnelly's *Beyond the Soundtrack* (2005). Brophy's is the only one aimed at the general filmgoer. I also consulted *Popular Music and Film* (ed. Ian Inglis, 2003), *Beyond the Soundtrack* (ed. Goldmark, Kramer and Leppert, 2007) and *Sound and Music in Film and Visual Media* (ed. Harper, Doughty and Eisentraut, 2009). All of them are appropriate additions to the film-studies section of a university library.

I found that by far the most useful resource in writing my book, apart from the films themselves, was the people I talked to. So I'd like to express my thanks to them, and particularly to the five directors and five composers who generously submitted themselves to my questions and came up with so many good answers. I'm also indebted to Penny Lomax and Jenny Parsonage for their careful work producing the six-part ABC radio series, *The Sound of Pictures*, which includes the interviews with Ennio Morricone, Sally Potter, Bruce Beresford, Richard Rodney Bennett and Peter Weir, and with the editor Rodney Holland.

I have a list of friends and colleagues I must thank for their suggestions of films to include and for pertinent remarks about sound and music (apologies to those I have left out): Roger Ashton-Griffiths, Angela Bennie, Martin Bresnick, Jon Burlingame, the late Tristram Cary, Maureen Cooney, Robert Davidson, Brett Dean, Paul Dean, Michael Dunn, Cesca Eaton, Yvonne Frindle, Anna Goldsworthy, Sandra Hall, Emily Heylin, Roy Howat, Mark Isaacs, Andrew Kelly, Oliver Knussen, James Ledger, Andy Lloyd-James, Claudio Marcello, Natasha Mitchell, Margaret Morgan, Ian Munro, Jessica Nicholas, Helen O'Brien, Federico Passi, Vincent Plush, Tim Pye, Robyn Ravlich, Jim Rolon, Alan Saunders, Sue Sinclair, Sue Smith, Christy Snelleman, Tim Stevens, Cathy Strickland, Robert Tims, Kim Waldock, Belinda Webster, Matthew Westwood, Tony Williams, Raff Wilson and Camille Williams at the video shop.

Finally, my wife, Anni Heino, watched most of these films with me and was, as always, my first and ideal reader. This book is all the better for her suggestions.

Films Mentioned in This Book

12 Angry Men (Sidney Lumet, 1957)
1900 (*Novecento*) (Bernardo Bertolucci, 1976)
2001: a Space Odyssey (Stanley Kubrick, 1968)
3:10 to Yuma (Delmer Daves, 1957)
39 Steps, The (Alfred Hitchcock, 1935)
42nd Street (Lloyd Bacon, 1933)
49th Parallel (Michael Powell & Emeric Pressburger, 1941)
55 Days at Peking (Nicholas Ray, 1963)
77 Sunset Strip (TV series, 1958–64)
8½ (Federico Fellini, 1963)
9 Songs (Michael Winterbottom, 2004)

Across the Universe (Julie Taymor, 2007)
Adventures of Robin Hood, The (Michael Curtiz, 1938)
Advise & Consent (Otto Preminger, 1962)
Ai no corrida (*In the Realm of the Senses*) (Nagisa Oshima, 1976)
Alexander Nevsky (Sergei Eisenstein, 1938)
Amadeus (Milos Forman, 1984)
Amarcord (Federico Fellini, 1973)
American Beauty (Sam Mendes, 1999)
American Graffiti (George Lucas, 1973)
Anatomy of a Murder (Otto Preminger, 1959)
And Starring Pancho Villa As Himself (TV film, Bruce Beresford, 2003)
And Your Mother Too (*Y tu mamá también*) (Alfonso Cuarón, 2001)
Angst des Tormanns beim Elfmeter, Die (*The Goalkeeper's Fear of the Penalty*) (Wim Wenders, 1972)
Another Woman (Woody Allen, 1988)
Apocalypse Now (Francis Ford Coppola, 1979)
Ascenseur pour l'échafaud (*Lift to the Scaffold*) (Louis Malle, 1958)
At the Circus (Edward Buzzell, 1939)
¡Átame! (*Tie Me Up! Tie Me Down!*) (Pedro Almodóvar, 1990)
Atonement (Joe Wright, 2007)
Away from Her (Sarah Polley, 2006)

Babes in Arms (Busby Berkeley, 1939)
Baby of Mâcon, The (Peter Greenaway, 1993)
Bad Boy Bubby (Rolf de Heer, 1993)
Bad Seed, The (Mervyn LeRoy, 1956)
Badlands (Terrence Malick, 1973)
Barry Lyndon (Stanley Kubrick, 1975)
Belly of an Architecht, The (Peter Greenaway, 1987)
Ben-Hur (William Wyler, 1959)
Bicycle Thieves (*Ladri di biciclette*) (Vittorio de Sica, 1948)
Big Chill, The (Lawrence Kasdan, 1983)
Big Country, The (William Wyler, 1958)
Big Easy, The (Jim McBride, 1986)
Billy Budd (Peter Ustinov, 1962)
Billy Liar (John Schlesinger, 1963)
Birds, The (Alfred Hitchcock, 1963)
Bis ans Ende der Welt (*Until the End of the World*) (Wim Wenders, 1991)
Black Narcissus (Michael Powell & Emeric Pressburger, 1947)
Black Robe (Bruce Beresford, 1991)
Blackboard Jungle, The (Richard Brooks, 1955)
Blackmail (Alfred Hitchcock, 1929)
Blair Witch Project, The (Daniel Myrick & Eduardo Sánchez, 1999)
Blood Simple (Joel & Ethan Coen, 1984)
Blow-Up (Michelangelo Antonioni, 1966)
Blue Velvet (David Lynch, 1986)
Boat That Rocked, The (Richard Curtis, 2009)
Body Snatcher, The (Robert Wise, 1945)
Bodyguard, The (Mick Jackson, 1992)
Boogie Nights (Paul Thomas Anderson, 1997)
Bourne Ultimatum, The (Paul Greengrass, 2007)
Brassed Off (Mark Herman, 1996)
Breaker Morant (Bruce Beresford, 1980)
Breakfast at Tiffany's (Blake Edwards, 1961)
Bride of Frankenstein (James Whale, 1935)
Brief Encounter (David Lean, 1945)
Britannia Hospital (Lindsay Anderson, 1982)
Broadcast News (James L. Brooks, 1987)
Broken Arrow (Delmer Daves, 1950)
Broken Flowers (Jim Jarmusch, 2005)
Buena Vista Social Club (Wim Wenders, 1999)
Bullitt (Peter Yates, 1968)

Films Mentioned in This Book

Bunny Lake Is Missing (Otto Preminger, 1965)
Buono, il brutto, il cattivo, Il (*The Good, the Bad and the Ugly*) (Sergio Leone, 1966)
Butch Cassidy and the Sundance Kid (George Roy Hill, 1969)

Ça commence aujourd'hui (*It All Starts Today*) (Bertrand Tavernier, 1999)
Californication (TV series, 2007–)
Call Northside 777 (Henry Hathaway, 1948)
Candy (Neil Armfield, 2006)
Canterbury Tale, A (Michael Powell & Emeric Pressburger, 1944)
Cape Fear (J. Lee Thompson, 1962)
Carrie (Brian De Palma, 1976)
Cars That Ate Paris, The (Peter Weir, 1974)
Casablanca (Michael Curtiz, 1942)
Casino Royale (Val Guest et al. 1967)
Casino Royale (Martin Campbell, 2006)
Cassandra's Dream (Woody Allen, 2007)
Castle, The (Rob Sitch, 1997)
Cat People (Jacques Tourneur, 1942)
Catch Me If You Can (Steven Spielberg, 2002)
Catch Us If You Can (John Boorman, 1965)
Celebrity (Woody Allen, 1998)
C'era una volta il West (*Once Upon a Time in the West*) (Sergio Leone, 1968)
Chariots of Fire (Hugh Hudson, 1981)
Children of Men (Alfonso Cuarón, 2006)
Cincinnati Kid, The (Norman Jewison, 1965)
Cinema Paradiso (*Nuovo cinema Paradiso*) (Giuseppe Tornatore, 1988)
Citizen Kane (Orson Welles, 1941)
Clockwork Orange, A (Stanley Kubrick, 1971)
Close Encounters of the Third Kind (Steven Spielberg, 1977)
Collateral (Michael Mann, 2004)
Coma (Michael Crichton, 1978)
Comfort and Joy (Bill Forsyth, 1984)
Conformist, The (*Il conformista*) (Bernardo Bertolucci, 1970)
Contract, The (Bruce Beresford, 2006)
Conversation, The (Francis Ford Coppola, 1974)
Cook, the Thief, His Wife & Her Lover, The (Peter Greenaway, 1989)
Cool Hand Luke (Stuart Rosenberg, 1967)
Cries and Whispers (*Viskningar och rop*) (Ingmar Bergman, 1972)
Crimes and Misdemeanors (Woody Allen, 1989)

Crimes of the Heart (Bruce Beresford, 1986)
Cross of Iron (Sam Peckinpah, 1977)
Curse of the Cat People, The (Gunther von Fritsch & Robert Wise, 1944)

Dangerous Liaisons (Stephen Frears, 1988)
Darjeeling Limited, The (Wes Anderson, 2007)
Darling (John Schlesinger, 1965)
Day for Night (*La nuit américaine*) (François Truffaut, 1973)
Day the Earth Stood Still, The (Robert Wise, 1951)
Days of Heaven (Terrence Malick, 1978)
Dead Poets Society (Peter Weir, 1989)
Dead Ringers (David Cronenburg, 1988)
Death in Venice (*Morte a Venezia*) (Luchino Visconti, 1971)
Deer Hunter, The (Michael Cimino, 1978)
Deliverance (John Boorman, 1972)
Departed, The (Martin Scorsese, 2006)
Devils, The (Ken Russell, 1971)
Die Hard (John McTiernan, 1988)
Dirty Harry (Don Siegel, 1971)
Distant Voices, Still Lives (Terence Davies, 1988)
Doctor Zhivago (David Lean, 1965)
Doll's House, A (Joseph Losey, 1973)
Dom za vesanje (*Time of the Gypsies*) (Emir Kusturica, 1988)
Don's Party (Bruce Beresford, 1976)
Don't Look Now (Nicolas Roeg, 1973)
Double Indemnity (Billy Wilder, 1944)
Double Jeopardy (Bruce Beresford, 1999)
Dr No (Terence Young, 1962)
Dr Strangelove or: How I Learned to Stop Worrying and Love the Bomb (Stanley Kubrick, 1964)
Draughtsman's Contract, The (Peter Greenaway, 1982)
Driving Miss Daisy (Bruce Beresford, 1989)
Du rififi chez les hommes (*Rififi*) (Jules Dassin, 1955)

East of Eden (Elia Kazan, 1955)
Easy Rider (Dennis Hopper, 1969)
Edge of Darkness (Martin Campbell, 2010)
Elephant God, The (*Joi Baba Felunath*) (Satyajit Ray, 1979)
Enchanted April (Mike Newell, 1992)
End of Violence, The (Wim Wenders, 1997)

Films Mentioned in This Book

Enfant sauvage, L' (*The Wild Child*) (François Truffaut, 1970)
Enfants du paradis, Les (Marcel Carné, 1945)
Equus (Sidney Lumet, 1977)
E.T.: the Extra-Terrestrial (Steven Spielberg, 1982)
Everyone Says I Love You (Woody Allen, 1996)
Exorcist, The (William Friedkin, 1973)
Eyes Wide Shut (Stanley Kubrick, 1999)

Fahrenheit 451 (François Truffaut, 1966)
Fall of the Roman Empire, The (Anthony Mann, 1964)
Family Plot (Alfred Hitchcock, 1976)
Fanny and Alexander (*Fanny och Alexander*) (Ingmar Bergman, 1982)
Far from Heaven (Todd Haynes, 2002)
Far from the Madding Crowd (John Schlesinger, 1967)
Faraway, So Close! (*Im weiter Ferne, so nah!*) (Wim Wenders, 1993)
Fearless (Peter Weir, 1993)
Fistful of Dollars, A (*Per un pugno di dollari*) (Sergio Leone, 1964)
Fistful of Dynamite, A (*Giù la testa*) (Sergio Leone, 1971)
Five Easy Pieces (Bob Rafelson, 1970)
Fly, The (David Cronenberg, 1986)
For a Few Dollars More (*Per qualche dollaro in più*) (Sergio Leone, 1965)
Force of Evil (Abraham Polonsky, 1948)
Foreign Correspondent (Alfred Hitchcock, 1940)
Four Musketeers, The (Richard Lester, 1974)
Four Weddings and a Funeral (Mike Newell, 1994)
From Russia with Love (Terence Young, 1963)
Frost/Nixon (Ron Howard, 2008)

Gallipoli (Peter Weir, 1981)
Genevieve (Henry Cornelius, 1953)
Getting of Wisdom, The (Bruce Beresford, 1978)
Ghost and Mrs Muir, The (Joseph L. Mankiewicz, 1947)
Gilda (Charles Vidor, 1946)
Giù la testa (*A Fistful of Dynamite*) (Sergio Leone, 1971)
Gladiator (Ridley Scott, 2000)
Glenn Miller Story, The (Anthony Mann, 1954)
Go-Between, The (Joseph Losey, 1970)
Goalkeeper's Fear of the Penalty, The (*Die Angst des Tormanns beim Elfmeter*) (Wim Wenders, 1972)
Godfather, The (Francis Ford Coppola, 1972)

Godfather: Part II, The (Francis Ford Coppola, 1974)
Gone with the Wind (Victor Fleming, 1939)
Good Night, and Good Luck (George Clooney, 2005)
Good, the Bad and the Ugly, The (*Il buono, il brutto, il cattivo*) (Sergio Leone, 1966)
Goodfellas (Martin Scorsese, 1990)
Gospel According to St Matthew, The (*Il Vangelo secondo Matteo*) (Pier Paolo Pasolini, 1964)
Graduate, The (Mike Nichols, 1967)
Great Dictator, The (Charles Chaplin, 1940)
Great Escape, The (John Sturges, 1963)
Gunfight at the O.K. Corral (John Sturges, 1957)

Hannah and Her Sisters (Woody Allen, 1986)
Hannibal (Ridley Scott, 2001)
Hard Day's Night, A (Richard Lester, 1964)
Hawaiian Eye (TV series, 1959–63)
Help! (Richard Lester, 1965)
Here We Go Round the Mulberry Bush (Clive Donner, 1968)
High Fidelity (Stephen Frears, 2000)
High Noon (Fred Zinnemann, 1952)
Hilary and Jackie (Arnand Tucker, 1998)
Hill, The (Sidney Lumet, 1965)
Holly and the Ivy, The (George More O'Ferrall, 1952)
Horloger de Saint-Paul, L' (*The Watchmaker of St Paul*) (Bertrand Tavernier, 1974)
Hotel Chevalier (Wes Anderson, 2007)
Husbands and Wives (Woody Allen, 1992)

if… (Lindsay Anderson, 1968)
Im weiter Ferne, so nah! (*Faraway, So Close!*) (Wim Wenders, 1993)
In Bruges (Martin McDonagh, 2008)
In the Realm of the Senses (*Ai no corrida*) (Nagisa Oshima, 1976)
Inglourious Basterds (Quentin Tarantino, 2009)
Inspector Morse (TV series, 1987–2000)
It All Starts Today (*Ça commence aujourd'hui*) (Bertrand Tavernier, 1999)
It's a Wonderful Life (Frank Capra, 1946)

Jaws (Steven Spielberg, 1975)
Joi Baba Felunath (*The Elephant God*) (Satyajit Ray, 1979)
Jules et Jim (François Truffaut, 1962)

Films Mentioned in This Book

Kaagaz Ke Phool (*Paper Flowers*) (Guru Dutt, 1959)
Kill Bill: Vol. 1 (Quentin Tarantino, 2003)
King Kong (Merian C. Cooper, 1933)
Knight's Tale, A (Brian Helgeland, 2001)

Ladri di biciclette (*Bicycle Thieves*) (Vittorio de Sica, 1948)
Lady Caroline Lamb (Robert Bolt, 1972)
Lady Chatterley (Pascale Ferran, 2006)
Lady Vanishes, The (Alfred Hitchcock, 1938)
Last Days of Disco, The (Whit Stillman, 1998)
Last Wave, The (Peter Weir, 1977)
Lawrence of Arabia (David Lean, 1962)
Leatherheads (George Clooney, 2008)
Leben der Anderen, Das (*The Lives of Others*) (Florian Henckel von Donnersmarck, 2006)
Lifeboat (Alfred Hitchcock, 1944)
Lift to the Scaffold (*Ascenseur pour l'échafaud*) (Louis Malle, 1958)
Lisbon Story (Wim Wenders, 1994)
Lives of Others, The (*Das Leben der Anderen*) (Florian Henckel von Donnersmarck, 2006)
Lodger, The (Alfred Hitchcock, 1927)
Lolita (Adrian Lyne, 1997)
Lord of the Rings: The Fellowship of the Ring, The (Peter Jackson, 2001)
Lord of the Rings: The Return of the King, The (Peter Jackson, 2003)
Lord of the Rings: The Two Towers, The (Peter Jackson, 2002)
Lost Horizon (Frank Capra, 1937)
Lost Weekend, The (Billy Wilder, 1945)
Love Actually (Richard Curtis, 2003)

M (Fritz Lang, 1931)
M. Butterfly (David Cronenberg, 1993)
M is for Man, Music, Mozart (TV film, Peter Greenaway, 1991)
Magnificent Ambersons, The (Orson Welles, 1942)
Magnolia (Paul Thomas Anderson, 1999)
Mamma Mia! (Phyllida Lloyd, 2008)
Man from Laramie, The (Anthony Mann, 1955)
Man Who Cried, The (Sally Potter, 2000)
Man Who Knew Too Much, The (Alfred Hitchcock, 1934)
Man Who Knew Too Much, The (Alfred Hitchcock, 1956)
Man Who Wasn't There, The (Joel & Ethan Coen, 2001)

Marie Antoinette (Sofia Coppola, 2006)
Master and Commander: the Far Side of the World (Peter Weir, 2003)
Match Factory Girl, The (*Tulitikkutehtaan tyttö*) (Aki Kaurismäki, 1990)
Match Point (Woody Allen, 2005)
Mean Streets (Martin Scorsese, 1973)
Melinda and Melinda (Woody Allen, 2004)
Midnight Cowboy (John Schlesinger, 1969)
Midsummer Night's Sex Comedy, A (Woody Allen, 1982)
Mission, The (Roland Joffé, 1986)
Mission: Impossible (TV series, 1966–73)
Mister Johnson (Bruce Beresford, 1990)
Moonraker (Lewis Gilbert, 1979)
Moonstruck (Norman Jewison, 1987)
Morte a Venezia (*Death in Venice*) (Luchino Visconti, 1971)
Mosquito Coast, The (Peter Weir, 1986)
Mouchette (Robert Bresson, 1967)
Mr Smith Goes to Washington (Frank Capra, 1939)
Mrs Doubtfire (Chris Columbus, 1993)
Mùi du du xanh (*The Scent of Green Papaya*) (Tran Anh Hung, 1993)
Murder on the Orient Express (Sidney Lumet, 1974)
Musa: the Warrior (Kim Sung-Su, 2001)

Naked Kiss, The (Samuel Fuller, 1964)
Nicholas and Alexandra (Franklin J. Schaffner, 1971)
Night of the Hunter, The (Charles Laughton, 1955)
No Country for Old Men (Joel & Ethan Coen, 2007)
Norma Rae (Martin Ritt, 1979)
North by Northwest (Alfred Hitchcock, 1959)
North West Frontier (J. Lee Thompson, 1959)
Notes on a Scandal (Richard Eyre, 2006)
Novecento (*1900*) (Bernardo Bertolucci, 1976)
Nuit américaine, La (*Day for Night*) (François Truffaut, 1973)
Number 13 (Alfred Hitchcock, 1922)
Nuovo cinema Paradiso (*Cinema Paradiso*) (Giuseppe Tornatore, 1988)

O Lucky Man! (Lindsay Anderson, 1973)
On Her Majesty's Secret Service (Peter R. Hunt, 1969)
On the Waterfront (Elia Kazan, 1954)
Once (Jim Carney, 2006)
Once Upon a Time in the West (*C'era una volta il West*) (Sergio Leone, 1968)

Films Mentioned in This Book

Orlando (Sally Potter, 1992)
Othello (Stuart Burge, 1965)
Outrage (Ida Lupino, 1951)

Paper Flowers (*Kaagaz Ke Phool*) (Guru Dutt, 1959)
Paradine Case, The (Alfred Hitchcock, 1947)
Paradise Road (Bruce Beresford, 1997)
Paranormal Activity (Oren Peli, 2007)
Paris, Texas (Wim Wenders, 1984)
Pather Panchali (Satyajit Ray, 1955)
Per un pugno di dollari (*A Fistful of Dollars*) (Sergio Leone, 1964)
Peyton Place (Mark Robson, 1957)
Peyton Place (TV series, 1964–69)
Pianist, The (Roman Polanski, 2002)
Piano, The (Jane Campion, 1993)
Pickpocket (Robert Bresson, 1959)
Pickup on South Street (Samuel Fuller, 1953)
Picnic at Hanging Rock (Peter Weir, 1975)
Pierrot le fou (Jean-Luc Godard, 1965)
Private Life of Don Juan, The (Alexander Korda, 1934)
Private Lives of Elizabeth and Essex, The (Michael Curtiz, 1939)
Prospero's Books (Peter Greenaway, 1991)
Psycho (Alfred Hitchcock, 1960)
Public Enemy, The (William A. Wellman, 1931)
Purple Rose of Cairo, The (Woody Allen, 1985)

Radio Days (Woody Allen, 1987)
Raging Bull (Martin Scorsese, 1980)
Ran (Akira Kurosawa, 1985)
Rashomon (Akira Kurosawa, 1950)
Rawhide (TV series, 1959–65)
Rear Window (Alfred Hitchcock, 1954)
Rebecca (Alfred Hitchcock, 1940)
Red House, The (Delmer Daves, 1947)
Red River (Howard Hawks, 1948)
Red Road (Andrea Arnold, 2006)
Repulsion (Roman Polanski, 1965)
Rififi (*Du rififi chez les hommes*) (Jules Dassin, 1955)
Ripley's Game (Liliana Cavani, 2002)
Road to Perdition, The (Sam Mendes, 2002)

Rollercoaster (James Goldstone, 1977)
Rome, Open City (Roberto Rossellini, 1945)
Rope (Alfred Hitchcock, 1948)
Rosemary's Baby (Roman Polanski, 1968)
Royal Tenenbaums, The (Wes Anderson, 2001)
Rushmore (Wes Anderson, 1998)

Saboteur (Alfred Hitchcock, 1942)
Salò o le 120 giornate di Sodoma (*Salò or the 120 Days of Sodom*) (Pier Paolo Pasolini, 1975)
Samson and Delilah (Warwick Thornton, 2009)
Sanders of the River (Zoltán Korda, 1935)
Savages, The (Tamara Jenkins, 2007)
Scarface (Howard Hawks, 1932)
Scent of Green Papaya, The (*Mùi du du xanh*) (Tran Anh Hung, 1993)
Schindler's List (Steven Spielberg, 1993)
Scoop (Woody Allen, 2006)
Screamers (Christian Duguay, 1995)
Se7en (David Fincher, 1995)
Sea Hawk, The (Michael Curtiz, 1940)
Seven Days in May (John Frankenheimer, 1964)
Seven Samurai (*Shichinin no samurai*) (Akira Kurosawa, 1954)
Seven Year Itch, The (Billy Wilder, 1955)
Seventh Victim, The (Mark Robson, 1943)
Shadow of a Doubt (Alfred Hitchcock, 1943)
Shadows (John Cassavetes, 1959)
Shadows and Fog (Woody Allen, 1991)
Shichinin no samurai (*Seven Samurai*) (Akira Kurosawa, 1954)
Shine (Scott Hicks, 1996)
Shining, The (Stanley Kubrick, 1980)
Shoot the Pianist (*Tirez sur le pianiste*) (François Truffaut, 1960)
Short Cuts (Robert Altman, 1993)
Shortbus (John Cameron Mitchell, 2006)
Silence of the Lambs, The (Jonathan Demme, 1991)
Silverado (Lawrence Kasdan, 1985)
Singin' in the Rain (Stanley Donen & Gene Kelly, 1952)
Six Feet Under (TV series 2001–05)
Sliding Doors (Peter Howitt, 1998)
Sling Blade (Billy Bob Thornton, 1996)
Soloist, The (Joe Wright, 2009)

Films Mentioned in This Book

Some Like It Hot (Billy Wilder, 1959)
Sopranos, The (TV series, 1999–2007)
Soul of a Man, The (Wim Wenders, 2003)
Sound Barrier, The (David Lean, 1952)
Spartacus (Stanley Kubrick, 1960)
Spellbound (Alfred Hitchcock, 1945)
Stage Fright (Alfred Hitchcock, 1950)
Star Wars (a.k.a. *Star Wars: Episode IV – A New Hope*) (George Lucas, 1977)
State of Play (Kevin Macdonald, 2009)
Stepford Wives, The (Bryan Forbes, 1975)
Sting, The (George Roy Hill, 1973)
Strange Interlude (TV film, Herbert Wise, 1988)
Strangers on a Train (Alfred Hitchcock, 1951)
Streetcar Named Desire, A (Elia Kazan, 1951)
Sunset Blvd (Billy Wilder, 1950)
Suspicion (Alfred Hitchcock, 1941)
Suspiria (Dario Argento, 1977)
Sweet and Lowdown (Woody Allen, 1999)
Symphony of Sorrowful Songs, The (Tony Palmer, 1993)

Take the Money and Run (Woody Allen, 1969)
Tale of Sweeney Todd, The (TV film, John Schlesinger, 1997)
Tango (Carlos Saura, 1998)
Tango Lesson, The (Sally Potter, 1997)
Taxi Driver (Martin Scorsese, 1976)
Tender Mercies (Bruce Beresford, 1983)
Third Man, The (Carol Reed, 1949)
Thirty-two Short Films About Glenn Gould (François Girard, 1993)
thirtysomething (TV series, 1987–91)
Thomas Crown Affair, The (Norman Jewison, 1968)
Three Colours: Blue (*Trois couleurs: Bleu*) (Krzysztof Kieslowski, 1993)
Tie Me Up! Tie Me Down! (*¡Átame!*) (Pedro Almodóvar, 1990)
Time of the Gypsies (*Dom za vesanje*) (Emir Kusturica, 1988)
Tirez sur le pianiste (*Shoot the Pianist*) (François Truffaut, 1960)
Titanic (James Cameron, 1997)
To Have and Have Not (Howard Hawks, 1944)
To Kill a Mockingbird (Robert Mulligan, 1962)
Torn Curtain (Alfred Hitchcock, 1966)
Touch of Class, A (Melvin Frank, 1973)
Touch of Evil (Orson Welles, 1958)

Tragedy of Othello the Moor of Venice, The (Orson Welles, 1952)
Trilogy: the Weeping Meadow (*Trilogia: To livadi pou dakryzei*) (Theodoros Angelopoulos, 2004)
Trois couleurs: Bleu (*Three Colours: Blue*) (Krzysztof Kieslowski, 1993)
Truly Madly Deeply (Anthony Minghella, 1990)
Truman Show, The (Peter Weir, 1998)
Tulitikkutehtaan tyttö (*The Match Factory Girl*) (Aki Kaurismäki, 1990)
Tunes of Glory (Ronald Neame, 1960)
Twisted Nerve (Roy Boulting, 1968)
Two Hands (Gregor Jordan, 1999)
Until the End of the World (*Bis ans Ende der Welt*) (Wim Wenders, 1991)

Vangelo secondo Matteo, Il (*The Gospel According to St Matthew*) (Pier Paolo Pasolini, 1964)
Vertigo (Alfred Hitchcock, 1958)
Vicar of Dibley (TV series, 1994–2007)
Viskningar och rop (*Cries and Whispers*) (Ingmar Bergman, 1972)
Voyage of the Damned (Stuart Rosenberg, 1976)

Watchmaker of St Paul, The (*L'horloger de Saint-Paul*) (Bertrand Tavernier, 1974)
Whatever Works (Woody Allen, 2009)
Whisky Galore! (Alexander Mackendrick, 1949)
Witchfinder General (Michael Reeves, 1968)
Withnail and I (Bruce Robinson, 1987)
Witness (Peter Weir, 1985)
Wiz, The (Sidney Lumet, 1978)
Wrong Man, The (Alfred Hitchcock, 1956)

Y tu mamá también (*And Your Mother Too*) (Alfonso Cuarón, 2001)
Year of Living Dangerously, The (Peter Weir, 1982)
Yes (Sally Potter, 2004)
Young and Innocent (Alfred Hitchcock, 1937)
Young Victoria, The (Jean-Marc Vallée, 2009)

Zelig (Woody Allen, 1983)

Index

Headings in italic followed by a name or names in italic refer to the titles of books or musical works. All other headings in italic refer to films unless otherwise indicated. Films which are identified by a title in English and a foreign language title are entered twice.

3:10 to Yuma 108–9, 173
8½ 137
9 Songs 135–6, 142
12 Angry Men 194
39 Steps, The 156–7, 175
42nd Street 141
49th Parallel 7–8
55 Days at Peking 16
77 Sunset Strip (TV program) 16
1900 (*Novecento*) 30
2001: A Space Odyssey 99, 100, 212, 263

Abba 142, 143
accents 172–3
Across the Universe 142–3
Adagio (Albinoni) 265
Adler, Larry 2
Adorno, Theodor W.
    Composing for the Films 5, 21
        need for film music to remain pure 11–13
Adventures of Robin Hood, The 15
Advise and Consent 173–4
Ai no corrida (*In the Realm of the Senses*) 3
'Ain't Too Proud to Beg' (The Temptations) 128
Albinoni, Tomaso, *Adagio* 265
Alexander Nevsky 253
    Prokofiev's music 12, 96, 98

'All Along the Watchtower' (Jimi Hendrix) 123–4
'All You Need Is Love' (The Beatles) 122
Allen, Woody 20–1, 229
    Dick Hyman's work with 55–9, 61–2
    Radio Days 113–14
    vocal personality 173
Almodóvar, Pedro
    music for *Tie Me Up! Tie Me Down!* 31–2
Also sprach Zarathustra (Strauss) 99, 263, 265
Amadeus 24
Amarcord 129
American Beauty 17
American Graffiti 112
An der schönen blauen Donau see *Blue Danube* waltz
Anatomy of a Murder 132
And Starring Pancho Villa As Himself 211
And Your Mother Too (*Y tu mamá también*) 169
Anderson, Lindsay 136–7
Anderson, Wes 120–1
Andress, Ursula 18–19
Andriessen, Louis 245, 255, 257–8
Angst des Tormanns beim Elfmeter, Die (*The Goalkeeper's Fear of the Penalty*) 240
Another Woman 20
Ant, Adam 125

Antonioni, Michelangelo 134–5
Apocalypse Now 3
'Arabesque No. 1' (Debussy) 149
Armfield, Neil 95
Ascenseur pour l'échafaud (*Lift to the Scaffold*) 13–14, 41, 71
Astatke, Mulatu 124
At the Circus 176
¡Átame! (*Tie Me Up! Tie Me Down!*) 31–2
Atonement 195–6
Atys (Lully) 94
Ave Verum Corpus (Mozart) 95
Away from Her 91
Aznavour, Charles 22

Babes in Arms 141
Baby of Mâcon, The 257
Bach, Johann Sebastian
   English Suite No. 2 in A minor, Prelude 87
   in *Fanny and Alexandra* 99–100
   Goldberg variations 89
   in *The Gospel According to St Matthew* 97–8
   Partita No. 2 in C minor 93
   Suite No. 5 in C minor for solo cello, Sarabande 177
   Well Tempered Clavier 91, 93
Bad Boy Bubby 138–9
Bad Seed, The 48
Badlands 21–2
'Ballad of High Noon' (Tex Ritter) 106–8
Ballade No. 1 in G minor (Chopin) 88
Barricades mystérieuses, Les (Couperin) 125
Barry Lyndon 4, 13, 99, 277
Bartók, Bela 67
   Music for Strings, Percussion and Celesta 99
'Be My Baby' (The Ronettes) 114–15
Beatles, The 135, 142
Beaver, Jack 150

Beethoven, Ludwig von
   Piano Concerto No. 5 in E flat (Emperor) 265–6
   String Quartet No. 14 in C sharp minor 89, 90
   Symphony No. 9 in D minor (*Choral*) 100, 101
   'Ode to Joy' 9–10
Belly of an Architect, The 245
Ben Hur 16
Benjamin, Arthur, *Storm Clouds* 158–9
Bennett, Richard Rodney 41–54
Bennett, Tony 115
Beresford, Bruce 201–17
Berg, Alban 73
   Wozzek 70
Bergman, Ingmar 20, 99–100, 185
Bicycle Thieves (*Ladri di biciclette*) 96
Big Chill, The 116–19, 128–9
Big Country, The 180–1
   music played in the concert hall 1–2
Big Easy, The 13
Bill Haley and the Comets 111–12
Billy Budd 168
Billy Budd (Melville) 167–8
Billy Liar 44
Birds, The 3, 149, 178
Bis and Ende der Welt (*Until the End of the World*) 240
Bizet, Georges, *The Pearl Fishers* 221, 232
Black Narcissus 14, 195
Black Robe 213, 216–17
Blackboard Jungle, The 111–12
Blackmail 147
Blair (pop artist) 10
Blair Witch Project, The 189
Bloch, Thomas 236
Blood Simple 183
Blow-Up 134–5
Blue Danube waltz (Strauss) 99, 100
Blue Velvet 276
Blues, The 243
Boat That Rocked, The 123, 142–3

Index

Body Snatcher, The 130, 163
Bodyguard, The 143–4
Bohème, La (Puccini) 59, 60
Bono 134
Boogie Nights 113
'Born to Be Wild' (Steppenwolf) 111
'Both Sides Now' (Joni Mitchell) 122
Bourne Ultimatum, The 201–2, 210
Bow Wow Wow (band) 125
Brando, Marlon 173
Brassed Off 2
Breaker Morant 201, 202–3
Breakfast at Tiffany's 110
Bregovich, Goran 245
Bresson, Robert 94–6
Bride of Frankenstein 16
Brief Encounter 101–4, 129–30
Britannia Hospital 136
Britten, Benjamin, *Hymn to the Virgin, A* 113
Broadcast News 128
Broken Arrow 14
Broken Flowers 124
Broughton, Bruce 17–18
Buena Vista Social Club 232, 237, 241–2
Bullitt 66
Bunny Lake Is Missing 135
Buono, il brutto, il cattivo, Il (*The Good, the Bad and the Ugly*) 29, 37, 38, 230
Butch Cassidy and the Sundance Kid 109–10

Ça commence aujourd'hui (*It All Starts Today*) 132, 169
Cabrel, Francis 128
Cage, John 245
Californication (TV series) 119
Call Northside 777 193–4
candles, development of 249
Candy 95
'Can't Take My Eyes Off You' (Frankie Vallie) 128
Canterbury Tale, A 22

Cape Fear 178
Carmichael, Hoagy 132–3
Carnival of the Animals (Saint-Saëns) 33
'Carnival of Venice' 151
'Caro mio bene' (Giordani) 130
Carrie 192–3
Cars That Ate Paris, The 261, 275, 277, 277–8
cartoons 72
Casablanca 16, 255
Casino Royale (1967) 18
  'Look of Love, The' (Dusty Springfield) 110
Casino Royale (2006) 18, 280
Cassandra's Dream 21
Castle, The 211–12
Cat People 130, 190
Catch Me If You Can 17
Catch Us If You Can 135
Cave, Nick 242
Celebrity 173
Cellier, Marcel 261
C'era una volta il West (*Once Upon a Time in the West*) 38
Chaplin, Charlie 64
Chariots of Fire 204
Chase, David 105
'Chi mi frena' (Donizetti, *Lucia di Lammermoor*) 155
Children of Men 114
Children of Paradise (*Les enfants du paradis*) 196
Chopin, Frédéric 87–8, 91, 223–4
  Ballade No. 1 in G minor 88
  Grand Polonaise Brillante 88
Choral Symphony (Beethoven) *see* Beethoven, Ludwig von, Symphony No. 9
Cincinnati Kid, The 66
Cinema Paradiso (Nuovo cinema Paradiso) 29–30
cinemagoing 251–2
Citizen Kane 19, 73, 178

classical music 87–104
Clément, René 73
clichés 12–13, 17–19
Clockwork Orange, A 100–1
Close Encounters of the Third Kind 3, 63
    musical MacGuffin 164–6
Coen, Ethan J. 89–90
Coen, Joel D. 89–90
Cohen, Leonard 123
Collateral 196
Coma 182–3
Comfort and Joy 13
Composing for the Films (Adorno and Eisler) 5, 21
    need for film music to remain pure 11–13
Concert champêtre (Poulenc) 45
'Concrete and Clay' (Unit 4 Plus 2) 120
Conformist, The 212
Contract, The 207, 215
Conversation, The 187, 188–9
'Conversation on a Barstool' (Annie Ross) 134
Cooder, Ry 232, 238–9
    Paris, Texas 240–1
Cook, the Thief, His Wife & Her Lover, The 245, 246, 256–7
Cool Hand Luke 73
Coppola, Sofia 124–5
Corbeil, Normand 215
Corbucci, Sergio 39
Couperin, François, *Barricades mystérieuses, Les* 125
Coward, Noël 102
Cries and Whispers (Viskningar och rop) 176–7
Crimes and Misdemeanors 20
Crimes of the Heart 213
Cronenberg, David 80, 81
    The Fly 83
Cross of Iron 4
'Cuddle Up a Little Closer' (Hoschna & Harbach) 61–2

culturally specific music 13
Curse of the Cat People 130
Curtis, Richard 121–3

Dallwitz, Burkhard 268–9
Dangerous Liaisons 13
Daniels, Melanie 149
D'Arienzo, Juan 236
Darjeeling Limited 120
'Dark Was the Night, Cold Was the Ground' (Blind Willie Johnson) 98, 242
Darling 144–5
    'Santa Lucia' 145, 281
    tone of voice 172
    voice over 171
Davies, Peter Maxwell, *The Devils* 13
Davies, Terence, *Distant Voices, Still Lives* 113–14
Davis, Miles 71
    Ascenseur pour l'échafaud 13–14, 41
Day, Doris 149
Day for Night (*La nuit américaine*) 137
Day the Earth Stood Still, The 165, 178
Days of Heaven 33, 171
Dead Poets Society 266, 276
Dead Ringers 83
Death in Venice (*Morte a Venezia*) 23–4, 103
Debussy, Claude 68, 73
    'Arabesque No. 1' 149
    Pelléas et Mélisande 70
Deer Hunter, The 128
Delerue, Georges 22, 212–13
Delius, Frederick, *Summer Night on the River* 89
Deliverance 3
'Departed Tango, The' (Howard Shore) 79
Departed, The 79, 110–11
Deutsch, Adolph 131
Devils, The 13
Dido (pop artist) 10

Index

Die Hard 9–10, 13
Dietrich, Marlene 149
Dion, Celine 111
Dirty Harry 66, 73–4
Distant Voices, Still Lives 113–14
'Do Not Forsake Me' (Tex Ritter) 106–8
Doctor Zhivago
    epic score 1
    'Lara's Theme' (Maurice Jarre) 262
'Dodo, l'enfant do' 130, 131
Dogme 95 8, 187, 229
    naturalism 233–5
    Sally Potter's views 233–5
    Wim Wenders's views 239–40
Doll's House, A 50
Domza vesanje (*Time of the Gypsies*) 228–9
Donaldson, Walter 62
Donizetti, Gaetano, *Lucia di Lammermoor*, 'Chi mi frena' 155
Don's Party 201
Don't Look Now 3–4, 175–6
Double Indemnity 16
    voice over 171–2
Double Jeopardy 209, 215–16
'Down Among the Sheltering Palms' (Abe Olman) 131
Dr No 18, 19
Dr Strangelove 99
Draughtsman's Contract, The 244
Dreyfus, George 203–4
Driving Miss Daisy 205–6
Du rififi chez les hommes (*Rififi*) 187
Duvall, Robert 203
DVDs 279
Dvořák, Antonin, *Rusalka* 'Song to the Moon' 207–9

'E lucevan le stelle', *Tosca* (Puccini) 221–2
East of Eden 42
Eastwood, Clint 243
Easy Rider 110, 111
Ecuatorial (Varèse) 20
Edge of Darkness 79
'Edition spéciale, L'' (Francis Cabrel) 128
Edwards, Ross 214
Eisenstein, Sergei 232–3, 255
    Alexander Nevsky 253
Eisler, Hanns
    Composing for the Films 5, 21
    need for film music to remain pure 11–13
electronics 82
'Elenore' (The Turtles) 123
Elephant God (*Joi Baba Felunath*) 121
Ellington, Duke 132
Enchanted April 51
End of Violence, The 238–9
Endelman, Stephen 211
Enfant sauvage, L' (*The Wild Child*) 93–4, 103, 173
Enfants du paradis, Les 196
Equus 47
Eshkeri, Ilan 92
ET 17
Everyone Says I Love You 61
Exorcist, The 21
Eyes Wide Shut 129, 170

Fahrenheit 451 169–70, 178
Fall of the Roman Empire, The 14, 16, 168
Family Plot 147
Fanny and Alexander 99–100
Fantasia on a Theme by Thomas Tallis (Vaughan Williams) 266
Far from Heaven 18
Far from the Madding Crowd 45–6
Faraway, So Close! (*Im weiter Ferne, so nah!*) 240
'Father and Son' (Cat Stevens) 123
Fearless 262–3, 266, 273–5, 280
Fellowship of the Ring, The 76
Fenton, George, *Dangerous Liaisons* 13
Figgis, Mike 243

film music 1–5
   clichés 12–13, 17–19
   decline 53–4
   its importance 49–50, 63–4
   music for film vs use of music 71–2
   role 7–25, 254
      Bruce Beresford's views 201–6, 209–10
      Peter Greenaway's views 246–7
      reinforcement of emotion 268–9
      storytelling 75–6
      Wim Wenders's views 238–9
films noirs 171–2
Fischer-Diskau, Dietrich 114
Fistful of Dollars, A (*Per un pugno di dollari*) 37
Fistful of Dynamite (*Giù la testa*) 39–40
Five Easy Pieces 90–1
Fly, The (film) 83
Fly, The (Shore) 83–4
Fonda, Henry 149, 173–4
For a Few Dollars More (*Per qualche dollaro in più*) 37–8
Force of Evil 89, 90
Foreign Correspondent 7
Foster, Stephen 13
Four Last Songs (Strauss) 265
Four Musketeers, The 66
Four Weddings and a Funeral 51–2
Franklin, Aretha 118
Freed, Arthur 141
Friedhofer, Hugo 8
Frith, Fred 226, 236
From Russia with Love 110
Frost/Nixon 17
Fuller, Samuel 185

Gabrieli, Giovanni 247–8
Gallipoli 265, 269
Galway, James 46
Gaye, Marvin 117
Gazza ladra, The see *Thieving Magpie*
Genevieve 2

Gershwin, George 20
Getting of Wisdom, The 201
Ghost and Mrs Muir, The 178
Gilda 13
Gillespie, Dizzy 67
'Gimme Shelter' (The Rolling Stones) 79
Giordani, Giuseppe, 'Caro mio ben' 130
Giù la testa (*A Fistful of Dynamite*) 39–40
Gladiator 205
Glass, Philip 1, 20, 245, 268–9
   Notes on a Scandal 20
Glenn Miller Story, The 24–5
'Gloomy Sunday' (Rezső Seress) 220–1
Go-Between, The 50
Goalkeeper's Fear of the Penalty, The (*Die Angst des Tormanns beim Elfmeter*) 240
Goblin (rock band) 21
Godard, Jean-Luc 254
Godfather, The 22–3, 55, 173, 194
Godfather II, The 23
Goldberg variations (Bach) 89
Goldsmith, Jerry 2
Golijov, Osvaldo 220, 236
Gone with the Wind 16
'Good Morning' (Nacio Herb Brown & Arthur Freed) 141
Good Night, and Good Luck 133
Good, the Bad and the Ugly, The (*Il buono, il brutto, il cattivo*) 29, 37, 38, 230
Goodfellas 115
Goodman, Benny 20
Goosens, Léon 43
Górecki, Henryk, Symphony No. 3 ('Symphony of Sorrowful Songs') 262–3
Gospel According to St Matthew, The (*Il Vangelo secondo Matteo*) 96–8
Graduate, The 110
Grand Polonaise Brillante (Chopin) 88
Granger, Farley 149
Grant, Cary 152, 153
Great Big Sea (band) 127

Index

Great Dictator, The 64
Great Escape, The 73
Greenaway, Peter 244–60
   Leonardo's Last Supper (installation) 244, 247
   Tulse Luper Suitcases (multimedia project) 252
Gunfight at the O.K. Corral 108
Gypsy music 219–20

Haazen, Guido, *Missa Luba* 98, 137
Haley, Bill, and the Comets 111–12
Hancock, Herbie 134
Handel, George Frideric 13
Hannah and Her Sisters 56
Hannibal 89
Hansard, Glen 141
Hard Day's Night, A 135
Harwood, Gwen 264
Hawaiian Eye (TV series) 16
Help! 135
Hendrix, Jimi 123–4
Here We Go Round the Mulberry Bush 135
Herrmann, Bernard 19, 32, 178
   comment on *Murder on the Orient Express* 48
   Fahrenheit 451 169
   Lalo Schifrin's comment 73
   Man Who Knew Too Much, The 159, 160
   Psycho 2, 151
   Vertigo 19
Heure espagnol, L' (Ravel) 70
High Fidelity 78, 116, 119
High Noon 106–8
Hilary and Jackie 146
Hill, The 38
Hirschfelder, David, *Sliding Doors* 10–11
Hitchcock, Alfred 276–7
   Birds, The 3
   Lifeboat 8
   on-screen appearances 148–9
   Strangers on a Train 21
   use of musical cues 146–66
   Vertigo 19
Hoffmann, Philip Seymour 127
Holland, Rodney 3–4
Hollingsworth, John 43
Holly and the Ivy, The 13
'Hong Kong Garden' (Siouxsie & the Banshees) 125
Hopkins, Anthony 168
Horloger de Saint-Paul, L' (*The Watchmaker of St Paul*) 168–9
Horner, James 111
Hoschna, Karl 61–2
Hotel Chevalier 120–1
human voices *see* voices
Hunt, Linda 265
Husbands and Wives 21
Hyman, Dick 55–65
Hymn to the Virgin, A (Britten) 113
hymns 138
   in *if...* 136–7
   see also songs

'I Don't Know You' (Annie Ross) 134
'I Heard It Through the Grapevine' (Marvin Gaye) 117
'I Want to Be Loved by You' (Marilyn Monroe) 131
'I Want Candy' (Bow Wow Wow) 125
'I Will Always Love You' (Dolly Parton) 143, 144
if... 136–7
'Il est né le divin enfant' 130–1
'I'm So Glad' (Skip James) 242–3
Im weiter Ferne, so nah! (*Faraway, So Close!*) 240
In Bruges 92
'In the End' (Scott Matthew) 139–40
In the Realm of the Senses (*Ai no corrida*) 3
Inglourious Basterds 119, 173
Inspector Morse (TV series) 146
Invaders, The 7–8
Irglová, Markéta 141

Isham, Mark 134
It All Starts Today (*Ça commence aujourd'hui*) 132, 169
It's a Wonderful Life 13, 16
'I've Got My Eyes on You' (Dianne Reeves) 133

Jackson, Peter 76, 77–8
James, Skip 242–3
Jamiroquai (pop artist) 10
Jarre, Jean Michel, *Oxygène* 269
Jarre, Maurice 262
  Dr Zhivago 1
  Lawrence of Arabia 1
  The Year of Living Dangerously 268
  work with Peter Weir 269–71
Jaws
  evocation of a shark 2
  Stravinsky and 16
'Jazz Meets the Symphony' 66, 70
Jewison, Norman 59
John Thomas and Lady Jane (Lawrence) 92
Johnson, Willie, 'Dark Was the Night, Cold Was the Ground' 98, 242
Joi Baba Felunath (The Elephant God) 121
Jules et Jim 109
'Jump' (The Pointer Sisters) 122

Kaagaz Ke Phool (*Paper Flowers*) 228
Kamen, Michael, *Die Hard* 9–10
Karas, Anton 2
Kaurismäki, Aki 186
Kempff, Wilhelm 265–6
Kieslowski, Krzysztof 24
Kill Bill movies 119–20
Kills (rock band) 114
Kindertotenlieder (Mahler) 114
King, B.B. 223
King Kong (1933) 16
Knight's Tale, A 125
  'We Will Rock You' (Queen) 280

Korngold, Erich Wolfgang 15
Kovacevich, Stephen 44
Kubrick, Stanley 98–9, 100–1
Kurosawa, Akira 81, 195
Kusturica, Emir 228–9

Ladri di biciclette (*Bicycle Thieves*) 96
Lady Caroline Lamb 46
Lady Chatterley 92–3
Lady Vanishes, The 149, 164
  MacGuffin 162–4
  musical clues 149
Laine, Frankie 106
'Lara's Theme', *Doctor Zhivago* 262
Last Days of Disco, The 113
Last Wave, The 271
Lawrence of Arabia, epic score 1
Lawrence, D.H., *John Thomas and Lady Jane* 92
Lean, David
  Dr Zhivago 1
  Lawrence of Arabia 1
Leatherheads 132
Leben der Anderen, Das (*The Lives of Others*) 187, 188
Legrand, Michel
  Doll's House, A 50
  Go-Between, The 50
  The Thomas Crown Affair 51, 110
  influence on Richard Rodney Bennett 51
Lehár, Franz, *The Merry Widow* waltz 152–4, 155, 157
'Leiermann, Der' (Schubert) 92
leitmotifs 14–15, 76, 180, 241
Lenoir, J.B. 242
  'Mama Don't Talk to Your Daughter' 243
Lenya, Lotte 127
Leonardo's Last Supper (installation, Greenaway) 244, 247
Leone, Sergio 37–8
Lewton, Val 130, 189–90

Index

Lievsay, Skip 82
Lifeboat 8, 87
Lift to the Scaffold (*Ascenseur pour l'échafaud*) 13–14, 41, 71
Ligeti, György 100
Lisbon Story 241
'Little Brown Jug' 278
Little Night Music, A (stage show; Sondheim) 49
Lives of Others, The (Das Leben der Anderen) 187, 188
Lobos, Los 242
Lodger, The 147
Lolita 33–4
'Look of Love, The' (Dusty Springfield) 110
Lord of the Rings, The 75–8, 83
Losey, Joseph 50
Lost Horizon 16
Lost Weekend, The 16
Love Actually 121–2
Lucia di Lammermoor (Donizetti), 'Chi mi frena' 155
Lully, Jean-Baptiste, *Atys* 94
Lumet, Sidney 47
Lutyens, Elisabeth 43–4
Lynch, David 276
Lyne, Adrian, *Lolita* 33–4
Lynn, Vera 99

M 155, 168
M. Butterfly 83
M is for Man, Music, Mozart (TV film) 257
MacGuffins 155, 157–8
 definition of, 157
 Close Encounters of the Third Kind 164–6
 Lady Vanishes, The 162–4
 North by Northwest 162
Magnificent Ambersons, The 189–90
Magnolia 139, 140–1
 soundscapes 169

Mahler, Gustav 24
 Kindertotenlieder 114
 'Symphony No. 5'
 Adagietto 103
Malick, Terence, *Days of Heaven* 33
Malkovich, John 173
'Mama Don't Talk to Your Daughter' (J.B. Lenoir) 243
Mamma Mia! 142, 143
Man Escaped, A 95
Man from Laramie, The 108
Man Who Cried, The 219–20, 232, 233, 236
Man Who Knew Too Much, The (1934), musical clues 158–9, 159, 161
Man Who Knew Too Much, The (1956) 149
 musical clues 158, 159–62
Man Who Wasn't There, The 90
Mancini, Henry 70
Mann, Aimee 140
Mann, Anthony 24–5
Marie Antoinette 124–5
Marriage of Christ, The (Gabrieli & Sollima) 247–8
Martin, Dean 60
Masonic Funeral Music (Mozart) 98
Mass in C minor (Mozart)
 Kyrie 95
Master and Commander 266
Match Factory Girl, The (Tulitikkutehtaan tyttö) 186
Match Point 21
Matheson, Muir 43
Matthew, Scott 139–40
Mayerl, Billy 147
Mean Streets 114
Melinda and Melinda 56
Melville, Herman, *Billy Budd* 167–8
Mendelssohn, Felix Bartholdy 21
 Songs Without Words 141
Merry Widow waltz (Lehár) 152–4, 155, 157

305

'Mešicku na nebi hlubokém'. *Rusalka* (Dvořák) 207–9
Messiaen, Olivier 68, 69, 258–9
Midnight Cowboy 110
Midsummer Night's Sex Comedy, A 21
Miley, Bubber 21
minimalism in music 252
mirrors 249–50
'Miss Up-to-Date' (Billy Mayerl) 147
Missa Luba (Haazen) 98, 137
Mission, The 36, 210
Mission: Impossible (TV series) 66
Mister Johnson 214–15
Mitchell, Joni 122
Mitchum, Robert 174
Monk, Theolonius 67
Monteverdi, Claudio
   Vespers for the Blessed Virgin
      'Magnificat' 95–6
'Moon River' (Henry Mancini & Johnny Mercer) 110
'Moonlight Serenade' (Glenn Miller) 25
Moonraker 110
Moonstruck 55, 59–60
Moreau, Jeanne 41
Moross, Jerome, *Big Country, The*, in the concert Hall 1–2
Morricone, Ennio 29–40, 204–5, 210, 230
   intricacy 36
   use of sounds 231
Morte a Venezia (Death in Venice) 23–4, 103
Mosquito Coast 276
Motion, David 226
Mouchette 95–6
Mozart, Wolfgang Amadeus
   Ave Verum Corpus 95
   Masonic Funeral Music 98
   Mass in C minor
      Kyrie 95
   Zaide 208
Mr Smith Goes to Washington 16

Mrs Doubtfire 75
Mùi đu đu xanh (The Scent of Green Papaya) 23
Murder on the Orient Express 47, 48
Musa: The Warrior 216
music
   experience of 218–19
   in films *see* film music
   on the set 272–3
musical clues 146–66
musical jokes 62
'My Baby Just Cares for Me' (Walter Donaldson & Gus Kahn) 62
'My Heart Will Go On' (Celine Dion) 111
Myer, Groove 271

Naked Kiss, The 14
'Natural Woman, A' (Aretha Franklin) 118
naturalism 233–5
Newell, Mike 51–2
Newman, Alfred 73
Newman, Randy 132
Newman, Thomas 17
Nicholas and Alexandra 46
Night of the Hunter 174
'Night Pat Murphy Died, The' (Great Big Sea) 127
No Country for Old Men 183
'No One Can Like the Drummer Man' (Sammy Lerner, Al Goodhart & Al Hoffman) 150
Norma Rae 3
North, Alex 212
North by Northwest 158
   crop duster scene 178, 181–2
   MacGuffin 162
North West Frontier 14
Notes on a Scandal 20
Novecento (1900) 30
Nuit américaine, La (Day for Night) 137
Number 13 147

Index

Nuovo cinema Paradiso (*Cinema Paradiso*) 29–30
Nyman, Michael 244, 245, 247, 253–4, 256
  references to 17th century music 248

O Lucky Man! 136, 137–8
O'Connor, Sinéad 111
'Ode to Joy' (Beethoven) 9–10
Odetta 98
O'Halloran, Dustin 126
Oldfield, Mike 21
Olman, Abe 131
On Her Majesty's Secret Service 110
On the Beautiful Blue Danube see *Blue Danube* waltz
On the Waterfront 42
Once 139, 141, 142
Once Upon a Time in the West (*C'era una volta il West*) 38
'Only You' (Sinéad O'Connor) 111
opera 70, 83–4, 255–9
Orff, Carl, *Schulwerk* 21–2
Orlando 218, 222–3
  score 226–8
Otello (Verdi) 70
Othello (1952) see *Tragedy of Othello Moor of Venice, The*
Othello (1965) 173
Outrage 194–5
Oxygène (Jarre) 269

panpipes 2–3, 261–2
Paper Flowers (*Kaagaz Ke Phool*) 228
Paradine Case, The 149
  Hitchcock's on-screen appearance 148
Paradise Road 213–14
Paranormal Activity 189
Paris, Texas 237, 238–9, 240–1
Partita No. 2 in C minor (Bach) 93
Parton, Dolly 143, 144
Pastoral Symphony, A (Vaughan Williams) 113
Patdeep (raga) 176

Pather Panchali 121
  music mirroring voices 176
Paz, Juan Carlos 68
Pearl Fishers, The (Bizet) 221, 232
Pêcheurs des Perles see *Pearl Fishers, The*
Peckinpah, Sam 4
Pélleas et Mélisande (Debussy) 70
Penderecki, Krystof 273
Per qualche dollaro in più (*For a few dollars more*) 37–8
Per un pugno di dollari (*A Fistful of Dollars*) 37–8
Peyton Place 16
Peyton Place (TV series) 16
Pheloung, Barrington 146
Pianist, The 87–8
Piano, The 3, 22
Pickpocket 94, 185
Pickup on South Street 184–5
Picnic at Hanging Rock 275, 277
  panpipes 3, 261–2
  Piano Concerto No. 5 (Beethoven) 265–6
Pierrot le fou 254
Pointer Sisters, The 122
Polanski, Roman 87–8
Pomus, Doc 134
pop music 105–26
Potter, Sally 218–36
Poulenc, Francis, *Concert champêtre* 45
Price, Alan 137–8
'Prisoner of Life' (Annie Ross) 134
Private Life of Don Juan, The 124
Private Lives of Elizabeth and Essex, The 15
Peter Sarstedt
Procol Harem 118
Prokofiev, Sergei 255
  Alexander Nevsky 96, 98, 253
  and *ET* 16–17
Prospero's Books 257
Psycho 2, 73
  black humour 151
  musical clues 151

Public Enemy, The 183–4
Puccini, Giacomo 70
   La Bohème 59, 60
   Tosca, 'E lucevan le stelle' 221–2
Pugliese, Osvaldo 236
Purcell, Henry 244, 247
Purple Rose of Cairo, The 58–9

Queen (band) 125, 280

Radio Days 113–14
Raging Bull 192
'Rags to Riches' (Tony Bennett) 115
'Raindrops Keep Fallin' On My Head' (Hal David & Burt Bacharach) 109–10
Raitt, Bonnie 242
Rakhmaninov, Sergei
   'Piano Concerto No. 2 in C minor' 101–4, 129–30
Ran 80–1
Rashomon 195
Ravel, Maurice 49, 68
   L'Heure espagnol 70
Rawhide (TV series) 106
Rear Window 63–4, 151
   Hitchcock's on-screen appearance 148–9
Rebecca 16
Rebennack, Mac 134
Red House, The 195
Red River 108
Red Road 187–8
Redgrave, Michael 149
Reed, Lou 242
Reeves, Dianne 133
Reich, Steve 245
Reinhardt, Django 57
Rembrandt Harmensz van Rijn 249–50
Repulsion 14
Return of the King, The 77
   beacon lighting scene 78
Rickman, Alan 2, 9, 122

'Ride of the Valkyries' (Wagner) 3
Rififi (Du rififi chez les hommes) 187
Ring of the Nibelung, The (Wagner) 14, 15
Ripley's Game 31
Rite of Spring, The (Stravinsky) 67
Ritter, Tex 106–7
Road to Perdition, The 192
'Rock Around the Clock' (Bill Haley an the Comets) 111–12
Rollercoaster 72
Rolling Stones 79, 114, 117
Rome, Open City 96
Ronettes, The (singing group) 114–15
Rope 149, 151
Rosa (Andriessen) 255
Rosemary's Baby 190
Ross, Annie 133
Rossini, Gioachino, *Thieving Magpie* overture 100
Royal Tenenbaums, The 121
Rózsa, Miklos 15, 16
'Ruby Tuesday' (The Rolling Stones) 114
Rusalka (Dvořák), 'Song to the Moon' 207–9
Rushmore 120
Ryder, Loren L. 63

Saboteur 89
Saint-Saëns, Camille, *Carnival of the Animals* 33
Salem's Lot 277
Salò o le 120 giornate di Sodoma (Salò or the 120 Days of Sodom) 22
Samson and Delilah 193
Sanders of the River 14
'Santa Lucia' 145, 281
Sarabande (Suite No. 5 in C minor for solo cello, Bach) 177
Sarstedt, Peter 120–1
Savages, The 127
Scarface 154–5
Scent of Green Papaya, The (Mùi đu đu xanh) 23

Index

Schifrin, Lalo 66–74
Schindler's List, use of classical music 87
Schlesinger, John 44–5
Schoenberg, Arnold 11, 42, 68
Schubert, Franz
    Piano Trio in E flat 99
    'Ständchen' (Serenade No. 4) 92
    String Quartet No. 9 in G minor 20
    Winterreise
        'Der Leiermann' 92
Schulwerk (Orff) 21–2
Scoop 21
Scorsese, Martin 243
    and temp tracks 80
    use of pop music 114–15
Screamers 215
Se7en 82, 83
Sea Hawk, The 15
Serkis, Andy 173
Seven Days in May 2
Seven Samurai (Shichinin no samurai) 195
Seven Year Itch, The 102
Seventh Victim, The 190
Shadow of a Doubt 157
    musical clues 152–4, 155
Shadows 14
Shadows and Fog 21
'Shepherds Shake Off Your Drowsy Sleep' 130
Shichinin no samurai (*Seven Samurai*) 195
Shine 22
Shining, The 99, 273, 277
Shoot the Pianist (*Tirez sur le pianiste*) 22
Shore, Howard 75–84
    'Departed Tango, The' 79
    The Fly (opera) 83–4
Short Cuts 133, 139
Shortbus 139, 140
Sibelius, Jean, *Valse Triste* 93
Siegel, Don 73–4
silence 178–92, 229, 274–5
Silence of the Lambs, The 75, 82
    use of classical music 89

silent films 8–9
Silverado 17–18
Singin' in the Rain 141, 142, 228
Siouxsie & the Banshees 125
Six Feet Under (TV series) 17
Skubiszewski, Cezary 132
Sliding Doors 10–11
Sling Blade 173
Smeaton, Bruce 261
'So Long, Marianne' (Leonard Cohen) 123
Sollima, Giovanni 247–8
Soloist, The 22
Some Like It Hot 131, 184
'Sometimes I Feel Like a Motherless Child' (Odetta) 98
Sondheim, Stephen, *A Little Night Music* 49
'Song to the Moon'. *Rusalka* (Dvořák) 207–9
songs 127–45
    function 105–6, 133–4, 137
    see also hymns
Songs Without Words (Mendelssohn) 141
Sopranos, The (TV series) 105, 111
Soul of a Man, The 237, 242, 243
sound
    a shared experience 279–81
    technical changes 237–8
    see also music; sound effects
Sound Barrier, The 170–1, 195
sound effects 229–30
    see also train whistles
Sound of Pictures (radio program) 3–4
spaghetti westerns 29, 204–5
Spartacus 14
    use of accents 172
Spellbound 16
    Hitchcock's on-screen appearance 148
Spielberg, Steven
    Close Encounters of the Third Kind 164–6
    musical MacGuffin 164–6

spotting 78, 206–8, 266–7
Stage Fright 149
'Stand By Your Man' (Tammy Wynette) 90
'Ständchen', Serenade No. 4 (Schubert) 92
Star Wars 15
State of Play 127
Steiner, George 222
Steiner, Max 16
Stepford Wives, The 170
Steppenwolf (band) 111
Stevens, Cat 123
Stewart, James 24–5
Sting, The 2
Storm Clouds (Benjamin) 158–9
storytelling 75–6
Strange Interlude (TV film) 53
Strangers on a Train 21
   Hitchcock's on-screen appearance 148
Strauss, Johann, II
   Blue Danube waltz 99, 100
   Vienna Blood waltz 152
Strauss, Richard
   Also sprach Zarathustra 99, 263, 265
   Four Last Songs 265
Stravinsky, Igor 11
   John Williams's debt 16
   The Rite of Spring 67
Streetcar Named Desire, A 42
Summer Night on the River (Delius) 89
Sunset Blvd 16
   voice over 171–2
Suspicion 153
   musical clues 152
Suspiria 21
Sweet and Lowdown 57
'Symphony of Sorrowful Songs' (Górecki) 262–3
Symphony of Sorrowful Songs, The 263

Take the Money and Run 20
Takemitsu, Tōru 80–1

Tale of Sweeney Todd, The (TV film) 45
Tango 69
Tango Lesson, The 236
Tarantino, Quentin 119–20
Taxi Driver 19, 178
   played in the concert hall 2
temp tracks (temporary music) 34–5, 45, 64–5
   Richard Rodney Bennett 45
   Bruce Beresford 210–11
   Dick Hyman 64–5
   Ennio Morricone 34–5
   Lalo Schifrin 71–2
   Martin Scorsese 80
   Howard Shore 80
   Peter Weir 264–5, 270
Temptations, The (singing group) 128
Tender Mercies 203, 204
'That's Amore' (Dean Martin) 60
Thieving Magpie overture (Rossini) 100
'Things to Come' (Dizzy Gillespie) 67
Third Man, The 2, 230, 231
Thirty-two Short Films About Glenn Gould 91
thirtysomething (TV series) 119
Thomas Crown Affair, The 51, 110
Thorn Birds, The 271
Three Colours: Blue (*Trois couleurs: Bleu*) 23–4
Threepenny Opera (Weill) 127
Tie Me Up! Tie Me Down! (*¡Átame!*) 31–2
timbre (vocal) 173–5
Time of the Gypsies (*Dom za vesanje*) 228–9
Tiomkin, Dimitri 16
   Fall of the Roman Empire, The 168
   High Noon 106–8
   Merry Widow, The 152–4
Tirez sur la pianiste (*Shoot the Pianist*) 22
Titanic 111, 230
To Have and Have Not 132–3
To Kill a Mockingbird 18, 171
tone of voice 171, 172

Index

Torn Curtain 158, 178–80, 187
Tosca (Puccini), 'E lucevan le stelle' 221–2
Touch of Class, A 102
Touch of Evil 64
Tragedy of Othello the Moor of Venice, The 173
train whistles
  12 Angry Men 194
  39 Steps, The 175
  Call Northside 777 193, 194
  Lady Vanishes, The 162–3
Trier, Lars von 8, 234, 239–40
Trilogy; The Weeping Meadow (*Trilogia: To livadi pou dakryzei*) 191–2
Troilo, Anibal 236
Trois couleurs: Bleu (*Three Colours: Blue*) 23–4
Trovatore, Il (Verdi) 221
Truffaut, François 93–4
Truly Madly Deeply 102, 122, 146
Truman Show, The 268–9
Tubular Bells 21
Tulitikkutehtaan tyttö (*Match Factory Girl*) 186
Tulse Luper Suitcases (multimedia project, Greenaway) 252
Tunes of Glory 2
Turtles, The (rock group) 123
Twin, Aphex 126
Twisted Nerve 120
Two Hands 132
Two Towers, The 77

Unit 4 Plus 2 120
Until the End of the World (*Bis ans Ende der Welt*) 240

Vallie, Frankie 128
Valse Triste (Sibelius) 93
Vangelis 268
Varèse, Edgard, *Ecuatorial* 20
Vangelo secondo Matteo (*Gospel According to St Matthew*) 96–8

Vaughan Williams, Ralph 7–8
  Fantasia on a Theme by Thomas Tallis 266
  Pastoral Symphony, A 113
Verdi, Giuseppe 73
  Il trovatore 221
  Otello 70
Veronese, Paolo, *The Wedding at Cana* 247–8
verse 224–5
Vertigo, Hitchcock's on-screen appearance 148
Vespers for the Blessed Virgin (Monteverdi) 'Magnificat' 95–6
Vicar of Dibley (TV series) 121
Vienna Blood waltz 152
Vinterberg, Thomas 8
Visconti, Luchino 24, 103
Viskningar och rop (*Cries and Whispers*) 176–7
Vitarelli, Joe 211
Vivaldi, Antonio 93–4
  'Mandolin Concerto in C' 94
vocal colour *see* timbre (vocal)
voices 167–77
  scoring 229
Voyage of the Damned 66–7

Wagner, Richard 16, 220
  Die Walküre, 'Ride of the Valkyries' 3
  Ring of the Nibelung, The 14, 15
  use of leitmotifs 14–15
Wain, Charles 271
'Wait' (The Kills) 114
Waiting for Godot (play), musical clues 151
Warren, Harry, 'That's Amore' 60
Washington, Ned 106
Watchmaker of St Paul, The (*L'horloger de Saint-Paul*) 168–9
Waxman, Franz 15, 16, 73
  The Paradine Case 149
'We Will Rock You' (Queen) 125, 280

Webb, Roy 130–1, 190
Wedding at Cana, The (painting, Veronese) 247–8
Weill, Kurt 21
   Threepenny Opera
      'Solomon's Song' 127
Weinstein, Harvey 211–12
Weir, Peter 261–78
'We'll Meet Again' (Vera Lynn) 99
Well Tempered Clavier (Bach) 91, 93
Wenders, Wim 237–43
'What Is This Thing Called Love' (Bubber Miley) 21
Whatever Works 20
'When a Man Loves a Woman' (Percy Sledge) 118
'Where Do You Go to My Lovely' (Peter Sarstedt) 120–1
Whisky Galore 174–5
'Whiter Shade of Pale, A' (Procol Harum) 118
Wild Child, The (*L'Enfant sauvage*) 93–4, 103, 173
'Wild Frontier' (Adam Ant) 125
Wilkinson, Marc 136
Williams, John 2
   debt to European composers 16–17
   great skill 17
   music for
      Close Encounters of the Third Kind 63, 165–6
      Jaws 2
      Star Wars 15
   use of leitmotifs 15

Williams, Lucinda 242
Wilson, Cassandra 242
'Windmills of Your Mind, The' (Michel Legrand) 110
Winterreise (Schubert)
   'Der Leiermann' 92
'Wise Up' (Aimee Mann) 140–1
Witchfinder General 184
Withnail and I 123–4
Witness 262, 270–1
Wiz, The 55
Wozzeck (Berg) 70
Writing to Vermeer (Andriessen) 255, 257–8
Wrong Man, The 149
Wynette, Tammy 90, 91

Y tu mamá también (*And Your Mother Too*) 169
Year of Living Dangerously, The 262, 265, 267–8
Yes 223–5, 231
Yo La Tengo 139
Yo-Yo Ma 266
'You Can't Always Get What You Want' (The Rolling Stones) 117, 119
Young and Innocent 153, 196
   musical clues 149–50
Young Victoria, The 92, 111

Zaide (Mozart) 208
Zamfir, Gheorghe 2–3, 261–2
Zelig 57, 58
Zimmer, Hans 17, 205–6

www.ingramcontent.com/pod-product-compliance
Lightning Source LLC
Chambersburg PA
CBHW060553230426
43670CB00011B/1810